PATTERNS OF
SEXUAL BEHAVIOR

D1571350

*the text of this book is printed
on 100% recycled paper*

Previous book by Frank A. Beach:

HORMONES AND BEHAVIOR

PATTERNS OF
SEXUAL BEHAVIOR

by CLELLAN S. FORD, Ph.D.

Professor of Anthropology, Yale University

and FRANK A. BEACH, Ph.D.

Professor of Psychology, Yale University

WITH A FOREWORD BY
ROBERT LATOU DICKINSON, M.D.

HARPER TORCHBOOKS
Harper & Row, Publishers
New York, Hagerstown, San Francisco, London

Contents

FOREWORD *by Robert Latou Dickinson*, M.D.   vii

I.   The Task and the Methods   1

II.   The Nature of Coitus   18

III.   Types of Sexual Stimulation   40

IV.   Circumstances for Coitus   68

V.   Attracting a Sex Partner   85

VI.   Sexual Partnerships   106

VII.   Homosexual Behavior   125

VIII.   Relations Between Different Species   144

IX.   Self-Stimulation   153

X.   Development in the Individual   167

XI.   Feminine Fertility Cycles   199

XII.   Other Physiological Factors in Sex Behavior   221

XIII.   Human Sexual Behavior in Perspective   250

GLOSSARY   268

BIBLIOGRAPHY   293

AUTHORS' NOTE   301

INDEX   303

This book is in part the outgrowth of the fourth Smith College Lecture Series delivered by Frank A. Beach in February, 1949.

Foreword

by Robert Latou Dickinson, M.D.

No contribution on the sex aspects of human life, save that of Kinsey, Pomeroy, and Martin appears as timely and important as this type of approach. It is a masterly assembly of data from the outer borders and from a large part of the antecedents of our own mores. The combination of sympathetic understanding and understatement with scientific detachment is noteworthy.

This is a time of wide demand for wise programs in sex education and marriage counseling, built upon basic studies, in the attempt to forestall the mounting breakup of homes. It is nothing less than an event, therefore, to discover an extensive and intensive analysis of the evidence on evolution of our sex behavior. And this from a team of collaborators with very special qualifications. From Professor Beach we have had half a hundred scientific papers and an earlier book; from Professor Ford, scholarly monographs based upon long investigations of preliterate peoples; both here applying their experience to a comparative examination of our own sex mores, in a fashion marked by freedom from bias and dogmatic statement.

One might call this text a sweeping and original analysis undating "original sin." Here the active awakening of sex awareness—in the Pentateuch pioneer and his mate—is moved backward from six thousand years to some million or more. This book depicts for one bodily function an evolution as drastic as Darwin's.

And a Paradise regained. So consistently has moralistic writing used "animal" and "beastly" as terms for the ultimate in damnation concerning byplays and frequencies in love-making; so dictatorially has much of our religious teaching classified all sex behavior; so unrelated to actuality is the bulk of our statutory law on these matters, that coverage such as this inquiry can hardly be too warmly welcomed as cogent, timely and most enlightening.

We *can* choose to dispute a distant common origin with certain primates. We *can* deny all evolution. We *can* refuse to recognize certain tribes as relevant relatives. *Or* we can give weight to studies concerning a wide variety of sex behavior. Only in this way may we claim open-mindedness in an evaluation of the sex prohibitions and restrictions which characterize our own society.

Certain wide areas of sex behavior have had to be passed over to make room for those adequately subjected to the following type of investigation. The Greek and Roman periods, the elaborate sex literature and sculptures of India, the multiple and unmatched pictured texts of the great Japanese artists have been subject to much comment in European writings, although their sequences and scope and intimacy have been scanted. Here review and inclusion would have required not one volume but several, and led into many bypaths.

Attitudes toward sex are rapidly changing in many ways, and we are forced to consider reorientation in several of our mores. I refer to confident progress toward utterly simple techniques of birth control. And I point to effective steps toward elimination of venereal disease through the application of modern hygienic methods combined with fearlessly frank sex education and general training in character and self-control. But unless we understand sex practices in evolutionary perspective we fail to comprehend the element of revolution in the present radical change in sex conditioning.

Although a strictly scientific study, recommending directly no practical applications, scholarship such as this has plain lessons. Through the development of scientific methods of research, morals can be based upon normals, theology can adopt physiology, and a workable code of ethics can mate with a sane understanding of sex.

PATTERNS OF
SEXUAL BEHAVIOR

Chapter I

The Task and the Methods

THIS book is about the sexual behavior of human beings and of lower animals. The people with whom it deals belong to 190 different societies, and these societies are scattered around the world from the edge of the Arctic Circle to the southernmost tip of Australia. Most of the animals whose behavior we describe are mammals and they represent many different species from rats and mice to man's nearest living relatives, the great apes.

DEVELOPING A THREE-WAY PERSPECTIVE

The biologist considers sexual behavior to be of fundamental significance because it leads to perpetuation of the species and thus to the continuity of life itself. The psychologist finds in the sexual impulse wellsprings of human conduct, deep reservoirs of motivation that impel men and women to action and furnish the driving force for many of their day-to-day activities. Sociologists recognize the integrating, cohesive functioning of sex as contributing to the stability of the family unit and thus to the entire structure of the social group. For the moralist, man's perpetual attempt to reconcile his basic sexual tendencies with the ethical standards and ideal demands of his social group presents a primary problem. And it is important to add that an objective interest in sexual behavior is not limited to specialists; a broad understanding of this subject is useful also for anyone who conceives of his own life as worthy of intelligent direction and management. Although the phrase "sexual behavior"

1

is part of our common vocabulary, it is likely to mean different things to different people. As used in this book, the term refers exclusively to behavior involving stimulation and excitation of the sexual organs. Since heterosexual coitus, i.e., intercourse between a male and female, is the means whereby the species is perpetuated, copulation between the sexes is taken as the core of our book. In addition, it has proved important to discuss certain kinds of behavior that occur just before coitus. These include various types of foreplay that initiate or increase sexual arousal and serve to prepare both partners for participating in the coital relationship. Finally, our consideration of sexual behavior encompasses such other common types of behavior as those involved in homosexual activities, in relations between animals of different species, and in habits of self-stimulation.

Men and women do not develop their individual patterns of sexual behavior simply as a result of biological heredity. Human sexual responses are not instinctive in the sense of being determined exclusively by the action of genes or chromosomes. On the contrary, from the first years of life every child is taught about sex, either directly or indirectly. And most significant is the fact that different societies teach different lessons in this regard. In some cultural settings children learn that sex is a subject to be avoided and that any form of sexual expression during childhood is wrong. In other societies boys and girls are taught that certain sexual activities are permissible whereas others are not. As the result of such divergent experiences in early life, the adult members of different societies have quite different opinions as to what is proper or normal in sexual relations, and what is immoral or unnatural.

Men and women in our own society who wish to understand their own sexual tendencies and habits cannot reach this goal merely by introspection. They can markedly increase their comprehension by learning how other members of the same society feel, believe, and act with respect to sex. Valuable for this level of understanding are careful interview studies such as those of A. C. Kinsey and his collaborators, W. B. Pomeroy and C. E. Martin. But the most complete knowledge of how Americans behave sexually would not in itself provide an adequate basis for a comprehensive understanding of human sexuality. This is true because of the facts just mentioned—namely, that human sex life is profoundly affected by social channelization and personal experience and therefore takes different forms under different social conditions.

It follows that a description of the sexual patterns of the human species can be truly representative and valid only after a large number of widely divergent cultures have been analyzed with a view to recognizing the similarities and differences in sexual codes and habits. In this manner and in this manner alone can the scientist discover which aspects of man's sexual reactions are determined primarily by training and experience. As we have noted, such a cross-cultural study reveals an impressive list of differences from one society to another. In the main, these differences are attributable to variation in the rules by which societies attempt to govern the behavior of their members. There are, of course, a number of similarities in the sexual behavior of human beings in all societies. Some of these similarities seem to reflect the fact that men and women everywhere have learned the same lessons from past experience. Life conditions have much in common regardless of the society in which a people live. Universal conditions of experience operating over a long period of social experimentation and learning may independently give rise to similar patterns of behavior. On the other hand, all human beings belong to the same species, and some of the intercultural similarities in behavior appear to arise from the fact that members of every society share a common species heredity.

In an attempt to determine which universal patterns of human sexual behavior are the result of common learning experiences and which are the result of genetically controlled biological tendencies, we have found it helpful to examine the evidence regarding the courtship and mating of lower animals. Because he is an animal, man shares with many other species certain basic behavioral traits. When it is found that a given type of sexual behavior is characteristic of human beings in many different societies and also is typical of all species of apes and monkeys, one is led to suspect that the common element is due to a common heredity.

This is the case, for example, in connection with habits of masturbation. Self-stimulation of the sexual organs is practiced by at least some members of every human society of which we have any knowledge. Some societies forbid such behavior, but it occurs nevertheless. The fact that masturbatory behavior appears in one society after another, whether or not the social code is opposed to the practice, is significant. Observations to the effect that many primates other than man display the same behavior suggest that the tendency toward this response is very primitive and firmly fixed in the hierarchy of human reactions. Male and female chimpanzees and monkeys engage in self-stimulation during early life, and to some extent in adulthood. The conditions under which this behavior appears suggest that it cannot be classified as an "abnormal" or "perverted" pattern as far as other animals are concerned. And with reference to human beings such categorization has meaning only in terms of a particular society's code of morals. When we affirm that certain habits such as that of masturbation must be regarded as one expected type of sexual expression we do not mean to imply that they are desirable types of response as far as human beings are concerned. But we do wish to argue for caution against interpreting such phenomena as "unnatural."

It is also worth noting that sexual relations sometimes occur between males or between females of many animal species. In men and women this sort of behavior is labeled "homosexual," and in our own society it is regarded as highly undesirable. Disregarding for the moment the social desirability or undesirability of homosexuality, we may say on the basis of the zoological evidence that human homosexual tendencies have a definite biological basis. Furthermore, and most important, there is little indication that these tendencies are restricted to a few deviant individuals. Instead they appear to exist in a large majority of both sexes, although they may not be recognized and although overt homosexual behavior may not occur. These matters receive detailed consideration in later chapters. They are mentioned here merely to explain why this book contains so much material pertaining to the sexual behavior of infrahuman animals.

Certain chapters in this book are concerned primarily with the physiological basis for sexual behavior. The reason for including this material is twofold. Some of the similarities between human sexual behavior and that of other animals are due to shared physiological factors. Differences in the sexual behavior of different species, on the other hand, can be partly explained as the result of evolutionary changes in the nature of the physiological controls involved. It is for these reasons that we have described briefly the ways in which the nervous system and various glandular secretions affect sexual behavior.

In summary of what has been said thus far, we have brought together evidence concerning the sexual behavior of human beings in a large number of different societies, and of animals belonging to many species. To this material we have added a knowledge of the several physiological factors involved in sexual behavior and their relative importance in different species. The purpose has been to provide a three-dimensional perspective or background against which the sexual life of any given species or of members of any particular society can be analyzed and understood. Comparisons and contrasts between man and other animals with respect to their sexual behavior and the physiological factors involved give some appreciation of the underlying biological tendencies upon which various kinds of sexual activities are based. Consideration of similarities and discrepancies between human sexual patterns in different cultural settings throws light upon the ways in which social conditions, acting through individual experience, mold and modify the inherited capacities.

IDENTIFICATION OF SOCIETIES AND SPECIES

This book is not intended to be an encyclopedia. We have not attempted to bring together all that is known about the sex life of animals and man. The data which we have included have been chosen because they fulfill the requirements imposed by the nature of our task, which is, first of all, to describe the basic sexual patterns of human beings and their closest animal relatives.

Human Societies. The necessity of including information concerning sexual behavior in a number of societies with quite different cultures has been stressed as essential to the objective of providing a cross-cultural perspective for an understanding of sexual behavior. In order to obtain such a perspective the number of societies examined is less important than the range of cultural differences included in the sample. The greater the variety of societies studied in terms of differences in environment, social organization, and religious codes and morals, the more adequate will be the resultant understanding of the extent to which human sexual behavior remains the same or is modified under varied conditions of experience.

Anthropologists classify the peoples of the earth in terms of their different societies, each of which is characterized by distinctive cultural patterns. This much is common knowledge, but what is perhaps less generally known is the great number of such societies and the extent to which they differ from one another. There are today some three to four thousand peoples whose cultures are sufficiently distinctive to be considered independent units.

A vast amount of information is available on the sexual behavior of people living in many of these societies. Literature containing the most complete and authentic accounts of behavior in societies with markedly different culture patterns has accumulated as the result of anthropological field research. For many years specialists trained in the observation of human behavior have been collecting comprehensive and detailed data on the customs, habits, and traditions of a great many contemporaneous societies. This literature has the great advantage of being based upon direct observation and investigation.

Anthropologists usually live for a year or more with the people they study, learn their language, talk with them and observe their behavior, and in some instances participate to a considerable degree in the life of the society. Thus they obtain their information at first hand and have opportunities to check and recheck their observations and conclusions. Moreover, many societies have been studied independently by several trained field workers, and this permits the independent verification of the description and interpretation of the behavior patterns of the people involved.

Anthropologists have investigated small isolated tribes such as the Siriono of eastern Bolivia, nomads who, in bands of less than a hundred persons, wander constantly over a vast area in search of food. And, in contrast, they have studied other people such as the Azande of Africa, a nation of over two million Negroes, skilled agriculturalists and craftsmen whose culture is characterized by a highly developed social and political organization. In short, anthropologists have observed representatives of a great many different societies.

Many of the peoples studied by anthropologists are "preliterate." These societies are usually referred to as "primitive," but the term is poorly chosen. They are not anachronistic examples of what our own society may have been thousands or hundreds of thousands of years ago. They are, on the contrary, just as highly "evolved" as European peoples. Cultural evolution has taken different directions in different societies. Instead of specializing in technology and the other trappings of what we are pleased to call "civilization," most preliterate peoples have elaborated other aspects of culture. The Australian Aranda, for example, have an extremely crude technology. But their kinship system is so elaborate and complicated that it exceeds the comprehension of any European or American unless he is a trained anthropologist.

In addition to the anthropological information on sexual behavior there exists a large body of material dealing with people in ancient societies, such as the Babylonians, the Greeks, and the Romans. These people, however, were not studied at first hand by trained investigators. Current knowledge of their sexual behavior depends upon fragmentary records which have come down from the past. It is nearly impossible to estimate the reliability and representativeness of the preserved descriptions of sexual behavior in ancient times. The class stratification that characterized most historical civilizations makes it probable that much of the available information concerning behavior actually refers exclusively to the upper social stratum. Particularly is this the case when the information is based upon the writings of individuals living at the time. Great literary figures such as Homer, for example, usually were members of an elite educated minority and the information they provide concerning the life of the times probably reflects the behavior of their associates rather than that of the masses of their society. For such reasons as these we have not included in this book materials on sexual behavior in ancient civilizations.

A comparable difficulty arises if one attempts to use the available information on complex modern societies such as that of the British or the Germans or the Poles. Information pertaining to our own society is a case in point. A major difficulty in specifying the sexual habits of Americans arises from the fact that ours is a complex society stratified into ethnic, regional, and social class divisions. Generalizations concerning the behavior of "Americans" are less meaningful than ones which relate to specific segments of our population. Yet most of the data on sexual behavior in the United States are available in relatively undifferentiated form.

The volume prepared by Kinsey, Pomeroy, and Martin furnishes a partial solution to this problem. These authors made an attempt to categorize the results of their survey by such indices as religion, income, and educational level. But even this leaves considerable room for improvement in the direction of being able to specify the social groups which constitute our society and the sexual behavior characterizing the members of each of these.

As a consequence of the difficulties involved in analyzing information about complex modern societies we have included only one of these, American society, in our sample. In addition we have employed data on 190 other peoples, all of which have been studied at first hand. If the world is divided into the five geographical areas of Oceania, Eurasia, Africa, North America, and South America (including Central America), the societies to which we shall refer are distributed as follows. The peoples most often referred to in the book are located on the maps of the world shown in Figures 1 and 2.

FIGS. 1 and 2. The locations of the Societies

OCEANIA	EURASIA	AFRICA	NORTH AMERICA	SOUTH AMERICA
Abelam	Ainu	Ashanti	Aleut	Abipone
Alorese	Andamanese	Azande	Apache	Apinaye
Aranda	Ao	Bena	Arapaho	Aymara
Balinese	Chenchu	Chagga	Arikara	Barama
Chamorro	Chukchee	Chewa	Cherokee	Cayapa
Dieri	Gilyak	Dahomeans	Cheyenne	Cherente
Dobuans	Gond	Fez	Chiricahua	Choroti
Dusun	Kazak	Ganda	Copper Eskimo	Colorado
Easter Is.	Khasi	Ila	Cree	Cuna
Futunans	Koryak	Jukun	Creek	Goajiro
Gilbertese	Kurd	Kababish	Crow	Haitians
Ifugao	Lakher	Kongo	Delaware	Jivaro
Kamilaroi	Lapps	Lamba	Flathead	Kaingang
Keraki	Lepcha	Lango	Fox	Macusi
Kiwai	Lhota	Lenge	Gros Ventre	Mataco
Kurtatchi	Mongols	Masai	Havasupai	Ramkokamekra

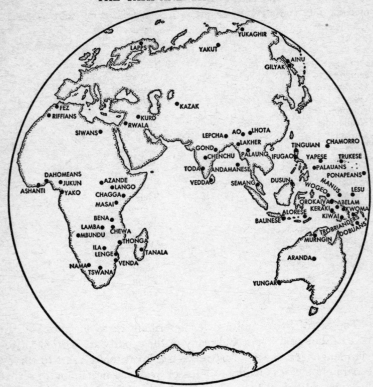

described in *Patterns of Sexual Behavior.*

OCEANIA	EURASIA	AFRICA	NORTH AMERICA	SOUTH AMERICA
Kusaians	Osset	Mbundu	Hidatsa	Rucuyen
Kwoma	Palaung	Nama	Hopi	Siriono
Lesu	Reddi	Nandi	Huichol	Taulipang
Loyalty Is.	Rengma	Pedi	Kansa	Tehuelche
Mailu	Rwala	Riffians	Kickapoo	Toba
Mangarevans	Samoyed	Siwans	Kiowa Apache	Tupinamba
Manus	Sema	Swazi	Klamath	Wapisiana
Maori	Semang	Tanala	Koniag	Witoto
Marquesans	Toda	Thonga	Kutchin	Yagua
Marshallese	Vedda	Tiv	Kutenai	Yaruro
Miriam	Yakut	Tswana	Kwakiutl	
Murngin	Yukaghir	Tuareg	Mandan	
Nauruans		Venda	Maricopa	
Orokaiva		Wolof	Menomini	
Palauans		Xosa	Naskapi	
Ponapeans		Yako	Natchez	

OCEANIA	EURASIA	AFRICA	NORTH AMERICA	SOUTH AMERICA
Pukapukans	Zulu		Navaho	
Purari			Ojibwa	
Rossel			Omaha	
Samoans			Oto	
Seniang			Papago	
Tasmanians			Penobscot	
Tikopia			Pima	
Tinguian			Ponca	
Tokelauans			Quinault	
Tongans			Sanpoil	
Trobrianders			Seminole	
Trukese			Sinkaietk	
Wogeo			Taos	
Yapese			Tarahumara	
Yungar			Thompson	
			Tlingit	
			Tolowa	
			Tubatulabal	
			Walapai	
			Wappo	
			Wintu	
			Yuma	
			Yurok	
			Zuñi	

The list of books and articles describing these societies runs to several thousand items, and many of the reports are written in foreign languages. It would have taken a great many years to survey separately every individual source of evidence pertaining to sexual behavior in each of the societies with which this book deals. Fortunately we have had access to the Human Relations Area Files, Inc., formerly known as Yale's Cross-Cultural Survey. These files include information on more than 200 different societies, so organized that the available data concerning any aspect of their culture can readily be located. By using these files the task of locating information pertaining to many of the peoples to which we shall refer has been greatly simplified. A selected bibliography of the sources used will be found at the back of this book.

Other Species.   Nearly all the animals referred to in this book will be partially familiar to most people. But the reader should also have at least a rudimentary understanding of the evolutionary relationships between various species. It is customary, for example, to refer to monkeys and apes as "man's nearest living relatives," and to consider other mammals as being more distantly related to our own species. The methods and criteria by which degrees of evolutionary relationship are determined have no pertinence to the present discussion. It will suffice to describe briefly the most generally accepted conclusions.

Men, apes, and monkeys combine to form the evolutionary order known as primates. Primates, in turn, are members of the class of animals known as mammals. Mammals are warm-blooded vertebrates distinguished primarily by the fact that they suckle their young. As a group, primates are the most highly evolved of the mammals. At the same time they share many general characteristics with other mammals. It is clear that man is also related, albeit more distantly, to subprimate mammals such as the dog, cat, horse, and even the rodents.

The subclass of mammals with which this volume is primarily concerned is called Eutheria and includes those species in which the young remain within the mother's uterus or womb for the full period of gestation. The Eutheria are divided into several orders. The ones with which we are most concerned in this book are the following:

1. Insectivora (e.g., mole, shrew)
2. Carnivora (e.g., cat, dog, weasel, bear)
3. Perissodactyla (odd-toed hoofed animals, e.g., horse, tapir, rhinoceros)
4. Artiodactyla (even-toed hoofed animals, e.g., pig, camel, deer, ox)
5. Proboscidea (elephant)
6. Rodentia (e.g., beaver, squirrel, mouse, rat, porcupine, guinea pig)
7. Lagomorpha (rabbit, hare)
8. Chiroptera (bat)
9. Cetacea (whale)
10. Edentata (e.g., armadillo, sloth)
11. Primates (man, ape, monkey)

The earliest ancestors of the primate order appeared some time before the Paleocene epoch which opened about 75 million years ago (see Figure 3. The following summary of trends in primate evolution is based upon G. G. Simpson's recent book, *The Meaning of Evolution*, Yale University Press, 1949). This type of mammal is called "prosimian." More than 60 million years ago a major evolutionary branch diverged from the prosimian stock and developed along somewhat specialized lines for approximately 30 or 40 million years. Then this branch subdivided and it was at this point that the

THE EVOLUTION OF PRIMATES

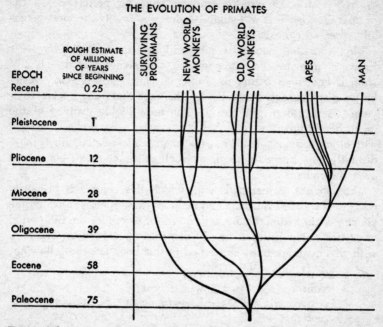

FIG. 3. Schematic representation of the evolution of primates from prosimian forebears. (Adapted from Fig. 17 in *The Meaning of Evolution*
by G. G. Simpson, Yale University Press, 1949.)

prehuman progenitors of our own species began to evolve separately
from any other type of primate. At the same time there emerged the
ancestral forms of the present-day apes which include the gorilla,
chimpanzee, and orangutan, and probably the gibbon and siamang.
Apes are therefore man's nearest living relatives; but measured in
terms of human generations the relationship appears quite distant,
since divergence between the original stocks occurred roughly 300
thousand centuries ago.

Now, to return to the changes that took place during the early
development of primates, during the Paleocene epoch another
branch separated from the same stem that later gave rise to men
and apes. This line of development eventually resulted in the appearance of certain other primates, the Old World monkeys. They
include the baboon, the macaque monkey of India, and several
other species. Old World monkeys are related to man much less

closely than are the apes, but more closely than one other group of primates known as New World monkeys.

The New World monkeys are evolutionary products of a line that arose from prosimian forebears some time during the Paleocene. They developed, as the name indicates, in what is now Central and South America. Because they did not derive from the same branch that produced men and apes, as did the Old World monkeys, this group is considered even further removed from our own species. They are, nevertheless, definitely primate in character and share with man many common anatomical and behavioral characteristics.

The primates other than man referred to in this book are classified below:

> Apes
>> Chimpanzee
>> Gorilla
>> Orangutan
>> Gibbon
>> Siamang
> Old World monkeys
>> Baboon
>> Macaque monkey (or rhesus monkey)
>> Pig-tailed monkey
>> Green monkey
>> Moore monkey
> New World monkeys
>> Howler monkey
>> Spider monkey

Data pertaining to the sexual behavior of animals below man have been gathered by one of us (Beach) over a period of approximately fifteen years. Much of the evidence derives directly from his personal research and the remainder has been summarized from a variety of other sources including technical journals, books, field studies by naturalists, practical accounts by commercial animal breeders, and reports by zoologists who have studied the habits of captive animals in zoological gardens.

LIMITATIONS

This book is subject to two types of limitations. In the first class are those which we have intentionally imposed upon the purpose and scope of the volume. Foremost among the self-imposed limitations are those arising from decisions as to what we would *not* try to accomplish.

The most significant of these is the avoidance of value judgments. We consistently eschewed any discussion of rightness or wrongness of a particular type of sexual behavior. Moral evaluations form no part of this book.

Another self-imposed limitation relates to the extent of theoretical interpretation in which we permitted ourselves to indulge. For example, much of the material presented in this book has implications for psychoanalytic and psychiatric theory. We have avoided the temptation to dwell at any length upon these implications because we feel that this is a task much more safely attempted by the psychiatrically trained specialist.

In this connection it should also be noted that we have virtually ignored a vast amount of available information relevant to sexual symbolism in different cultures. The literature on the societies with which we deal abounds in myths, magical formulas, dream interpretations, and the like which clearly relate to sex. The significance of this information to an ultimate understanding of human sexual behavior is unquestionably great. But the difficulties of assessing this significance are numerous. To interpret the sexual symbolism appearing in dreams among members of our own society is hard enough. When one attempts to extend such an analysis to the symbolism reported for a people who live in a different culture, speak a different language, and operate on the basis of a different value system, problems become too complex for either of us to solve.

Many unavoidable limitations have been forced upon us by the nature and extent of the evidence. It is, in the first place, disappointingly incomplete. In many cases it is impossible to find answers to simple but fundamental questions of fact. The reasons for this seem to be of two types. Some of the information which we hoped to obtain is lacking because of difficulties of observation. For example, it is almost impossible to observe the behavior of some wild animals in their native habitats. And of course it is equally difficult to observe directly sexual behavior in human societies which insist upon extreme privacy in matters pertaining to sex.

A second type of reason for lacunae in the evidence depends upon the fact that investigators have failed to make certain observations, although they could have done so quite easily. In their study of human societies, for example, anthropologists could readily list and analyze the physical characteristics of the men and women who were most eagerly sought after as sexual partners. Yet in many instances this information is omitted from otherwise admirable ethnographic accounts. And, to take a quite different example, students of animal behavior consistently fail to report such easily obtainable information as the extent of sexual activities in the lactating female.

A major gap in our information on human beings is the almost complete lack of any sort of experimental data. This is understandable. Few people like to be the subjects of experimentation, least of all in matters that pertain to sex. We feel that the scarcity of experimental data greatly increases the importance of the cross-cultural approach employed in this book. The varied cultures which characterize different societies provide, as it were, natural experiments. If one wishes to learn the effects of socially approved premarital sexual freedom upon marital fidelity he cannot set up an experiment in our own society to find the answer, but he can compare the behavior of people in cultures that permit some sexual liberty before marriage and in those that do not. To be sure, the variety of experiences in different societies has not come about as a result of the planned direction and careful control which characterize experimental procedures. But these natural "social experiments" do give us some perspective on human sexual behavior which is not at present available within the framework of any single society.

IMPLICATIONS

This book has certain practical implications for future research in the study of human and animal sexual behavior. One important point is that investigators of human sexual behavior can learn much from their co-workers in the field of animal research. If the anthropologist is familiar with the problems and observations which occupy the investigator of primate behavior he will be better equipped to make parallel investigations in his own field research. Conversely, research concerning animal behavior will be broadened and its significance increased if the investigator has before him a picture of the interests and problems of the anthropologist.

The theoretical contributions of this book will of course be discussed in detail in the following chapters. They arise primarily from the broad background which it provides for the fuller understanding of sexual behavior. An appreciation of the patterns of sexual behavior which primates share with other mammals provides a sound basis for the analysis of human sexuality. For example, the fact that there is a universal tendency among mammals to indulge in sexual play in childhood, long before fertility is achieved, sheds new light upon the behavior of youngsters in our own and other societies that restrict the sexual activities of children.

Another type of insight derives from a knowledge of the evolutionary changes which have occurred in the biological basis for sexual behavior. Thus, appreciation of the fact that the lower mammals are more dependent upon "sex hormones" than are the primates adds considerably to our understanding of human sexual activities. Accompanying this relative lessening of hormonal control is an increase in the importance of the role of the cerebral cortex in the direction and control of sexual behavior. This finding in turn relates to our conclusion that learning and experience are significantly more powerful in controlling the behavior of primates than that of the lower mammals. Particularly in the case of man, the role of learning is paramount. Moreover, human beings learn much of what they know, not by solitary experimentation but by being taught and by observing the behavior of other members of their society. Consequently, the nature of the society in which a people live clearly plays a significant part in shaping the patterns of human sexual behavior.

The fact that many societies vary markedly in their attitudes, beliefs, and morals helps to explain many of the intercultural differences in observed patterns of human sexual behavior. Such differences are best interpreted in terms of the ways in which the various societies channelize the sexual activities of their members. At the same time the observation that there are many similarities in respect to sexual behavior among the members of all human societies provides a framework of cultural universals which arise as a consequence of man's mammalian heritage and of certain learning experiences that are commonly involved in the social lives of all human beings.

Finally, through a combination of the perspectives outlined above, a frame of reference is provided within which the sexual behavior of any individual person can be analyzed. As a representative of one mammalian species each person shares with other members of this class a basic pattern of sexual behavior. As a representative of the primates each person reflects the evolutionary changes which have occurred in the biological factors influencing sexual behavior. As a human being and thus a member of some society each person lives under the conditions laid down by a universal culture pattern as well as by the specific social structure and traditional rules of behavior that characterize his particular group. Along with other members of his society each person finds certain opportunities and restrictions provided by his culture which tend to mold his sexual behavior into a particular pattern. Given this frame of reference, then, the specific behavior patterns exhibited by an individual can be analyzed in terms of his own particular biological heredity and life experiences.

Chapter II

The Nature of Coitus

THIS chapter presents factual information concerning the nature of heterosexual intercourse. We deal here with the coital act as it is performed by mature males and females in different societies and by animals of different species. Forms of copulatory behavior vary from species to species and from one human society to another. But at the same time certain basic similarities that emerge from these comparisons give an essential unity to intercourse as it is practiced in all societies and throughout the scale of mammals.

THE MOST PREVALENT FORM OF SEXUAL ACTIVITY

Two generalizations that can be made concerning heterosexual coitus are that it is the prevalent form of sexual behavior for the majority of adults in all human societies of which we have any knowledge, and that it is rarely if ever the only type of sexual activity indulged in. Every human being grows up in a community of adults whose notions of right and wrong exert a profound influence upon his behavior, and all known cultures are strongly biased in favor of copulation between males and females as contrasted with alternative avenues of sexual expression. This point of view is biologically adaptive because it favors perpetuation of the species and of the social group. Any society with a culture that favored some nonreproductive form of sexual activity would be unlikely to survive for many generations. The predominance of heterosexual intercourse over other kinds of sexual expression probably is due to a combination of two factors, biological and social. It cannot be understood solely in terms of either one alone. Human societies appear to have seized upon and emphasized a natural, physiologically determined inclination toward intercourse between males and females, and to have discouraged and inhibited many other equally natural kinds of behavior. We believe that under purely hypothetical conditions in which any form of social control was lacking, coitus between males and females would prove to be the most frequent type of sexual behavior. At the same time, however, several other types of sexual activity would probably occur more commonly than they do in the majority of existing societies.

In later chapters we will present considerable evidence to support the conclusion that noncoital sexual relations do occur even in those societies that exert the most extreme pressures against such behavior. There are some peoples who do not strictly forbid homosexual relations, autoerotic practices, or animal intercourse; and under such conditions one or the other of these alternative sexual patterns often constitutes an important secondary form of sexual expression for part of the population. Nevertheless, regardless of social approval or disapproval, the significant fact is that noncopulatory patterns always remain secondary for the group as a whole. They never supplant heterosexual intercourse in the life span of any large segment of the group.

Among animals other than man sexual activity is less affected by the attitudes and behavior of other individuals (although it is not to be imagined that such influences are completely lacking) and one might logically expect the zoological evidence to provide some indications concerning the biologically "natural" forms of sexual expression for mammalian organisms. Interestingly enough, the picture does not differ greatly from that presented by the cross-cultural evidence. In all infrahuman animals heterosexual intercourse is the most frequent form of sexual behavior. To be sure, autoerotic and homosexual activities occur among animals, but they are less numerous than coitus despite the absence of cultural restrictions. Apes and monkeys indulge in a variety of sexual habits in addition to copulation. The sexual play of young primates often involves various experimental or indiscriminate contacts which outnumber copulatory interactions between males and females; but with the advent of maturity, heterosexual coitus assumes the dominant position. No alternative form of sexual behavior takes permanent precedence over heterosexual contact in any animal species.

Anatomical Factors Involved in Intercourse

Before proceeding to a more detailed consideration of the coital act, it is necessary to outline briefly the anatomical factors involved, particularly in human beings and other primates. Some knowledge of these matters will assist the reader to assess the behavioral significance of the different positions that may be assumed in intercourse and of many of the activities associated with coitus.

The most sensitive part of the masculine copulatory organ is the glans, certain regions of which contain many nerve endings that may be stimulated by either light touch or heavy pressure. According to Dickinson, there is relatively little variation in the size of the human penis in comparison with the range of variability of other bodily characters such as body height and weight. In the fully erect condition this organ has an average total length of six and one-fourth inches. The glans makes up approximately one-quarter of the length. The average circumference of the tumescent penis at the base is four inches and its diameter is one and five-eighths inches.

There are no measurements of the engorged gorilla phallus, but in two dead specimens this structure was found to have a length of about three-quarters of an inch and a diameter of approximately one inch. This is much smaller than the human penis, but in gross structure the phallus of the gorilla resembles that of the human male more nearly than does that of any other primate. The copulatory organ of the male chimpanzee has no well-developed glans and it possesses a long slender shaft. Yerkes and Elder estimated the length of the erect penis in three adult chimpanzees as ranging from six to eight inches, with a diameter at the base of about three-quarters of an inch. Both gorillas and chimpanzees possess a penile bone. In the latter species the os penis is located in the lower part of the organ and measures approximately three-quarters of an inch in length.

The most prominent parts of the feminine genitalia are the labia majora or outer lips of the vulva. Within these are the labia minora which usually are not visible unless the outer lips are parted. Between the labia minora lie the vaginal opening, the urinary opening, and the clitoris. The clitoris is the feminine counterpart of the masculine penis. It is a miniature phallus, having a shaft, a glans, a prepuce or foreskin, and sometimes showing the capacity for erection. In five of the 100 women examined by Dickinson the clitoris measured two-sixteenths of an inch in height. In 75 cases the dimension was from two-sixteenths to one-fourth of an inch. And in the remaining 20 women the range was from five-sixteenths to one-half of an inch in length. Dickinson states that the size of this organ is not necessarily any index to its sensitivity.

The clitoris is located in front of or, if the woman is lying on her back, above the urinary opening which in turn is above the vaginal opening. In most women the distance from the meatus (external opening of the urinary tract) to the clitoris is less than one and one-half inches. The location varies in different individuals; too high a clitoris is believed by some investigators to reduce the capacity for orgasm during intercourse. Landis measured the meatus-clitoris distance in several hundred women and concluded that individuals in whom this distance is greater than one and one-half inches are less likely to experience orgasm than are women in whom it is less. This opinion is not shared by all investigators. Dickinson, for example, believes that the location of the clitoris is much less important than its susceptibility to displacement. He says that the most reliable index to clitoral function is the extent of its displacement under appropriate conditions of stimulation.

The external sexual parts of the female gorilla resemble those of a woman in having recognizable labia majora and minora, and a fairly prominent clitoris. In the adult chimpanzee the labia majora are rudimentary, although at one stage of fetal development these structures are present in much the same form as they assume in human females. Because the labia majora are vestigial in adult chimpanzees, the labia minora and the clitoris are constantly exposed. The inner lips of the vulva and the clitoris are both large. In these anthropoid apes the vaginal opening is directed more toward the rear than anteriorly as it is in human beings.

Old World monkeys have no labia majora whatsoever and the labia minora and clitoris are prominent. The clitoris of New World monkeys is quite large and tends to increase in size at the time of estrus. A large clitoris is considered by Zuckerman and other authorities to be phylogenetically a primitive character. It is probably of considerable behavioral significance that neither monkeys nor apes possess a hymen. This potential obstruction to successful initial intercourse is found only in our own species.

It is well known that at least the majority of women derive sexual excitement from clitoral stimulation. During intercourse this structure may be stimulated in several ways, but the most common sources of excitation involve rhythmic pressures exerted upon the clitoris as it is seized between the pubic bones of the man and woman, and the displacements induced in it by rubbing against the upper surface of the male organ. It is obvious that the amount and intensity of stimulation that occur depend in part upon the positions assumed during copulation.

POSITIONS ASSUMED FOR COITUS

As far as the masculine climax is concerned, the most important single source of genital stimulation involves activation of sensory receptors in the glans penis. Individual differences exist, of course, but for most human males the sensations derived from gentle friction exerted upon the glans as it rubs against the moist vaginal walls are basic to the occurrence of ejaculation and orgasm. The bodily adjustments that give rise to these sensations involve merely insertion of the phallus followed by piston-like thrusts within the vagina. Any position that permits intromission and movement is favorable for climax.

In women, on the contrary, the sensory basis for satisfaction in intercourse is much less obvious. There is considerable evidence to support the belief that distention of the vaginal walls resulting from penile insertion is an important factor. Although the sensory supply to the interior vagina is scant, some women describe distinct sensations referable to the anterior wall. There is some question as to whether clitoral stimulation is usually necessary for complete climax. Certainly this is not the case for every human female. Nevertheless, as noted above, there is no doubt that for a large proportion of women the clitoris serves as one important locus of sexual stimulation. This being the case, it is worth while to examine the kinds and degrees of clitoral stimulation that are likely to occur when different positions are adopted during sexual intercourse.

Possibilities for Clitoral Stimulation. The pubic bone, or symphysis, is located directly above the base of the penis in men and beneath the fatty mound of tissue that lies above the vulva in women. When a man and woman lie or sit in a face-to-face position with their bodies pressed tightly together, the pubic bones of the pair are more or less in opposition. In most women the clitoris is situated slightly below or to the rear of the symphysis. But during the act of intercourse in the positions mentioned there is a very high probability that the clitoris will be subjected to rhythmic pressures as the fatty tissue above it is alternately compressed and released.

In addition, if the man moves backward and forward while executing copulatory thrusts, the upper surface of the penis is likely to rub against the clitoris, displacing it first in one direction and then in another. As the woman lies beneath the man, appropriate movements on her part can increase the amount of friction exerted upon her clitoris. Even greater control over clitoral stimulation is possible when the woman lies upon her partner or kneels over his body. Under such conditions the intensity of pressure and the magnitude of the displacements are or can be made maximal.

When intercourse is practiced in any position other than some variant of the face-to-face relationship, the possibilities for stimulation of the clitoris are greatly reduced. Particularly is this true of those positions in which the woman's back is toward the man and he achieves intromission from the rear. Here the pubic bones of the male and female are widely separated and the clitoris is subjected to no pressure whatsoever. Furthermore, since the clitoris lies above the vagina, it will not, under such circumstances, come into contact with the male organ.

There are, to be sure, a few variants of the rear entry method that do provide for clitoral pressure and friction. One of these occurs when the man lies on his back and the woman sits above him with her face toward his feet. In this instance the woman, leaning forward and moving back and forth, can cause the clitoris to rub heavily against the underside of the penis. The masculine organ is forced flat against the male's abdomen and thus offers some resistance to the pressure of the feminine sexual parts.

With few exceptions, however, face-to-face copulation undoubtedly affords the greatest opportunity for the woman to derive stimulation of the clitoris. Now, if such stimulation is satisfying and desirable, it might be expected that this type of coital position would be preferred by most people in most societies. It does not follow, of course, that a demonstrated preference for this sort of copulation, if it exists, is to be explained solely in terms of the kinds of stimulation it makes possible. Nevertheless, an examination of the cross-cultural evidence on this subject is worth while.

Preferred Positions in Human Intercourse. In our own society the most common coital position is one in which the woman lies upon her back while the man lies above and facing her. Kinsey, Pomeroy, and Martin estimate that 70 per cent of American couples have never experimented with any other method. When any alternative is tried, the most popular position is that in which the man lies on his back and the woman sits or lies above him in a face-to-face position. Kinsey and his collaborators found that their subjects considered this position the one most likely to produce orgasm in the woman; as noted earlier, it is one that affords the greatest opportunity for clitoral excitation. Still other positions such as lying side by side, standing face to face and various forms of rear entry are, of course, known in this society. But they are practiced sparingly and by relatively few couples.

Coitus in which the woman lies upon her back with the man above and facing her is the usual pattern in many societies other than our own.[1] In some of these societies[2] the man squats or kneels before the supine woman and draws her toward him so that her legs straddle his thighs. As the act proceeds the man may pull the woman up so that they embrace one another in a semierect squatting or kneeling position. It is interesting that this particular variation is predominantly an Oceanic pattern. The anatomical relationship in such a position is such as to result in vigorous clitoral stimulation.

Lying side by side, face to face, is the preferred position among the Goajiro, Kwakiutl, and Masai. Intercourse in the sitting position, the woman squatting over the man, is the dominant pattern only on Palau and Yap. An alternate form of this occurs among the Pukapukans, in which the man folds his legs under him and the woman faces him with her legs on his thighs. Coitus with the man entering the woman from the rear does not occur as the usual practice in any of the societies in our sample, and this may well be due in part to the fact that stimulation of the clitoris is minimal when this position is employed.

Although one position for coitus is preferred and dominant, in most of these societies other postures are used under certain circumstances. The variant with the woman squatting upon the man is a secondary position for a number of peoples,[3] and it is significant that they describe this method of copulation as the one which brings

---

[1] Alorese, Aranda, Azande, Balinese, Barama, Chagga, Chenchu, Colorado, Crow, Hopi, Ifugao, Kaingang, Kurtatchi, Kusaians, Lepcha, Lesu, Marshallese, Penobscot, Ponapeans, Pukapukans, Ramkokamekra, Rucuyen, Rwala, Siriono, Tikopia, Trobrianders, Trukese, Wogeo.

[2] Balinese, Chenchu, Kurtatchi, Kusaians, Lepcha, Lesu, Siriono, Trobrianders, Trukese.

[3] Crow, Hopi, Murngin, Ponapeans, Pukapukans, Trobrianders, Trukese, Wogeo.

the greatest satisfaction to the woman. Quite a few people[4] have intercourse in the side-by-side position either when being discreet or when the woman is pregnant. Usually intercourse occurs face-to-face, but occasionally in some of these societies intercourse may take place while lying side by side, the man entering the woman from the rear. In some societies[5] coitus occasionally occurs with the man standing behind the woman while she bends over or rests on her hands and knees. This method is apparently confined to brief and sudden encounters in the woods. On Truk for quick copulation a standing position is used in which the woman is said to "rest her foot on the man's shoulder."

It is a stereotype of our society that during copulation the male is active and the female plays a relatively passive role. Any woman who takes too active a part in coitus may be accused or feel guilty of displaying a masculine trait, and the man who is relatively passive during the sex act is likely to be considered somewhat feminine. The extent to which these matters are culturally conditioned is made clear by data on other societies. Several peoples in addition to ourselves consider the appropriate sexual role for the female to be a passive one, the male being supposed to be active and aggressive. The Chiricahua, for example, feel not only that a woman should not be forward, but she must not even display any emotion during intercourse. The Colorado Indian woman always plays a passive role during coitus. And among the Kaingang and the Lepcha women take no initiative in sexual activity, but submissively respond to the man's desires. However, in other societies such as the Hopi, Trukese, and Trobrianders passivity is not demanded of the woman, and under these conditions she is far from relaxed and suppliant. Among these peoples, both partners are equally aggressive and vigorous; an inactive woman is considered apathetic and undesirable as a sex partner.

Coital Positions in Other Primates. The copulatory position of adult apes and monkeys of all species is essentially the same and it differs markedly from those preferred in any human society. The basic pattern consists of the female's turning her back to the male and bending sharply forward at the hips while elevating her hinder

[4] Alorese, Azande, Crow, Goajiro, Kurtatchi, Kwakiutl, Lepcha, Masai, Murngin, Ramkokamekra, Trobrianders, Trukese.
[5] Crow, Dobuans, Hopi, Kurtatchi, Kwoma, Lepcha, Marshallese, Wogeo.

parts, thus exposing the genitalia. The male stands behind the female, either in a semierect posture or bending forward over her back, and the penis is inserted in the vagina from the rear. Because the vaginal opening is placed more posteriorly than in the human female, rear entry is the easiest and simplest approach.

Before describing in detail the coital techniques of different primate species it is necessary to mention the few exceptions to the foregoing generalizations concerning the prevalence of rear entry. The male howler monkey of Central and South America normally copulates from the rear and in a standing position, but on a single occasion Carpenter observed a highly receptive female seated across a male's legs with her back to him. In this case the male apparently was sexually fatigued and the female unusually aggressive. There is no proof that intromission was effected.

Montane has described an individualistic method of copulation which was devised by one adult male chimpanzee: ". . . He sits on the floor, his legs extended and together, and pounds on the floor with the backs of his hands. . . . the female . . . goes to the male . . . turns her back (to him), seats herself upon his thighs with her legs separated and at the same time leans toward [his] feet,—prostrated so to speak,—and in the attitude of a Mohammedan at prayers." (Quoted in Bingham, 1928, p. 29.) During coitus the female remained motionless and all activity was shown by the male. It will be noted that this posture involved rear entry and it should be added that the same male was often observed to mate in more normal chimpanzee fashion, mounting the stooping female from the rear.

To add another exception to the general rule of rear entry copulation for subhuman primates it is necessary to mention face-to-face coitus in captive orangutans. Mr. Frederick A. Ulmer, Jr., Curator of Mammals at the Philadelphia Zoological Gardens, has kindly given us permission to quote his own description of such behavior.

I have seen them in coitus with the female in either the supine or prone position. Actually the supine position seems to be the preferred one, for the female often presents to the male by lying on her back, grasping her hind feet with her hands, and pulling them forward over her abdomen to expose the genital opening. Recently Guarina had her seventh baby and has been separated from Guas. As a replacement for her, we substituted their daughter Ivy, who likewise presents by the method described above. She will also grasp the bars in a corner of the cage and hang head downward with her buttocks projecting upward and outward in presentation.

Another position in coitus occurs when Ivy attempts to elude Guas' amorous advances and climbs the cage bars. Guas reaches up with his enormous arms and gently but firmly pulls her down to him so that they are in a sitting position with her back to his abdomen.

According to Ulmer, the same animals copulate at other times in what we have described as the normal or usual anthropoid position employing rear entry. It is impossible to determine how general or infrequent the face-to-face position may be for orangutans since there are no records of mating under natural conditions. It is worth noting, however, that at least some pairs are capable of copulating in a position similar to that employed by many human beings.

In view of the possibility that some apes may learn to copulate in a fashion that differs from the usual pattern for their species it is important to discover in so far as possible how such personal idiosyncrasies might arise. Bingham studied the sexual play of immature male and female chimpanzees when the little animals were three to four years old. This life stage is appropriately labeled "childhood" because in this species adolescence begins during the seventh or eighth year or even later. The first instance in which ventral (face-to-face) coital adjustments were noted occurred just after a male and female had been climbing about on a vertical wire grill. The male had an erection and the female took the masculine organ in her hand and manipulated it for several minutes. Presently the pair descended to the floor.

As they descended, he continued, with considerable interruption [by other chimpanzees], to keep an arm about her. His erection remained pronounced. . . . After considerable shifting on the floor, during which each sat upright, they pushed close together in ventral position and embraced by putting both arms about the body of each other. [These sitting embraces were repeatedly interrupted by other young apes in the room, but the pair renewed contact each time.] . . . Once more they put their arms about each other with bellies mutually pushed close together. Wendy continued to hitch forward, her knees clasping closely at Billy's sides, until her hips were so far advanced that she actually leaned over backwards. She clung to Billy more and more for support as she continued to force her hips forward. . . . Billy was thus drawn forward as Wendy leaned backward . . . they went over in a lying embrace. . . . During the entire adjustment, Billy maintained the same front to front position, and as she rolled on her back he shifted also until he was lying directly on her. Wendy seemed to do most of the squirming that brought about this adjustment. She then raised her feet from the floor until her legs tended to encircle his back in an embrace about his flanks. She thus exposed the ano-genital region, while her pelvis curled upward and forward appropriately for coition. . . . His feet remained flat on the floor. His knees were bent, and his upper legs embraced her pelvis, hips, and thighs. In this position he made relatively slow, forward curling movements of the pelvis which brought his penis against her body. (Bingham, 1928, pp. 83-84.)

The similarity between the coital posture assumed by these young apes and the position described earlier as an Oceanic pattern is striking. Intromission was not achieved in the relationship described in this quotation; but on later occasions when the same posture was employed, Bingham noted that copulatory thrusts increased in vigor and believed that the penis was at least partially inserted. As the result of considerable experimentation and growing experience the immature animals are said to have become more and more adept at ventral copulation. Females frequently took the initiative, as in the incident described above, but young males began to behave more and more aggressively, often pushing the female into the recumbent position and lying down upon her. Interspersed with the ventral contacts there often occurred dorsoventral copulations in which the female crouched or stooped and the male approached from the rear.

As the apes studied by Bingham grew older, the frequency of ventral copulatory contacts appears to have decreased. At any rate some of these same animals have been observed to mate many times during adulthood and in each instance the customary chimpanzee position has been employed. The possibility remains, however, that as the result of early experimentation and learning a given pair of individuals might form the habit of copulating in the face-to-face position. It should be added that this apparently has not actually occurred, and according to some authorities the posterior placement of the chimpanzee's vagina renders regular intromission from the anterior approach highly unlikely.

The foregoing evidence deals, as has been indicated, with what appear to be exceptional modes of coitus as far as subhuman primates are concerned. It is probably much more important that the vast majority of matings for all apes and monkeys involve rear entry by the male. The female chimpanzee who is sexually receptive crouches low upon the ground, with limbs flexed and with her exposed genitalia directed toward the male. In response to this "sexual presentation" the male rises on his hind legs and bends over the stooping female with his hands on her shoulders or sides, or touching the floor. He presses his abdomen against the female's hind quarters and forces the penis into the vagina. Pelvic thrusts follow and, if the female remains motionless long enough, ejaculation takes place within the vagina.

The gibbon is one species of ape that spends most of its time in the trees, and coitus appears to be an exclusively arboreal affair. Male and female approach one another and embrace momentarily. Then the female bends sharply forward, elevating her hind quarters. The male investigates the feminine genitalia and proceeds to copulate. Insertion is achieved from the rear while the male partly stands and partly swings from a higher branch. During intercourse, the female may reach backward with one arm and hold the male close to her.

The copulation of monkeys invariably involves rear entry. Zuckerman, who has observed hundreds of matings among adult baboons, states that copulation from the rear is the only method employed. The following description of a typical mating between a male and female macaque is taken from the report of G. V. Hamilton, one of the pioneer workers in this field.

She observed his approach from her shelf, and as he ascended toward her, smacking his lips, she, too, smacked her lips. As soon as the male clambered upon the shelf the female assumed the sexual position, viz.; Hind legs fully extended to an almost vertical position; forelegs sharply flexed; tail erect; body inclined forward and downward from the hips; head sufficiently extended and rotated to enable the female to direct her gaze upward and backward. The male grasped the female at the angles formed by the juncture of hips and body with a hand on either side, and in mounting her, he clasped her legs just above the knees with his feet. He leaned forward and downward during copulation, smacking his lips violently. The female seemed to invite contact with his mouth, for she persistently thrust her smacking lips towards the male, until he leaned still further downward and touched her lips with his own. Shortly before copulation ceased, the male uttered a succession of shrill little cries, and greatly increased the vigor of his copulatory movements. (Hamilton, 1914, pp. 300-301.)

E. J. Kempf has published descriptions of macaque copulation that agree substantially with those of Hamilton. H. C. Bingham, however, states, "A striking difference in the subjects [monkeys] observed by me from those observed by Hamilton and Kempf is the absence of 'kissing' during intromission." All three of these investigators studied captive monkeys. C. R. Carpenter's accounts of sexual behavior in the macaque are based upon observation of free-living animals. The behavior appears to be the same as it is in caged monkeys. Carpenter notes the "squeal" of the male when ejaculation is imminent—a response described by Hamilton as "shrill cries." In addition, Carpenter writes, "the female turns her head to the right and upwards as if trying to put her mouth to that of the male." Probably the type of "kissing" recorded by Hamilton may occur upon occasion if the male is sufficiently responsive, but it may not be a common accompaniment of coitus.

In closing this discussion of the coital positions employed by sub-human primates we wish to suggest one rather interesting line of thought. An apparent difference between males and females of many primate species lies in the occurrence, or at least in the ease with which the human observer can identify the occurrence, of sexual climax. The behavior of most male apes and monkeys clearly reveals the exact moment at which ejaculation and orgasm take place. As the event approaches, copulatory movements become increasingly vigorous and rapid. Climax usually is accompanied by a mild convulsive spasm and is followed by a period of relative unresponsiveness to sexual stimuli.

In the behavior of the female there is no such reliable indicator of orgasm. To be sure, Carpenter has described a spasmodic arm reflex on the part of the sexually excited female macaque, and this may increase in intensity during coitus. But in the main the receptive female primate appears to indulge in one coital act after another, giving little or no indication that she experiences any explosive, temporarily exhausting, release of built-up excitement.

It was pointed out above that for many human females the occurrence of orgasm seems to be greatly facilitated by the stimulation of the clitoris during intercourse. We noted that female apes and monkeys have a well-developed clitoris, and evidence to be summarized in Chapter III strongly suggests that stimulation of this organ has a sexually exciting effect upon females of several sub-human primate species. But clitoral stimulation is minimal or lacking when coitus is accomplished by rear entry, the habitual position employed by all primates except our own species. These items of information lead to the interesting but highly speculative hypothesis that orgasm is rare or absent in female apes and monkeys because their method of mating deprives them of one very important source of erotic stimulation. Orgasm does occur in males of the same species because, just as in human beings, they receive the necessary type of penile stimulation. As long as intromission is effected, the bodily positions assumed for intercourse are relatively unimportant to the male.

Coital Positions in the Lower Mammals. So far as is known, all subprimate terrestrial mammals copulate in essentially similar fashion. The female flattens or arches her back concavely, thus exposing and elevating her external genitals. The male mounts from the rear, resting his forefeet upon the female or clasping them about her sides. In most cases penetration is achieved by the male's pelvic movements, although in some species, including bats and elephants, the penis is independently mobile and appears to enter the vagina without the occurrence of pelvic movement. Females of most species stand quietly during coitus, although in some cases the female sways to and fro or pushes actively against the male's copulatory thrusts.

There are many anecdotal accounts of ventral copulation in various lower mammalian species, but these appear to involve either inaccurate observations or erroneous deduction. Actually, the anatomical position of the vagina in these animals precludes penetration from the anterior approach. Many animals engage in mock fighting or wrestling just prior to mating. In such instances one partner occasionally falls or lies temporarily upon the other in a prone, face-to-face position, and the casual observer may be excused for confusing this behavior with actual coitus. In his *Historia Animalium* Aristotle stated that the hedgehog copulates belly to belly; this myth, which is also applied to porcupines, has survived to the present day. The persistence with which amateur and even professional naturalists describe ventral copulation in animals whose backs are covered with spines or quills is amusing. It reflects, one must conclude, the limitations of human imagination or the ubiquitousness of anthropocentrism in human thought. At any rate, careful laboratory studies show beyond question that these animals mate in much the same manner as other quadrupeds (Shadle, Smelzer, and Metz, 1946). The female porcupine's tail is curled upward and forward and the male enters from the rear, resting his forefeet on the undersurface of her tail.

DURATION OF INTERCOURSE

Human Societies. The most important single factor controlling
the duration of the coital relationship between a man and woman
is the speed with which the male achieves orgasm. For a large
majority of men this is followed fairly promptly by loss of the erection and at least temporary impotence. Dickinson questioned 362
married American couples concerning the length of time from the
beginning intromission to the occurrence of the husband's ejaculation. The replies are summarized in Table 1. (Dickinson and Beam,
1931, p. 59.) Eleven husbands (3 per cent) were reported to be able
to copulate as long as they wished and to reach orgasm at any time.

TABLE 1

Estimates of Average Time from Beginning of Intromission to
Husband's Ejaculation in 362 Married Couples

TIME	PER CENT OF TOTAL CASES
Less than 5 minutes	40
5-10 minutes	34
15-20 minutes	17
30 minutes or more	9

According to Kinsey, Pomeroy, and Martin, most males in our
society normally reach a single orgasm and do not attempt to continue intercourse beyond that point. Approximately three-quarters
of the American men who attempt to delay orgasm are not able to
do so for more than two minutes, and for a "not inconsiderable
number" the climax is reached within a minute or less. These figures
and those of Dickinson exclude any time that is devoted to precopulatory stimulation (see Chapter III).

Information concerning the length of time ordinarily consumed
in coitus in societies other than our own is meager. The Hopi Indians
prolong the precoital period and attempt to delay orgasm as long
as possible after intromission. Foreplay and intromission consume a
considerable amount of time in the sexual behavior of the Panopeans
and Trobrianders. Marquesan men learn to control the muscles
involved in emission so that they can maintain an erection for a
considerable period and ejaculate at will. The Balinese believe that
too hasty intercourse results in a deformed child. In contrast, Ifugao
men, particularly if young and inexperienced, rarely indulge in

much precoital activity and achieve orgasm almost immediately after intromission.

In our own and many other societies it is generally believed that the majority of women need more protracted stimulation than men if they are to experience sexual climax. Many American women who rarely or never have orgasms during intercourse blame their failure upon the fact that the husband ejaculates quickly, loses the erection, and terminates intromission after too short a time. Dr. Katharine Davis compiled statistics dealing with a large number of college-educated American wives who at some time during their marriage had found sexual relations distasteful. Excluding those individuals who cited ill health as the reason for their negative reaction, the most common explanations in order of their frequency were physical repulsion ("vulgar, disgusting, nasty, revolting, brutish"), lack of physical desire, intercourse too frequent or too painful, failure to achieve orgasm, intercourse too exhausting (meaning, perhaps, climax too difficult to achieve), fear of pregnancy, and psychic inhibition ("whole life built on thought that it was wrong").

Landis and his collaborators interviewed 44 "normal" married women and found that 3 in this group had never experienced orgasm. An additional 10 women rarely or never reached orgasm, but "carried on sexual relationships because they felt this was expected of them." Fourteen others regarded sexual relations as pleasant, sometimes had orgasm but most of the time did not. And only 17 of the 44 wives described sexual relationships as satisfying experiences usually accompanied by orgasm. Dickinson and Beam gathered evidence on this point from several hundred married women. The results are incorporated in Table 2. (Dickinson and Beam, 1931, p. 63.)

Attitudes of people in other cultures toward this problem are of interest. But references to orgasm in the female in societies other than our own are relatively rare. This probably reflects a failure on the part of investigators to obtain such information, since no statements could be found which indicate that the women of any society fail to experience a sexual climax. Crow Indian women expect and desire orgasm and are reported to achieve one more often while sitting on top of the man, whereas when the man lies on top he usually ejaculates before the woman reaches a climax. On Truk and on many of the other Caroline Islands the woman is expected to have an orgasm as the consequence of coitus. If a Trukese man reaches climax before his partner, she may laugh at him and request him to try again. It is stated that the woman is relatively unlikely to attain a climax unless she adopts the superior position, squatting upon the man. In this coital position women achieve an orgasm which is said to be accompanied or preceded by urination on their part.

In this connection it may be significant that a relation between

TABLE 2

Wife's Experience with Orgasm as Reported in 442 Cases

WIFE'S REPLY	PER CENT OF TOTAL GROUP
Orgasm during coitus	
"Yes" (frequency not stated)	40
Usually	2
Sometimes	15
Rarely	10
Formerly, not now	4
Following coitus by masturbation involving clitoral stimulation	3
Not experienced with husband	26

sexual arousal and micturition is apparent in the behavior of some infrahuman mammals. Female howler monkeys invite coition by assuming the mating position before a male. Sometimes this reaction is accompanied by urination on the female's part and this occurrence appears to increase her stimulative value for the male. Female chimpanzees often display erection of the clitoris while they are urinating, and the sight of a urinating female serves, upon occasion, to evoke copulatory attempts by the male. Reliable indicators of sexual receptivity in the mare include frequent urination and movements of the clitoris. The ewe that is in heat reacts to the ram's investigations of her vulva by urinating, and he responds by intensifying his sexual approaches. Females of many wild species such as the marten urinate very often while they are in season. The excretions are deposited on stones or other objects and they serve, presumably, to attract any passing male. It is known that male dogs are attracted by the urine of the bitch in heat

In a few species micturition forms a regular element of the male's precoital pattern. The sexually excited male porcupine rears upon his hind legs and walks toward the female. If she is in an advanced stage of heat, the female also assumes an upright posture and faces the male. As they stand facing each other a few inches apart, the male begins to discharge urine in frequent, short spurts which in less than a minute may thoroughly wet the female from nose to tail. Shadle, Smelzer, and Metz, who described this behavior, were impressed by the force under which urine was expelled. They found that the stream may be projected as far as six and one-half feet from the spot where the male stands.

Duration of Coitus in Other Species. The sexual intercourse of most anthropoid apes is a very brief affair. Yerkes presents the results of 95 timed matings involving three adult male chimpanzees and six different females. The data are summarized in Table 3.

TABLE 3

Duration of Intromission and Number of Thrusts in the Copulatory Acts of 3 Male Chimpanzees Mated with 6 Different Females

Male	Seconds of Intromission		Number of Thrusts	
	Average for All Females	Range of Averages for Different Females	Average for All Females	Range of Averages for Different Females
Bokar	9.8	8.0-15.3	19.7	13.3-29.0
Jack	6.7	6.0- 7.1	12.4	10.7-15.0
Pan	8.0	6.5- 9.7	19.1	13.5-25.0

(Yerkes, 1939, p. 103.) It will be seen that the most protracted intromissions barely exceeded 15 seconds and the average duration of insertion was less than 10 seconds. The average number of copulatory thrusts exhibited by the different males ranged from 12.4 to 19.7. Although these are even shorter than the usual human copulations, they are, from the biological point of view, highly adaptive. It is physically impossible for a male ape to force the female to continue genital contact if she vigorously attempts to escape. Therefore, once intromission is achieved, a male who ejaculates quickly has a better chance to fertilize his mate before she terminates the union.

For some lower primates the pattern of coitus is such that the male's ejaculation may be delayed for some time. The copulatory behavior of macaques and some other monkeys consists of a series of mounts in which intromission is achieved, several pelvic thrusts are made by the male, and contact is terminated within a few seconds. The number of such acts that occur before ejaculation is

36

achieved varies from as few as 3 to more than 100, depending upon the current excitability of the male. Intervals between sexual mounts range from 1 to 20 minutes and reflect the strength of desire in both partners. During the mount in which ejaculation occurs there are more thrusts and insertion is maintained for a longer time, though rarely for more than 30 seconds.

Figure 4, based upon data published by Carpenter (1942), shows the normal structure of a copulatory series in free-living macaques. Time is represented along the base line in intervals of 30 seconds, and each vertical bar represents a single mount by the male. The height of the bar indicates the number of copulatory thrusts executed during that mount. The total time from the first mount to discontinuation of sexual activity was 40 minutes. The male mounted

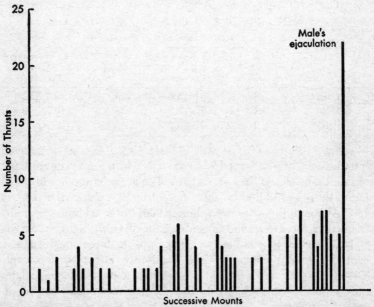

FIG. 4. Pattern of a "copulatory sequence" in the macaque monkey. Time is represented along the base line and the number of copulatory thrusts on the vertical axis. The male mounts, delivers several thrusts and then dismounts. A series of such responses precedes the occurrence of the male's ejaculation, which is accompanied by a large number of thrusts and temporarily terminates his sexual responsiveness. (Based upon data reported by Carpenter, 1942.)

37 times and showed a total of 161 thrusts, a frequency which Carpenter describes as above average but not extreme. Subtracting the sum of all intercopulatory intervals from the total time consumed shows that the time for all intromissions amounted to only 6.9 minutes. This is an average of less than 11 seconds per intromission, and if it were possible to exclude the final mount, in which insertion was relatively prolonged, the average intromission time would be further reduced. Examination of the figure shows that as orgasm was about to occur the intervals between copulations were shortened and the number of thrusts tended to increase. Ejaculation was accompanied by 22 very rapid and vigorous thrusts.

Carpenter also observed coitus in free-living howler monkeys and reports that for this species the average duration of intromission is 22 seconds. Males show from 8 to 28 thrusts (average 17) during a single intromission. The time interval between successive intromissions varies from 6 to 45 minutes. The published account contains no mention of the occurrence of ejaculation.

Among subprimate mammals most of the larger quadrupeds copulate very quickly. Bulls, stallions, and rams usually ejaculate shortly after penetrating the female. The male elephant achieves intromission, ejaculates, and withdraws within a period of 30 seconds. For the boar, only a few minutes elapse after intromission before ejaculation takes place.

Male lions and house cats maintain genital insertion only for 5 to 10 seconds, but the coital pattern of some other carnivores such as dogs, foxes, and wolves is relatively protracted because of the occurrence of genital "locking." Only after intromission has been achieved does the penis become fully tumescent, and erection includes swelling of a large bulb situated at the base of the masculine organ. This engorged structure completely fills the vulva of the female. Until detumescence occurs, separation is likely to be painful and injurious and the pair remains tied from four or five minutes to more than an hour.

The longest mammalian matings occur in the mink and sable. There is no locking, but once intromission has been achieved it is maintained for very long periods and several ejaculations appear to take place, with rest periods occurring in between. Timed matings of the sable have lasted for as long as 8 hours from the moment of original insertion until withdrawal.

SUMMARY

In this chapter we have noted that heterosexual coitus is the prevalent form of sexual activity for adults of all human societies and of all mammalian species. All mammals except man customarily copulate in a rear entry position; exceptions are rare. By contrast, there is no known human society in which rear entry is the usual pattern of intercourse. The universality of some variant of face-to-face intercourse in human beings reflects in part the anatomical fact that the vaginal opening of the human female is farther forward than it is in other mammals. Face-to-face copulation affords a better opportunity for intense stimulation of the woman's sexual organs, particularly the clitoris, than does rear entry, and is therefore more apt to bring her to orgasm. In this connection it is of importance to note that positive indication of a sexual climax has not been detected in females of any infrahuman species.[6] This emphasizes the possibility that stimulation of the clitoris plays a highly significant role in female sexuality, since intercourse with rear entry gives no opportunity for direct clitoral stimulation.

The duration of the copulatory act depends predominantly upon the speed with which the male achieves orgasm after intromission. Most men in American society appear to reach a climax in a matter of minutes; it is unusual for a man to maintain an erection for as long as half an hour once intromission has been effected. Very little information relative to the duration of intercourse is available for members of other human societies. However, we do know that among some peoples, the Marquesans for instance, men learn to prolong intromission for a considerable period of time by delaying ejaculation. Intercourse among the anthropoid apes is a very brief affair, averaging less than 10 and barely exceeding 15 seconds. In some lower animals intromission is achieved several times in succession before the male ejaculates. Most of the larger quadrupedal mammals copulate very quickly, the elephant for example ejaculat-

---

[6] One possible exception to this generalization is seen in the postcoital behavior of the domestic cat. As soon as the male dismounts after copulation many females display a series of "after reactions," which include violent twisting and rolling about in semiconvulsive fashion. The vulva is licked repeatedly and the female usually refuses to accept the male until the "after reactions" are completed. Whether this behavior actually reflects a climax of excitement comparable to the masculine orgasm it is impossible to decide. It does, however, clearly depend upon genital stimulation, for "after reactions" are lacking in females whose genitalia have been rendered insensitive bv transection of the afferent nerves.

ing within half a minute after penetration. The longest mammalian matings occur in the mink and sable, some of which have been timed at eight hours from the moment of original insertion until withdrawal.

This chapter has been concerned with the basic patterns of coital behavior and has ignored certain activities which precede copulation as well as others that accompany the sex act proper. The next chapter deals with a description of the types of sexual stimulation which are characteristically associated with coitus in various different human societies and in animals of different species.

Chapter III

Types of Sexual Stimulation

IN MANY human societies and in numerous animal species certain forms of bodily stimulation are so intimately associated with heterosexual intercourse that they may be considered integral parts of the total coital pattern. They range from primitive responses like biting and scratching to such highly socialized patterns as mutual grooming of the partner's body. The nature of these various activities and their distribution among human societies and infrahuman animals form the subject matter of this chapter.

DIFFERENCES IN VARIETY AND DURATION OF SEXUAL FOREPLAY

In our society the characteristic amount and variety of sexual foreplay vary from couple to couple and from one set of external circumstances to another. In interviews with 526 American husbands and wives, Dickinson found that some men and more women consider any sexual behavior except actual coitus to be a perversion and to be distasteful. The only genital stimulation these people regard as normal and moral is that derived from intromission. But Dickinson's group also included other couples whose intercourse was occasionally preceded by oral stimulation of the partner's genitals. And there were ten married pairs whose copulation was habitually prefaced by stimulation of the penis by the woman's mouth (fellatio), of the woman's clitoris by the man's lips and tongue (cunnilinctus), or by the simultaneous performance of both of these activities (soixante-neuf).

Kinsey, Pomeroy, and Martin have reported a relationship between the educational level of American husbands and the amount and kinds of sexual techniques involved in their marital relations. Manual and oral stimulation of the masculine or feminine genitalia and of the woman's breasts occurs more frequently in marriages where the man, at least, has attended college. These forms of behavior tend to appear much less often if the husband has had less than nine years of formal schooling. The greatest discrepancy between these two educational-level groups is in attitudes toward oral stimulation of the feminine breasts and genitals.

According to Landis and his co-workers, poor sexual adjustment in marriage tends to be positively correlated with unwillingness to engage in any sexual activity save coitus. This generalization must be viewed with caution. The population to which it refers was highly selected. In any event one should guard against a converse application of the interpretation. Unwillingness to experiment with extracoital techniques does not necessarily reflect inadequate sexual adjustment. Landis feels that in his subjects the primary cause of the maladjustment was an unfavorable attitude toward intercourse which, in turn, was generalized to include a negative attitude toward any sort of intimacy.

There are several societies in our sample in which couples indulge in a minimum of sexual foreplay. The general pattern among the Lepcha, for example, is for a man and woman to proceed immediately to copulation, although the man may fondle the woman's breasts just prior to intromission. Similarly, the Kwoma engage in very few preliminaries and almost no embracing occurs before coitus. On Ponape, by way of contrast, precopulatory stimulation is quite extended, and hours may be consumed in working up to actual intercourse. The Trobrianders also devote a considerable period to precoital activities. In none of these societies, however, does any type of foreplay serve as a substitute for intercourse. The closest approach to such a situation is found in those societies where pseudocoitus is customary under certain circumstances, as for example in extramarital or premarital relations.

In animals other than man the duration of precopulatory play varies markedly from one species to another. In some cases several days of mutual stimulation may be necessary before males and females become capable of fertile mating. This is particularly true of certain birds, but it is generally believed that females of several

mammalian species come into heat earlier than they would otherwise if they are kept with males who provide frequent stimulation
in the form of sexual courtship. For this reason ewes are often
penned with a "teaser" ram in order to bring them into estrus as
quickly as possible. The fox vixen may become sexually receptive
after one or two hours of "heckling" by the male. And commercial
fox breeders affirm that vixens which are allowed to run with the
dog fox become receptive earlier in the year than do isolated females.

Proximity to an individual of the opposite sex may produce
noticeable bodily changes in receptive female chimpanzees. The
following quotation is from Yerkes and Elder's study of this species.
"Our experiments have provided evidence that placement of a male
with or in a cage adjoining that of a female who for some time has
been isolated may induce genital swelling.[1] Even a few minutes
may suffice for noticeable change, and within an hour or two the
swelling may be from one-fourth to one-half maximal size." (Yerkes
and Elder, 1936, p. 14.)

Some animals will not copulate until after a preliminary period
of association during which mutual stimulation usually occurs. Even
visual familiarity may be important. Shadle, Smelzer, and Metz
found that male porcupines did not respond to receptive females
unless they had lived in adjacent cages for several days. One male
inhabited a cage between those of two females, and when they
came into season he copulated with both individuals. Other males
whose cages were kept at a distance from the females failed to
cover them in mating tests. It is of interest to note that no comparable selectivity is shown by females of this species. When she
is fully receptive, the female porcupine will accept any sexually
aggressive male.

The duration and variability of the sexual play that precedes
coitus are not the same for all individuals within a given species.
Some male dogs regularly indulge in prolonged courtship of the
female before attempting to mate, whereas other individuals mount
the bitch immediately. Male apes are reported to develop highly
individualistic sexual patterns. Some appear to enjoy a protracted
period of gentle play followed by intercourse, whereas others habitually rush to the female and attempt to copulate without indulging
in any preparatory measures.

[1] The periodic swelling of the skin surrounding the genitals is described in detail in
Chapter XI. It is controlled by ovarian hormones, coincides with the period of fertility,
and can usually be taken as an indication of readiness to mate.

FUNCTIONAL SIGNIFICANCE

Before proceeding to a detailed discussion of the various types of stimulation that precede the occurrence of sexual intercourse it will be profitable to consider briefly the functional significance of all such behavior. This is most obvious in the performance of lower animals. Much of the preparatory activity of human beings takes place on the symbolic level and may consist primarily of language responses. Animals that lack such highly developed intellectual capacities are proportionately more dependent upon direct bodily stimulation for the arousal and maintenance of erotic excitement.

If fertile mating between a male and female animal is to occur, two requirements must be met. Both individuals must attain the requisite degree of emotional excitement, and their actions must be temporally and spatially synchronized. Precoital courtship and play serve these ends. In most cases the activities involved are mutual and reciprocal. One partner stimulates the other and is then stimulated in return. The result of this continuing interaction is an increasing level of excitement in both individuals. The pair remains in close proximity for longer and longer periods of time and attention is focused more and more intensively upon the genitals. Eventually mounting activity appears. At first it may be perfunctory or incomplete, but with each successive attempt both male and female show increasing excitement and vigor and eventually the serial pattern culminates in a completed copulation.

The outstanding difference between the sexual foreplay of human beings and that of other animals lies in the intentional or consciously directed nature of such behavior in our own species. The male dog who repeatedly licks the enlarged vulva of the estrous bitch does so because that bodily region is covered with secretions that attract his attention and compel him to investigate. His activities are not carried out with the knowledge that they will increase his partner's receptivity. They do so, nevertheless, and at the same time they exert a parallel effect upon his own level of excitement.

The human male or female can in many instances determine the sexual availability of a potential partner without engaging in any physical contact. Language often suffices. In some cases, however, an individual who is reluctant to copulate may become eager to do so after a period of preliminary stimulation has aroused his or her desire. And even when both parties are anxious for intercourse, the degree of arousal resulting from purely symbolic stimulation usually can be enhanced by the direct activation of critical sensory receptors. In essence the foreplay of human lovers serves the same functions as the courtship of lower animals. It increases the level of precoital excitement and prepares both partners for a fuller degree of participation in the coital relationship which is to follow.

In the following pages we shall discuss the various kinds of stimulation by which these goals are achieved in different human societies and different animal species.

GROOMING AND DELOUSING

Grooming and delousing are widespread forms of behavior that frequently lead to sexual relations. Among the Siriono, Dusun, Plains Cree, and Trobrianders, men and women often groom one another for some time before beginning to copulate. Holmberg has described such behavior on the part of Siriono couples: "Lovers also spend hours in grooming one another—extracting lice from their hair or wood ticks from their bodies, and eating them; removing worms and spines from their skin; gluing feathers into their hair; and covering their faces with uruku . . . paint. This behavior often leads up to a sexual bout, especially when conditions for intercourse are favorable." (Holmberg, 1946, p. 182.)

Grooming behavior is not limited to the human species, but instead is characteristic of most if not all kinds of apes and monkeys. In fact, it appears to be a basic pattern for primates. Carpenter's observations of rhesus monkeys indicate that in this species grooming is properly classified as a form of secondary sexual activity, apparently affording erotic stimulation and often intimately associated with coitus. The initial arousal of sexual interest is sometimes traceable to grooming of one partner by the other. Grooming typically occurs during the intervals between the successive intromissions which precede ejaculation (see Chapter II), and either male or female may utilize this kind of behavior to reawaken or intensify the partner's sexual responsiveness.

The sexual connotations of grooming are also apparent in the behavior of baboons. Zuckerman has shown that any female who is in estrus temporarily assumes the position of "chief wife" (see Chapter VI). Upon this female the male overlord concentrates his sexual activities, and she always grooms him more frequently than do other females who are not eager for copulation. Yerkes states that the less acceptable a male chimpanzee is to a female, the more eager he is to groom her. This is interpreted as a method of currying favor. For the female ape, in contrast, grooming sometimes appears to be a way of diverting the male from primary sexual behavior, although it may also constitute a means of continuing contact with him after copulation has occurred.

Yerkes sees the grooming activities of primates as possessing more than merely sexual significance.

"Flea-picking"[2] in monkey, "grooming" in chimpanzee, and "delousing" in man, are functionally identical patterns of response. They are complex expressions of the visual acuity and manual skill which are peculiar to the primates. They may well be basically natural or inherited and only secondarily cultural; but in either event they are biologically important as conditioning comfort and health, highly socialized, strongly motivated, and accompanied by marked positive effects. The student of phylogenesis, with special interest in the evolution of human social service, may well suspect that cultural developments and transformations of the variously named forms of grooming in infra-human primates have given origin to the tonsorial artistry, nursing, surgery, and other related social services of man. (Yerkes, 1933, p. 12.)

The broader implications of this type of interpersonal behavior are of general interest, but for the purposes of this discussion it is sufficient to remember that the human beings and other primates who indulge in grooming responses at any time are likely to do so in connection with primary sexual activity.

Lower mammals that have no prehensile forelimbs are incapable of the elaborate grooming responses typical of primates, but even in such animals various forms of general bodily stimulation customarily precede coitus. The following description of mating in the meadow mouse offers one illustration of the type of interaction which may occur: "The female started licking the male about the ears and down one side of the neck. The male remained perfectly motionless, then raised his left front leg and slowly rolled over to the right onto his back, with the female continually licking about the region of the neck, and apparently helping to push him onto his

[2] As Yerkes points out, this term is poorly chosen because in actuality no parasites need be present in order that grooming shall occur. "Skin dressing" would be a much more appropriate phrase.

back with exaggerated vertical movements of her head. . . . [Finally the male got up and] this procedure ended in copulation." (Hatfield, 1935, cited in Reed, 1946, pp. 188-189.)

Although most male minks and sables initiate the mating relationship with extreme vigor and aggression, this is not always the case. In some instances the male is gentle, licking and nuzzling the female for long periods of time until she becomes active. Eventually both animals begin to play and roll about on the ground, gradually exciting each other to the point of copulation.

STIMULATION OF THE FEMALE BREASTS

In American Society. One type of precoital activity, extremely common among human beings but rare in other species, is stimulation of the feminine breast by the male. Manual or oral manipulation of the woman's breasts by the man frequently precedes or accompanies intercourse in the United States. Most of the married couples interviewed by Dickinson said that the husband habitually caressed his wife's breasts manually before having coital relations. Sucking or titillating the nipples with the tongue was less common but not infrequent. A few wives reported that the stimulus provided by nipple suction was sufficient to produce a climax without any genital contact, and orgasms resulting from nursing an infant were occasionally described.

According to Kinsey and his co-workers, the frequency with which married couples indulge in this particular form of sexual play depends in part upon the educational level of the husband. Manual manipulation of the breasts was the rule in 96.3 per cent of all college graduates interviewed by these workers, but in only 78.6 per cent of men who had not gone to high school. The proportion of the college-educated group reporting frequent mouth contact with the breasts was 81.6 per cent, whereas only 33.2 per cent of the males from lower educational levels employed this technique.

In Other Societies. Stimulation of the woman's breasts by her partner is a common precursor or accompaniment of intercourse in some societies other than our own,[3] and for some peoples this form of activity constitutes the only form of precoital sex play. Gorer's description of the Lepcha is a case in point: "Courtship barely exists among the Lepchas and no preliminary stimulation in the way of

[3] Alorese, Apache, Dusun, Gilyak, Haitians, Ifugao, Lakher, Lepcha, Mailu, Marquesans, Sema, Trobrianders, Trukese.

kisses or embraces are employed, though a man may fondle a woman's breasts immediately before copulation; fondling of the breasts in public is considered slightly shameless but rather funny; it is the equivalent to a direct invitation." (Gorer, 1938, p. 329.)

There are a few societies in which breast stimulation is reported to be completely lacking.[4] Among these peoples, however, a copulating couple may lock in a tight embrace as climax approaches and the woman's breasts are then pressed close to the man's chest. Failure to practice breast stimulation does not necessarily imply the existence of specific prohibitions against the custom. The Siriono, for example, do not engage in this form of precoital activity although they appear to be almost completely uninhibited in sexual matters.

For most of the societies in which the man customarily stimulates the woman's breasts, the behavior is confined to manual manipulation, but in some cases the mouth is used. Oral stimulation of the breasts invariably accompanies coitus among the Trukese, and they report that suction on the nipple facilitates the attainment of the woman's climax. Among some of the natives of the east central Carolines the man rubs his nose against the woman's breasts while making love.

Relatively few societies insist upon concealment of the woman's breasts by clothing, and in the great majority of cases the bare bosom is not inconsistent with ideals of feminine modesty. Furthermore, even for those peoples who prefer that women keep the breasts covered, the custom is usually restricted to the period between puberty and the birth of the woman's first child. An outstanding exception is represented by the Ainu, whose women always conceal their breasts; when forced to nurse a child in the presence of men they do so covertly, exposing only enough of the breast to let the child take the nipple.

The habit of concealing the breasts during everyday life bears no direct relation to the importance assigned to breast stimulation as a form of erotic play. The Apache, Trukese, and Dusun cover the female breast and this area is stimulated during sexual activities. With these few exceptions, however, in all the societies which use this form of caress the upper part of the woman's body is usually bare. Among the societies that do not employ breast contact as a source of arousal, only the Kwakiutl cover the breasts, and the Lesu

[4] Kurtatchi, Kwakiutl, Kwoma, Lesu, Manus, Siriono.

often do so; none of the other peoples in the same category ever conceal the bosom.

For many of the societies which include prolonged breast stimulation as part of the standardized coital pattern, caressing the breast has become an erotic symbol. For example, Du Bois writes of the Alorese:

> Intercourse is solicited of young women by touching their breasts. A common euphemism for intercourse is "to pull a girl's breasts," since it is supposed that no woman can avoid being aroused by such a caress or would be able to resist a man who approached her in this fashion. Opportunities for this sort of approach are offered at dances and in the roughhousing that occurs among young people when they are away from their elders. In describing this situation one young man said, "Our hands move about at random and touch a girl's breast. That makes her spirit fly away and she has to sleep with a man." (Du Bois, 1944, p. 98.)

Squeezing a woman's breasts has definite sexual connotations among the Dusun; and a characteristic approach in seduction, as practiced by Ifugao men who are experienced in love-making, is to touch the woman's nipples. The Lakher have greatly elaborated this type of symbolism, and many of their love songs include the refrain, "Oh my love, let me fondle your breasts." In practice the Lakher lover puts his arms around the girl, caresses her breast, and, if no objection is forthcoming, proceeds to make further advances. In those societies in which breast stimulation is absent from the coital pattern there are no symbolic invitations involving this part of the body.

In Other Species. Special investigation or stimulation of the female's mammary regions by the adult male occurs rarely if at all in the sexual behavior of subhuman animals. This may be related to the fact that in most mammals these structures are well developed only while the female is suckling young and not when she is desirous of intercourse. Some primate females possess recognizable breasts, but they do not seem to attract the attention of the male and are rarely accorded more than passing attention. The only suggestion that nipple stimulation may have a sexual effect is found in Carpenter's description of some female monkeys that were observed during estrus to pull and suck at their own nipples. He believes that this behavior may validly be interpreted as autoerotic because the nipple is an erogenous zone in the human female. According to Carpenter, nipple sucking by female monkeys may be comparable to the masturbation shown by the males of the same species.

KISSING AND MOUTHING

In Human Beings. Kissing is a ubiquitous item in the sex play that accompanies heterosexual intercourse in our own society. Many couples supplement simple lip contact with the "deep kiss," which involves thrusting the tongue of one partner into the mouth of the other. Some of the husbands and wives in the group studied by Dickinson reported that mouthing or nibbling the neck or ear of the spouse provided an extra source of erotic arousal. Kinsey and his collaborators found that the deep kiss was practiced frequently by 77.3 per cent of the well-educated American males they interviewed, but that it was much less common (40.5 per cent) among husbands whose schooling had not extended beyond the eighth grade.

Some form of kissing accompanies sexual intercourse in many other societies.[5] For the Kwakiutl, Trobrianders, Alorese, and Trukese kissing consists of sucking the lips and tongue of the partner, permitting saliva to flow from one mouth to the other. Among the Lapps, kissing is performed with the mouth and nose at the same time.[6] By contrast there are some peoples among whom kissing is unknown.[7] When the Thonga first saw Europeans kissing they laughed, expressing this sentiment: "Look at them—they eat each other's saliva and dirt." The Siriono never kiss, although they have no regulation against such behavior. The Tinguian, instead of kissing, place the lips near the partner's face and suddenly inhale. Concerning the Balinese, Covarrubias writes as follows: "The love technique of the Balinese is natural and simple; kissing, as we understand it, as a self-sufficient act, is unknown and the caress that substitutes for our mode of kissing consists in bringing the faces close enough to catch each other's perfume and feel the warmth of the skin, with slight movements of the head . . . in the manner which has been wrongly called by Europeans 'rubbing noses.'" (Covarrubias, 1937, p. 144.)

In Other Species. Behavior bearing some resemblance to kissing is seen in a few subhuman animals. Bingham noted that when immature male and female chimpanzees are playing they occasionally press their mouths together, and this reaction is often followed by mutual investigation of the sexual organs. While prepuberal apes are en-

[5] Alorese, Chiricahua, Cree, Crow, Gros Ventre, Hopi, Huichol, Keraki, Kwakiutl, Lapps, Tarahumara, Trobrianders, Trukese.

[6] Struthers (cited in Reed, 1946) reports that male and female Canadian porcupines rub noses frequently when the female is receptive and copulation imminent.

[7] Balinese, Chamorro, Chewa, Lepcha, Manus, Siriono, Thonga, Tinguian.

gaged in copulatory play, the male may take the edge of the female's ear between his teeth or draw the hair of her shoulder through them. On some occasions the males studied by Bingham took the female's protruding lower lip between their own lips and sucked strongly during copulation.

Descriptions of coitus as performed by macaque monkeys were presented in Chapter II, and it will be recalled that some observers have reported the occurrence of lip contact between the male and female during intercourse. Other authorities state that although the female often turns her head backward and upward to gaze at her partner, the male rarely leans downward and puts his mouth upon that of his mate. The receptive female howler monkey solicits coitus with rhythmic tongue movements, and if a male is slow to respond she may lick his face and hands. The lingual gestures apparently carry definite sexual significance, for even during copulation the female may turn her face to the male and continue them.

Mouth-to-mouth contact is not common among subprimate mammals, although in some cases it does occur, as when for example the male house mouse licks the female's mouth prior to coition. The precopulatory courtship of southern sea lions occurs as the animals sit facing one another, rubbing their necks together. The front and sides of the neck are thus caressed and, according to Hamilton, occasionally one member of a pair rubs its mouth against that of the partner. Although the behavior does not involve mutual oral contact, it is of interest to note Neumann's report that prior to coitus male and female elephants often insert the tip of the trunk into the mouth of the sexual partner.

STIMULATION OF THE PARTNER'S GENITALS

Men. This is a very widespread type of extracoital sexual activity for human beings and all other kinds of mammals. Handling, stroking, and rubbing of the woman's sexual parts was practiced frequently by 89.6 per cent of the college-educated American men interviewed by Kinsey, Pomeroy, and Martin. The same behavior was characteristic of 74.8 per cent of the males at a low educational level. Dickinson describes fifteen wives who were able to have orgasm during coitus only if intromission was supplemented by manual stimulation of the clitoris, and the same authority notes that some women who cannot reach climax in intercourse are regularly brought to orgasm afterward by the husband's manipulation of the clitoris.

Manual stimulation of the feminine genitalia by the male is a common preliminary to coitus in several societies other than our own.[8] Among the Crow, men ordinarily finger the woman's clitoris prior to intercourse, and before copulating with a virgin the man customarily stretches the hymen with his finger. Dahomean men play with a woman's labia before coitus, and young girls attempt to thicken and lengthen the labia in order to increase their sexual attractiveness. In the Marianas it is believed that the woman's pleasure in intercourse is greater if the clitoris is large; hence a girl's lover attempts to increase the size of this organ by rubbing and pulling it.

Fingering the feminine genitalia serves in some societies as a stereotyped erotic advance. The Crow, for example, have a custom of crawling up to the lodges at night, locating the women's beds, thrusting their arms under the tent and trying to stimulate a woman's genitals. If he is successful, a man may by this device persuade the woman to have intercourse with him later on. The Trobrianders believe that if a man can insert in a woman's vagina a finger which has been magically charmed, she will find him irresistible as a lover.

Oral stimulation of the female genitalia prior to coitus is practiced at least occasionally by a considerable number of American husbands, according to Kinsey, Pomeroy, and Martin (45.3 per cent of the well-educated and 4.1 per cent of the poorly educated men). This practice is reported to occur in a few other societies as well,[9] predominantly in Oceania. It is considerably elaborated on Ponape, where the men stimulate the labia with their tongue and teeth. In this same society the clitoris is titillated by the penis which the man holds in his hand before attempting full insertion. After a period of such foreplay the woman urinates and only then does intromission occur. Another custom reported of the Ponapeans is for a man to place a fish in the woman's vulva and then gradually to lick it out prior to coitus. Alorese men occasionally stimulate the woman's genitals orally, although the custom is frowned upon.

Women. American women are slightly less likely to handle the penis than are men to manipulate the feminine sexual parts. How-

[8] Aranda, Aymara, Azande, Chamorro, Crow, Dahomeans, Hopi, Koryak, Ponca, Siriono, Trobrianders.

[9] Alorese, Aranda, Kusaians, Marquesans, Ponapeans, Trukese.

ever, this practice is performed frequently by the wives of 75.3 per cent of the college-educated husbands and 57.1 per cent of the grade-school-trained men whose behavior was analyzed by Kinsey, Pomeroy, and Martin. Application of the woman's mouth to the phallus is much less common in our society, being completely avoided in approximately 58 per cent of the cases and taking place only occasionally in most of the remainder. As stated above, however, there are some American couples who habitually employ fellatio or soixante-neuf before copulating.

Manual stimulation of the male genitals by the woman occurs among the Alorese, Aranda, Crow, Hopi, Siriono, Tikopia, Trobrianders, and Wogeo. On Tikopia a man is forbidden to touch either his own or the woman's genitals, and she often guides his penis into her vagina. A similar custom is practiced by the Wogeo, whose code forbids men to touch the feminine genitalia; women generally fondle the penis and assist their partners to achieve intromission. Oral stimulation of the penis by the female occurs among the Aranda, Ponapeans, Trukese, and Wogeo.

Males of Other Primate Species. Male apes and monkeys often stimulate the female's genitalia in the course of the precopulatory investigations. The following description of behavior displayed by a pair of immature chimpanzees illustrates the kinds of reactions that can occur:

. . . Wendy was turning so that her face was away from Billy and her posterior parts were turned conspicuously towards him. . . . Billy showed interest in the protruding genitalia [and] . . . gradually the manipulations of his free hand became directed more and more [toward them]. . . . He picked at them with his fingers and several times took them in his lips. Shortly after this manipulation began it became apparent that Wendy was sexually stimulated. The clitoris became noticeably erect, and I could detect occasional surges as though she were voluntarily increasing the erection. There were at least a half dozen such propulsions coming at varying intervals, perhaps from one to ten seconds apart. (Bingham, 1928, pp. 98-99.)

The foregoing behavior occurred while the two animals were clinging to a vertical grillwork. After approximately five minutes of such sexual interaction the young apes descended to the floor and went through the motions of copulation. On other occasions it was observed that males not only took the feminine genitalia in their lips, but definitely sucked at them, a procedure to which the female "responded with evident satisfaction." Zuckerman describes a young male orangutan whose cagemate was a female chimpanzee. The male often took the female's external genitals in his mouth and sucked at them for long periods of time.

Genital manipulation frequently accompanies copulation between captive male and female macaque monkeys. Hamilton noted that perfunctory attempts at coitus are often followed by inspection of the female's genitals on the part of the male, who uses his mouth and fingers and, presumably, increases the state of excitement in his partner as well as himself. Copulations occurring immediately after such stimulation are particularly vigorous. Of considerable interest is Hamilton's statement that the amount of precopulatory stimulation necessary for completed intercourse increases if the period of cohabitation is prolonged. Heterosexual couples that have been caged together for several days rarely mate without protracted preliminary genital manipulation. But if either the male or the female is allowed access to a new mate, coitus tends to occur promptly without any sort of foreplay. Kempf has made essentially the same observation, namely, that when two monkeys have lived together for some time sexual excitement does not occur through stimulation of the distance receptors alone (vision and hearing), but that additional stimulation involving touch, taste, and smell is necessary for full arousal.

The copulation of baboons is often preceded by manual and oral investigation of the female's vulva by the male. A masculine overlord confronted with an estrous female whose sex skin is swollen frequently manipulates the labia and clitoris with his lips and tongue, thus stimulating a sexual response. In most cases this activity is followed immediately by copulation. The clitoris of the spider monkey is greatly elongated and prior to coition the male stimulates this organ manually.

Females of Other Primate Species.   From the scientific literature a reader gains the impression that females of most infrahuman primate species are much less likely to stimulate the male's genitals than is the male to react to the vulva. There is, however, ample indication that the former response can and sometimes does occur.

Female chimpanzees occasionally grasp the erect or semierect penis of a potential sex partner and squeeze or pull it rhythmically. This stimulation sometimes induces the male to attempt copulation. When a male is trying to effect intromission, the female may reach backward and handle the phallus, pulling it toward the vaginal opening. Although some female chimpanzees inspect the male organ with the nose and lips, there are no clear-cut reports of genuine fellatio for this species.

The macaque female occasionally touches or smells the male's penis. Female howler monkeys that are desirous of intercourse solicit the male with characteristic calls and gestures. If a male is not immediately responsive the female may lick his copulatory organ, a procedure which usually evokes increased excitement and leads to attempts at coition.

Males and Females of Subprimate Species.   Subprimate mammals often engage in precoital activities that result in stimulation of the genitalia of one or both partners. Species that possess prehensile appendages characteristically employ them in such behavior. The female elephant, for example, may manipulate the male's penis with her trunk; and males touch the tip of the trunk to the female's vulva and anus, often displaying a partial erection at the same time. The female's response is to extrude the vulva and to push her hind quarters toward the male.

Males of many quadrupedal species, and females of some, use their mouth parts or forefeet to stimulate the sexual organs of a potential mate. It is not implied that the behavior of the active partner is "intentional" in the sense that it is calculated to produce a response in the individual who is acted upon. The odoriferous genital region has a high attractive value which calls for intensive investigation; and this investigation, consisting of touching, pulling, nibbling, nosing, or biting, may constitute a source of erotic stimulation for the animal that is being investigated. That the significance is genuinely sexual is shown in many cases by the nature of the observable response.

Male skunks, for example, respond to the female that is in heat by scratching her swollen vulva with the claws of one forefoot. The resulting excitation of touch receptors in her genitalia causes the female to adopt the bodily posture necessary for coition. The sight of the female in this pose then stimulates the male to mount her. Male dogs lick the congested genitalia of the bitch in heat, providing her with intense stimulation which produces a prompt rise in her blood pressure and causes her to move the hind quarters convulsively from side to side. Very often a female that is in heat, but not immediately receptive, eventually permits the male to mate after a prolonged period of such genital stimulation. The estrous bitch often sniffs at and licks the male's reproductive organs, and in some instances this evokes a partial erection and encourages a sluggish male to become more aggressive in his mating responses.

Before copulation, the male African lion frequently licks the female's vulva and this stimulus often affects her in such a way that she promptly attempts to force herself underneath the male in the mating position. Female and male rodents practice genital stimulation of the partner. For example, female rice rats and kangaroo rats that are sexually receptive follow the male about, nosing and licking the scrotum and penis until he is sufficiently aroused to assume the sexual initiative.

Male and female farm animals of several species engage in protracted genital investigation and stimulation before attempting to copulate. The ram, for example, investigates the ewe's vulva repeatedly until she is ready to stand and accept service. In general the results of this type of behavior are twofold. The individual carrying on the investigation derives olfactory and gustatory stimulation which increases his or her state of arousal; and at the same time, tactile stimulation of the sex organs tends to increase sexual excitement in the animal that is being investigated.

Painful Stimulation

Human Societies. Among some members of our own society intense sexual arousal may lead a man or woman to pinch, scratch, bite, or otherwise bring pain to the partner. And for at least some individuals a mildly painful stimulus can, under certain conditions, result in increased sexual excitement. There are a few men and women in whom the tendency to inflict pain or to seek painful stimulation is so strongly developed that their habitual patterns of sexual behavior are widely deviant from those of the general population. Within the framework of our culture such elaborations are considered by most people to be abnormal and perverted. They represent, however, magnifications of tendencies which are more generally present in many, if not all, human beings.

In some societies other than our own there occurs a surprising amount of behavior that involves the infliction of pain in association with coital activities.

Holmberg's description of love-making as practiced by the Siriono leaves no doubt concerning its aggressive components:

Although love is not idealized in any romantic way by the Siriono, a certain amount of affection does exist between the sexes. This is clearly reflected in the behavior that takes place around the hammock. Couples frequently indulge in such horseplay as scratching and pinching each other on the neck and chest, poking fingers in each others' eyes, and even in making passes at each others' sexual organs. (Holmberg, 1946, p. 182.)

The sexual act itself . . . is a violent and rapid affair. There are few if any preliminaries. Kissing is unknown, but oral stimulation is not absent; lovers have the habit of biting one another on the neck and chest during the sex act. Moreover, as the emotional intensity of coitus heightens to orgasm, lovers scratch each other on the neck, chest, and forehead, so that they often emerge wounded from the fray. Although people are proud of them, these love-scars sometimes cause trouble (in cases of extramarital intercourse), because they are visible evidence of the infidelity of a husband or wife. (Holmberg, 1946, p. 184.)

Choroti women spit in their lover's face during coitus, and the Apinaye woman may bite off bits of her partner's eyebrows, noisily spitting them to one side. Ponapean men usually tug at the woman's eyebrows, occasionally yanking out tufts of hair. Trukese women customarily poke a finger into the man's ear when they are highly aroused. Women of many societies bite the skin of the partner's neck, shoulder, or chest when sexual excitement is at its height. The red marks left on the skin may be a subject of jest; the Toda greet any person who is so marked with the quip, "You have been bitten by a tiger."

The following description of the coital practices of Trobriand Islanders is taken from Malinowski:

A mat is usually spread on the boards or on the earth, and, when they are sure of not being observed, skirt and pubic leaf are removed. They may at first sit or lie side by side, caressing each other, their hands roaming over the surface of the skin. Sometimes they will lie close together, their arms and legs enlaced. In such a position they may talk for a long time, confessing their love with endearing phrases, or teasing each other. . . . So near to each other, they will rub noses. But though there is a good deal of nose-rubbing, cheek is also rubbed against cheek, and mouth against mouth. Gradually the caress becomes more passionate, and then the mouth is predominantly active; the tongue is sucked, and tongue is rubbed against tongue; they suck each other's lower lips, and the lips will be bitten till blood comes; the saliva is allowed to flow from mouth to mouth. The teeth are used freely, to bite the cheek, to snap the nose and chin. Or the lovers plunge their hands into the thick mop of each other's hair and tease it or even tear it. (Malinowski, 1929, pp. 332-333.)

On the whole, I think that in the rough usage of passion the woman is the more active. I have seen far larger scratches and marks on men than on women; and only women may actually lacerate their lovers. . . . The scratching is carried even into the passionate phases of intercourse. It is a great jest in the Trobriands to look at the back of a man or a girl for the hallmarks of success in amorous life. (Malinowski, 1929, p. 334.)

Malinowski's conjecture that in Trobriand culture the woman is likely to be more violently aggressive than is her lover deserves particular attention because it is not in complete accord with evidence pertaining to other species which will be discussed subsequently. Questions concerning a possible difference between the sexes in tendencies toward the infliction or acceptance of painful stimulation during erotic arousal have certain theoretical implications. From the evolutionary point of view it would be valuable to know whether the Trobriand man's relative restraint and the woman's relative aggression reflect a biological difference or whether this behavior is predominantly the consequence of cultural conditioning.

Other Species. The fact that many human societies implicitly recognize a connection between sexual excitement and the infliction of pain upon one's partner is particularly interesting in view of the fact that fighting and mating are so closely related in a large number of vertebrate species. It is not an exaggeration to state that physically aggressive behavior forms an integral part of the sexual pattern for vertebrates of every major phyletic class, although it does not follow that this is true of every species. A few examples illustrating the behavior of representative species from several major classes will demonstrate the evolutionary spread of this phenomenon.

The male jewel fish that is ready to breed assumes possession of a small territory and defends it against all comers. If a second male intrudes, the resident promptly launches an attack, nipping at the newcomer and striking him with the tail. The attacked individual usually flees without retaliating. If he does not do so, the battle continues until one male or the other is vanquished. When a fertile female enters the territory of a breeding male she is accorded the same treatment as a member of his own sex. The female, however, neither retreats nor attempts to return the attack. The male's aggressive reactions become less and less intense until finally he shifts from the fighting pattern to the one of courtship, and spawning then occurs.

Male fence lizards and American chameleons are also territorial creatures who react against any intruder that encroaches upon their private preserves. The initial reaction is one of "bluffing," in the course of which the challenger executes a stereotyped pattern of bodily movements that may cause the intruder to withdraw before the battle can be joined. Sometimes, however, a wandering male will accept the challenge; and when this occurs the two lizards rush together, each attempting to seize the other's neck or head in his jaws. The encounters are far from mild and serious injury may be inflicted.

When a receptive female approaches a territory-holding male he responds with the "bluffing" reaction. She continues to advance, but does not give any sign of readiness to fight. Her passive actions cause the male to change from an attack posture to one of preparation for copulation. He moves toward the female and, as she passes him, her neck is flexed laterally in a signal of sexual readiness. The male responds by seizing the female's neck in his jaws. Then, wrapping his tail around hers, he attempts to force his sexual organ into her genital opening. If she does not spontaneously adopt the coital position, the male releases the female's neck and nips sharply at her flanks—a performance that induces her to assume a more receptive posture.

Many mammals bite their partners in connection with sexual intercourse. Male shrews, bats, and rabbits mount the female from the rear, and during copulation they seize the skin or fur of her neck or back in their teeth. Male fishers bite the female's shoulders while copulating. Biting and holding the female's neck skin is an indispensable element in the coital patterns of some species. Just before he mounts the receptive female, the male domestic cat grips the loose skin of her neck in his teeth. This behavior has these three results: (1) It produces an erection in the male. (2) It causes the female to lower her fore quarters and assume the mating position. (3) Since the grip is maintained after the male has mounted, it assists him in making the bodily adjustments essential to achieving intromission. Cats that fail to grip and hold the female's neck rarely succeed in completing the copulatory act. Male lions bite the neck of the lioness after mounting her. The neck grip may be relaxed after intromission has been achieved, but if the female shifts her position the male may bite her again.

A certain degree of aggression characterizes the sexual approach of many domestic animals. Male sheep, for example, bite the ewe's wool and skin during precoital play. The stallion often nips at the withers of the receptive mare and frequently bites her neck while he is mounted in the position for service. The courtship and mating of some fur-bearing cetaceans involves a good deal of painful stimulation. During copulation, the male elephant seal holds the female by biting her neck. Female sea lions grip the male's neck in their teeth before copulating.

The normal mating pattern of the mink, marten, and sable begins when the male springs upon the female and seizes the skin of her neck in his mouth. His long, sharp canine teeth pass completely through her pelt and his jaws may remain locked for most of the copulatory period. The female's initial response consists of a vigorous attempt to escape, and for a considerable length of time the two animals engage in what appears to be a violent battle. The male is much larger than his mate and when her struggles grow less marked he gets into a position that will permit intromission. Eventually insertion is accomplished, and, as indicated in Chapter II, it may be maintained for several hours. Only after he has penetrated the female is the male likely to relax his grip on her neck, and if she tries to terminate the mating before he is ready to do so, he promptly secures another neck-hold and prevents her from escaping.

This description might appear to justify application of the term "rape" to copulation in these animals, and the comparison has been proposed many times. In actuality, however, males of these species can never copulate with a female who is truly nonreceptive. The female must respond appropriately to the male, and nonestrous females fail to do so. The violent behavior has an important biological function. Many males refuse to mate with females that are too compliant and therefore fail to offer the normal amount of resistance. If coition takes place without the usual conflict, conception rarely occurs. Stimuli which the female receives during the vigorous fighting are necessary for the release of ripe eggs from her ovaries; and therefore, in the absence of this stimulation, intercourse is sterile. The functional importance of the aggressive encounter is further emphasized by the fact that some minks have been known to ovulate *without copulating*, after they have engaged in a protracted struggle with an active male.

As far as an evolutionary interpretation of human behavior is concerned, the most significant evidence pertaining to painful stimulation and its effects upon sexual performance is found in descriptions of behavior among infrahuman primates. There are some species for which violent aggression constitutes a normal element in the sexual pattern. Two examples are the macaque and the baboon. It may be of considerable importance that in both of these kinds of monkeys males are invariably dominant over females in nonsexual as well as sexual situations. Of added significance is the fact that it is the male who injures the female, almost never the reverse.

According to Zuckerman, adult male baboons continuously dominate the females that form their harems. When food is made available the male assumes possession of every morsel, even if he cannot consume it; nonestrous females must get along on the scraps he leaves or must snatch their nourishment at moments when the overlord is not watching. When she is not in estrus, a female tends to remain somewhat apart from her overlord, but if he desires intercourse she accommodates him. Females that are in estrus stay close to the ruling male and may be permitted to eat some small part of his food. When a male is sexually aroused by a female he often chases her about, alternately biting and copulating with her. The female makes no attempt to defend herself. She neither retaliates nor refuses to mate with the overlord who has just injured her.

Pronounced aggression often accompanies sexual behavior in the macaque monkey. Here again, as in the case of baboons, males are always socially dominant over females, although there are no sexual partnerships except when the female is in heat (see Chapter VI). Hamilton found that nearly all of his mature males chased and bit their mates "in apparent preparation for copulation." And in several cases, females that were not initially receptive became eager for intercourse after having been pursued and injured by a male. This change in the female's attitude appeared to reflect genuine sexual arousal rather than self-protective submission to the masculine partner. The latter type of response is seen in females who are not in estrus, but at that time the behavior is perfunctory and lacks the

usual signs of excitement such as vigorous lip smacking and convulsive arm movements.

Carpenter's field studies of free-living macaques show that sexual
aggression is not confined to captive animals. As indicated earlier,
nonreceptive females rarely approach a male closely; but monkeys
that are in estrus repeatedly attempt to establish physical contact
with a masculine consort. As a consequence they are often severely
bitten. The females do not launch a retaliatory attack but persistently
return to the male who has inflicted pain upon them. Eventually the
relationship becomes somewhat more pacific and copulation follows.
By the end of her nine- or ten-day estrous period a macaque female
is likely to be covered with scars and wounds inflicted by a succession
of erstwhile sexual partners.

In contrast to the type of relationship described in the preceding
paragraphs, there are other monkeys whose sexual patterns include
relatively little infliction of bodily injury upon either partner.
Howler and spider monkeys are two cases in point. In both species
males usually tend to be socially dominant over females, but the
divergence is less extreme than in the macaque or baboon. Furthermore, dominance is much less marked during sexual interaction than
it is in the latter two species. The female spider or howler monkey
actively solicits the sexual favors of the male. He may claw and bite
her; and when this happens she retreats and then returns after a
short interval. But the infliction of pain is not an invariable or even
a frequent accompaniment of intercourse.

Female macaques and baboons also assume the initiative in seeking intercourse while they are in estrus; but the nature of the male's
response makes it clear that his initial reactions are highly charged
with an element of aggression. In both of these species, furthermore,
dominant males demand and often receive sexual satisfaction from
females that are not in heat and are not anxious to copulate. The
feminine response in such cases has the appearance of submissive
acquiescence to a potential enemy. Spider and howler females, in
contrast, have not been seen to permit coitus save when they were
physiologically in estrus. They do not employ sex as a social device
to avoid injury by a male.

The situation is even more complicated in the case of chimpanzees.
During copulation males of this species often grip the skin of the
female in their teeth, but the action is rarely violent enough to in-

duce pain. It is clear that by virtue of his superior size and strength, the male ape is capable of winning a fight with the female. It is obvious, also, that some males are quite dominant over some females in nonsexual as well as sexual situations. However, the reverse situation also obtains; certain males may be subordinate to a particular female at all times. In a very general way it appears that when two apes who are strangers to each other meet, it is usually the male who assumes the commanding role. But most pairs that live together for some time tend to become socially adjusted. This adjustment may take the form of permanent dominance by the male, or equalization of social status may finally become the fixed pattern. In either instance, however, it is very likely that the female will temporarily become dominant over her mate during the times that she is in estrus and her sex skin is swollen. If she does not spontaneously assert her dominance at such times, the male may encourage and urge her to do so. This obviously differs greatly from the types of relations seen in monkeys.

If a male chimpanzee is definitely dominant over a given female he may induce her to copulate while she is not physiologically in heat (see Chapter XI). Sometimes this is achieved by persistence and persuasion, and sometimes apparently by threat of punishment. Between partners who are socially well adjusted and of approximately equal dominance, sexual relations tend to be confined to the female's period of estrus. Most of the exceptions that occur take place when the female offers herself sexually to divert the male from appropriating a desired prize such as a bit of food. In such instances it is the female who takes the sexual initiative and her response is hardly interpretable as one of protective submission.

As far as human beings are concerned, we have pointed out that for some societies the infliction of a certain degree of physical pain regularly accompanies erotic arousal. Under such conditions it seems probable that sensations of pain actually heighten the state of sexual excitement. In this connection comparison of men and women with males and females of other species proves informative. As propounded by certain of its adherents, psychoanalytic theory classifies masochistic tendencies as normal and useful components of feminine sexuality. Dr. Helene Deutsch has written as follows concerning this subject:

Woman's entire psychologic preparation for the sexual and reproductive functions is connected with masochistic ideas. In these ideas, coitus is closely associated with the act of defloration, and defloration with rape and a painful penetration of the body. The sexual readiness, the psychologic pleasure-affirming preparation for the sexual act, draws its masochistic components from two sources—one infantile, regressive and dispositional, and the other *real*. For defloration is really painful and involves the destruction of a part of the body. . . . Acceptance of pain associated with pleasure, or of pleasure associated with pain, may result in such a close connection between the two that the sexual pleasure becomes dependent upon pain. Thus feminine sexuality acquires a masochistic character. Actually a certain amount of masochism as psychologic preparation for adjustment to the sexual functions is necessary in woman. . . . (Deutsch, 1945, Vol. II, p. 277.)

Dr. Deutsch does not mention the masculine sex, but it would be difficult to apply the foregoing interpretation to males of our species. Freud and many of his followers appear to believe that the masochistic element plays a much less prominent and basic role in the sexual life of men than in that of women. But if men are to be credited with any masochistic impulses whatsoever, the genesis of such tendencies in the male must be explained in an entirely different fashion.

Furthermore, cross-cultural evidence presented in the present chapter does not support the belief that women react sexually to pain in a different or more intense fashion than do men. Several generalizations can be made concerning employment of painful stimulation as a sexual response in various human societies. The first point is that when such behavior appears as a general cultural pattern, it inevitably is mutual to both partners. If the husband bites his wife during intercourse, she also bites him. If a wife scratches or pinches her mate, the action is reciprocated. Under special circumstances physical force and perhaps pain may on occasion be inflicted upon a woman by a man in an attempt to compel sexual acquiescence. But, save in rare and extreme cases, the behavior does not contribute to the sexual arousal or satisfaction of either partner. Only when the interaction is bilateral does it generally assume the proportions of a genuine sexual stimulus.

In this characteristic of mutuality the infliction of painful stimuli in human sexual patterns differs markedly from its occurrence in most lower animals. For nearly every other species in which comparable behavior appears, infliction of pain is the prerogative of the male, and only the female appears to be sexually aroused by painful stimuli. There are, however, one or two instructive exceptions. The female sea lion bites her mate's neck before, and sometimes during, copulation. Male seals are not attacked by the female, but they do engage in frequent and violent battles with other bulls. And after every such encounter the male displays a wave of sexual excitement that leads to copulation with one or several of the cows in his harem. Male rats that are subjected to an electric shock just before copulating with the female tend, in subsequent tests, to mount her very rapidly and to display unusually violent coital responses.

It might be conjectured that males as well as females of other species are susceptible to increase in sexual arousal through the effects of painful stimulation. The absence of regular behavior patterns involving infliction of injury upon the male by the female may be due to the fact that usually she is smaller and weaker than her partner. Furthermore, the coital position common to infrahuman mammals makes it difficult for the female *in copulo* to assault the male, although she is especially vulnerable if the male wishes to bite her.

A second general point concerning human behavior is that widespread habits of inflicting pain upon the sexual partner appear to be formed in certain societies and not in others. And societies in which intercourse is regularly associated with biting, scratching, or hair pulling prove inevitably to be ones in which children and adolescents are allowed a great deal of sexual freedom. There are, to be sure, some "permissive" societies whose coital techniques involve no painful stimulation. But wherever this kind of stimulation is considered normal and desirable by the group as a whole, the regulations governing the behavior of immature persons are always found to be relatively free and nonrestrictive. Furthermore, if the cultural stereotype of satisfactory intercourse includes a considerable amount of moderately painful interaction, it also represents the woman as an active, vigorous participant in all things sexual—she is accorded equal rights of initiative and is expected to experience orgasm as a result of coitus.

For all animals, including man, sexual excitement is closely related to other forms of intense emotional arousal. Sensations of pain associated with the mating relationship may inhibit sexual reactivity and divert the individual from sexual activities, or the emotional response to pain may summate with the effects of other stimuli to produce an increased sexual fervor. Which effect will be produced depends upon the physiological constitution and previous experience of the individual under consideration.

It seems probable that any man or woman is physiologically capable of positive erotic responses to mild degrees of pain, but this underlying capacity is usually shaped in one direction or the other from early childhood. In societies where the sexual act is thought of as a relationship in which biting or scratching is an essential element, the pain produced by such activities will be seen as a desirable and pleasant contributor to the full response. As has been noted, such societies always provide ample opportunity for males and females to learn, during their early life, the possibility of deriving sexual satisfaction from being bitten or pinched, or from having one's hair pulled. For societies that do not incorporate mutual physical aggression in their concepts of normal heterosexual relations there will be no association of pain with sexual arousal and satisfaction. Members of such societies will learn to expect a painless form of precoital and coital activity. And for them, the occurrence of pain in connection with sexual excitement will tend to have an inhibiting, distractive effect. We should expect, of course, that some couples in such societies will learn through experimentation that mild pain can have a positive sexual value. And there may be some individuals whose life experiences are such that the infliction of pain (or the receipt of it) comes to have a special stimulus value in sexual arousal and satisfaction. But they will be the exceptions to the cultural norm.

SUMMARY

For nearly every human society and for all species of infrahuman animals sexual intercourse usually is preceded and accompanied by certain types of sensory stimulation in addition to those resulting directly from contact between the masculine and feminine genitals. Among societies there is great variability in the amount and kinds of sexual foreplay, some peoples indulging in a minimum of such activity and others characteristically devoting long periods of time to intimate physical preparations for copulation. There are also marked differences within certain societies. A case in point is our own society, in which some couples regularly practice elaborate forms of genital stimulation before engaging in intercourse, whereas others disapprove of and avoid any genital contact save that involved in coitus proper.

The functional significance of sexual foreplay is most apparent in the behavior of lower animals. The physical stimulation derived from this type of activity serves two biologically important purposes. It tends to increase the initial level of excitement, thus raising the probability that coitus will be attempted. It also synchronizes the reactions of the male and female and in this fashion renders it more likely that when copulation is attempted it will be successfully completed. Comparable functions are served by the sexual play that precedes human intercourse. The erotic excitement aroused by symbolic (language) interaction is heightened and intensified by direct physical stimulation, with the result that ensuing coital relations are more likely to be mutually satisfactory and complete.

Perhaps the most widespread form of precopulatory stimulation for both men and animals involves handling or mouthing the sexual organs of the partner. In all species this form of approach is employed much more frequently by males than by females, although it is not absent in the behavior of the latter sex. Another extremely common type of preliminary to intercourse is grooming of the partner's body. This seems to be a basic primate trait, appearing in all monkeys and apes and in many of the societies covered in this book.

Mouth-to-mouth kissing, a very common though definitely not a universal precursor of coitus in human societies, is rarely if ever seen in any other species. Some monkeys occasionally press their lips against those of the sexual partner during the act of intercourse, but it is questionable whether this practice occurs with regularity in any primate species save our own. Even more restricted, as far as the zoological evidence is concerned, is stimulation of the female breast by the male. This behavior seems almost totally absent in all subhuman forms, although it is common among the members of many different human societies.

In view of the data summarized thus far, we are tempted to speculate that breast stimulation and kissing as forms of sexual stimulation are more or less restricted to the human species, whereas preliminary stimulation of the genital organs has a much more ancient phylogenetic origin extending far down into the lower levels of the mammalian scale.

One final type of stimulation associated with sexual excitement involves the infliction of physical pain. The occurrence of such activities is regular and characteristic in many human societies. There are a number of peoples whose stereotype of intense love-making includes scratching, biting, and pulling the hair of the sexual partner. In contrast, there are other societies in which these forms of stimulation appear to be totally lacking. It is our conclusion that for most people high levels of erotic arousal tend to generate moderately assaultive tendencies. And, furthermore, that for the majority of human beings painful stimulation which is not too intense is likely to increase rather than decrease the level of sexual excitement. The inherited capacity to derive satisfaction from this kind of stimulation is greatly modified by learning and experience. Our cross-cultural evidence strongly suggests that societies which incorporate painful stimulation in the approved forms of foreplay also provide ample opportunity for the developing individual to learn the facilitative effects of the resulting sensations.

The evolutionary background for assaultive behavior associated with sexual arousal is clear in some ways but not in others. Male mammals of many species attack and injure the receptive female before or during coitus. The female's response in such cases usually indicates that the pain which she experiences actually increases the level of her arousal. There is, however, one important difference between men and all other animals in this connection. All human societies that encourage the infliction of mild pain in connection with intercourse take the attitude that such behavior should be bilateral or mutual. If the man bites the woman, she is permitted and expected to bite in return. If the girl scratches her lover, he retaliates. This is not true of the lower animals. In their case it is almost always the male who wounds the female, very rarely the reverse.

The kinds of behavior discussed in this chapter do not occur indiscriminately at any time that a male and female may desire to engage in sexual relations. They take place only at certain times, in certain places, and under certain circumscribed conditions. The purpose of the next chapter is to consider the conditions under which sexual relations occur in different human societies and in different animal species.

Chapter IV

Circumstances for Coitus

IN EVERY human society and in all species of animals sexual intercourse occurs under certain types of circumstances, and under others it takes place rarely or not at all. The importance of particular conditions varies from society to society and from one animal species to another. In this chapter we shall examine the circumstances under which coitus does or does not occur in various human societies and subhuman animals.

PLACE OF OCCURRENCE

Human Societies.   In the United States marital intercourse generally takes place in the privacy of the bedroom. Premarital and extramarital relations may occur in a variety of places as a matter of expediency, but in such cases the basic desire for privacy is maintained and even augmented by the need for secrecy. Occasionally intercourse takes place out of doors in the open, but far more often it occurs behind closed doors.

In most other societies couples normally seek seclusion for sexual intercourse. There are, however, a few exceptions. In the summertime some Formosan natives copulate out of doors and in public, provided there are no children around. Yapese couples, though generally alone when they engage in intercourse, copulate almost anywhere out of doors and do not appear to mind the presence of other individuals.

In some societies[1] as in our own, the dwelling affords the seclusion required for marital intercourse. Among most of these peoples, however, men and women intent upon unlawful liaisons steal off into the bush or forest rather than risk discovery indoors. In Lesu, for example, married people copulate indoors and lovers in the bush. The Pukapukans and the Trukese exhibit a similar discrimination; premarital and extramarital affairs are the only instances in which intercourse takes place out of doors. In seeming recognition of this tendency a few peoples, like the Hopi, Lamba, and Lango, insist that the only legitimate place to copulate is in the dwelling. The Lepcha, however, prefer to have intercourse indoors for reasons of comfort regardless of the legitimacy of the relationship.

The living quarters of some people are such that intercourse within the dwelling would inevitably be a public affair. Under such conditions the customary site for coitus is out of doors where a certain measure of privacy can be assured. For example, Holmberg writes of the Siriono:

Much more intercourse takes place in the bush than in the house. The principal reason for this is that privacy is almost impossible to obtain within the hut where as many as fifty hammocks may be hung in the confined space of five hundred square feet. Moreover, the hammock of a man and his wife hangs not three feet from that of the former's mother-in-law. Furthermore, young children commonly sleep with the father and mother, so that there may be as many as four or five people crowded together in a single hammock. In addition to these frustrating circumstances, people are up and down most of the night, quieting children, cooking, eating, urinating, and defecating. All in all, therefore, the conditions for sexual behavior in the house are most unfavorable. Consequently intercourse is indulged in more often in some secluded nook in the forest.

Between married couples a good deal of sexual intercourse takes place in the late afternoon in the bush, near the water hole or stream upon which the band is camped. It is rarely indulged in more than once a day. When the afternoon meal has been eaten, and before retiring, couples often proceed to the water hole to bathe and, after bathing, indulge in sexual intercourse. Unmarried couples and potential spouses, of course, must take advantage of whatever opportunities arise. A favorite spot for sexual indulgence between potential spouses, when there is one near the camp, is a patch of ripening maize, which is generally both near at hand and secluded. (Holmberg, 1946, p. 183.)

[1] Alorese, Barama, Chenchu, Colorado, Copper Eskimo, Cuna, Hopi, Kwakiutl, Lamba, Lango, Lepcha, Lesu, Seniang, Trukese, Yagua.

Living under comparable conditions the Rucuyen usually, and the Witoto always, have intercourse in the bush. The Marshallese, Semang, and Taulipang also prefer to have intercourse out of doors because their dwellings are crowded.

Two tribes, the Gond and the Yurok, advance a different and curious reason for using the forest rather than the house for their sexual engagements. These people live in single-family dwellings and no lack of privacy accounts for their reluctance to copulate indoors, but they believe that coitus in the house will result in poverty. The Yurok believe that sexual activities have an adverse effect upon the accumulation of wealth and it is within the dwelling that all objects of value are kept. The Gond say that the goddess of wealth resides in the dwelling and would be annoyed by the proximity of a copulating pair.

Members of a few societies seem to show a preference for the out of doors simply because they find such settings more agreeable. Only during inclement weather do the Wogeo seek shelter for their sexual indulgence. Similarly, the Pukapukans prefer some soft bank or secluded nook. Malinowski writes of the Trobrianders:

The scrub surrounding the village, which is periodically cut for gardens, grows in a dense underbrush and does not everywhere offer a desirable resting place. Here and there, however, a large tree . . . is left behind for the sake of its perfumed flowers, or there may be a group of pandanus trees. Pleasant shady places, too, can be found under an old tree in one of the groves which often mark the site of a deserted village, whose fruit trees, coco-nut palms, and big banyans make an oasis within the stunted tropical undergrowth of recent cultivation. On the coral ridge (raybwag) many spots invite a picnic party. Cavities and hollows in the coral, rocks of queer or attractive shape, giant trees, thickets of fern, flowering hibiscus make the raybwag a mysterious and attractive region. Especially delightful is the part which overlooks the open sea towards the east. . . . The roar of the breakers on the fringing reef, the dazzling sand and foam and the blue sea, provide the favourite surroundings for native love-making, and also constitute the scene in which the mythical drama of incestuous love has been laid by native imagination. . . . (Malinowski, 1929, pp. 326-327.)

Although there are exceptions, some of which we have previously discussed, it seems clear that possibility of seclusion generally determines whether human intercourse takes place within the dwelling or out of doors. This generalization is borne out by the sample of societies on which we have adequate information. These societies can be divided into the peoples who habitually have intercourse indoors and those who repair to the bush, and they are further divisible into those who live as single families in a private dwelling (or in houses provided with partitioned rooms), and those who live in unpartitioned houses containing many families. The result of this type of analysis is shown in Table 4.

TABLE 4

Preferred Location for Intercourse in 25 Societies as a
Function of Type of Living Quarters

	PRIVATE FAMILY DWELLING OR PARTITIONED ROOMS	UNPARTITIONED MULTIPLE DWELLING
Outdoors	3	9
Indoors	12	1

A particularly interesting society in this connection is the Kiwai. Formerly these people lived in long, unpartitioned houses which contained several families. In those days intercourse regularly took place in the bush. Today they live in small one-family dwellings, and marital intercourse within the house is becoming the customary pattern.

Other Species. A desire for privacy during sexual intercourse seems confined to human beings. Male-female pairs of other animal species appear to be unaffected by the presence of other individuals and to mate quite as readily in a crowd as when they are alone. As a matter of fact, their behavior often indicates that sexual excitement is enhanced rather than inhibited by proximity to other animals, particularly when the others are also engaging in sexual relations. The only exception to this generalization is seen when relations between a male and female are interfered with by a third individual. If a potential rival attempts to intervene in the coital relationship, a pair may move away and thus avoid further interruption.

This is not to say that physical surroundings have no effect upon the mating reactions of subhuman animals. Quite to the contrary, certain aspects of the environmental setting are often of paramount importance.

In some animals sexual activity does not take place until a suitable site for courtship and mating has been discovered. Many fishes, amphibians, and birds are capable of fertile union only in certain environmental settings. In certain cases males and females do not become physiologically prepared for reproduction until they have selected and prepared the spot where mating is to take place. Some birds, such as the arctic tern, begin to build nests before they are completely ready for mating. If an unseasonal snow covers the nesting materials and thus halts construction, copulatory behavior is concomitantly delayed and does not appear until nesting can be resumed.

Examples of a preference for certain localities as a setting for intercourse are found in the habits of those territorial mammals which establish and maintain rights of ownership over special geographical areas. In some species the female fulfills this function. Wild minks live solitary lives and each individual inhabits a den on the bank of some river or stream. Throughout most of the year these animals avoid one another, but during the breeding season the female exposes herself at the entrance of her burrow. Males patrol the waterways and approach any female they see. As a male draws near, the female retreats and the male pursues her into the den, where the actual mating takes place. Male mammals of many species actively defend their individual territories. Intruding males are driven away; but receptive females, once they have crossed its boundaries, are permitted or even compelled to remain within the male's private domain. Under these conditions sexual intercourse takes place exclusively within the confines of the area possessed by the masculine partner.

Some animals display no original choice of a particular location but come to prefer surroundings in which successful intercourse has previously occurred. Many males are sexually inhibited in a new and strange environment. Under such conditions, instead of responding to the receptive female they spend their time exploring the novel setting in which they encounter her. But males that have mated with females in a particular place, such as a breeding crate, an experimental observation cage, or a particular pasture, often show signs of sexual arousal the next time they are taken to the same enclosure. There soon develops a strong tendency to approach and remain within the setting previously associated with sexual satisfaction, and to respond sexually to any other individual met there. As far as mammals are concerned there is less indication that females are strongly affected by the immediate environment.

TIME OF OCCURRENCE

Human Societies. For most couples in our society intercourse takes place most frequently at night. According to Kinsey, Pomeroy, and Martin, more American males prefer to copulate in the light, and more females in the dark. These authors suggest that this variance is due to basic differences in the neural organizations involved in masculine and feminine sexual responses. Most men are said to be more aroused by the sight of things associated with sex than are the majority of women. Therefore, men should find intercourse in the light more stimulating than do females. This interpretation is not supported by the cross-cultural or the zoological evidence.

An examination of data from human societies other than our own indicates that if differences between male and female actually exist, cultural factors override them. Some peoples regard night and the dark to be the only proper conditions for intercourse. Thus, the Alorese, the Kwakiutl, the Hopi, and the Crow distinctly prefer the dark of night, because to be seen copulating is for them a source of great shame and daytime coitus is too risky. The Cuna, the Semang, and the Lango also copulate only at night. The Masai of Africa confine sexual intercourse to the evening for fear that if it takes place during the day all of the man's blood will flow into the woman's womb, leaving only water in his veins.

In contrast, however, when there is no expressed cultural preference for night or day, either time may be chosen for sexual activities. The Pukapukans, the Trobrianders, and the natives of the Carolines have no bias in this matter, and among them sexual intercourse occurs as often in the daylight as at night. The Trukese copulate both at night and during the day, although, if it is the latter, the woman will not remove her lava lava (skirt) during intercourse. Some societies express a specific choice for daylight engagements. The Rucuyen and the Yapese much prefer the daytime to night for love-making, and the Siriono routinely have intercourse in the late afternoon after bathing. The Chenchu consider it dangerous to have intercourse in the dark. They believe that any child conceived under such conditions is apt to be born blind.

Other Species. Observation of various animal species suggests that the human preference for nocturnal intercourse (where it exists) depends primarily upon learning and cultural pressures. The mating of animals regularly occurs during the part of the diurnal cycle in which the species is most active. Man's nearest living relatives, the anthropoid apes, are creatures of the light. They wake early and retire when it grows dark. Their sexual activities are confined entirely to the daylight hours. The rest of the time the chimpanzee, gorilla, or orangutan is sleeping.

The same thing is true of monkeys. Only those primitive primates that sleep during the day and forage at night engage in sex play or mating after dark. Comparable generalizations can be applied to lower mammals, birds, reptiles, and fishes. Rats are primarily nocturnal creatures. They sleep most of the day and become active in the early evening. Females tested under laboratory conditions are found to come into heat from about 10 P.M. until 4 A.M. and to be unreceptive before and after this period. Males of the same species are relatively unresponsive sexually during the day but are easily aroused during the night and early morning.

The explanation of the diurnal variation in sexual excitability of the male rests upon the fact that the rat is a nocturnal animal, normally active during the dark hours and inactive when it is light. This behavioral cycle is correlated with a basic rhythm that involves the entire metabolism of the organism. During the day the rat's temperature is lower, oxygen consumption decreases, and general activity is minimal. Accordingly, the animal is less responsive to any sort of stimulation in the daytime than at night. The nocturnal rise in reactivity to all kinds of stimuli is, therefore, reflected in a greater tendency to be sexually active at this time. The cycle is not specifically a sexual one and should not be compared to the female's rhythm of receptivity.

Pigeons, chickens, and other diurnal birds court and mate only while it is light, whereas nocturnal species such as the owl engage in sexual activities exclusively after dark. Trout, bass, and other fishes that depend heavily upon vision for finding food tend to be strictly diurnal and to spawn during the day. Eels, catfish, and other piscine species that rely less upon vision and more upon chemical and tactile sensitivity may mate at night.

The zoological evidence suggests that human sexual behavior might be expected to occur primarily while it is light, if other factors were not operating in favor of nocturnal sexual activity. Man is primarily diurnal and ill equipped to get about in a dark or poorly lighted world, but he has developed sources of artificial illumination which permit him to establish nocturnal behavior patterns. Another factor conducive to nocturnal sexual relations is the concealment afforded by darkness, a desideratum which is rendered important in most societies by custom and law. In societies where it is customary to copulate at night and in the dark, satisfactory sexual activities soon become associated with the absence of light. Under these circumstances darkness may well tend to acquire a stimulating value and to facilitate prompt arousal and sexual responsiveness.

FREQUENCY

One circumstance affecting the occurrence of sexual intercourse is the recency with which it has previously occurred. For this reason the subject of frequency of sexual relations is discussed at this point. The matter is more complicated than it might at first appear, however, for in human beings frequency is rarely a simple function of the degree of readiness, desire, or potency of the two partners. On the contrary, every society imposes restrictions upon a couple's sexual activity and enforces various periods of abstinence which have nothing to do with the man's or woman's capacity for erotic responsiveness or sexual performance.

It is necessary, therefore, to examine the major types of social restrictions before treating the cross-cultural evidence pertaining to frequency of intercourse. In Chapter XI we discuss at length a certain class of these restrictions, namely, those imposed upon the menstruating, pregnant, or lactating woman. In addition to these, there are many other occasions when coitus is forbidden.

Occasions When Coitus Is Forbidden.   In many societies, including those that normally condone certain extramarital relations, the surviving partner of a deceased wife or husband is not supposed to copulate for a certain period of time. The abstinence continues only a few days in some societies, but lasts several months or even years in others. There may be a difference in the duration of this period depending upon the sex of the survivor, the widow usually refraining for a longer interval. Among the Siriono, in whom personal ties between husband and wife seem to be especially weak, the survivor of a deceased spouse will usually abstain from coitus for two to three days. The Kongo, in contrast, demand that a widow mourn her husband for one to two years, depending upon his social status. A widower in this same society is permitted to remarry as soon as the former wife has been buried and certain rites have been performed, a matter of a few months. The Ashanti widow abstains from sexual intercourse for a year after her husband has died lest he return and, by sleeping with her, cause her to become barren or to die. When one of an Ashanti man's wives dies he is not allowed to have intercourse with his other wives for a few weeks until the final obsequies for the dead woman have been held. Should this rule be violated, any infant upon whom the widower looked would perish.

In some societies restrictions on coitus after a death extend to persons other than the surviving marital partner. These individuals usually are the relatives of the deceased, or persons otherwise closely associated with him. Among the Jivaro of South America, for example, copulation is forbidden to close relatives for several days after a death. The Bena of Africa debar from sexual intercourse relatives of anyone who has died, until the funeral rites are over and the spirit safely away in the Land of the Shades. In the western Carolines, men who have been pallbearers are taboo to women for four days. The Lesu require sexual continence of all members of the community during the interval between any death and burial.

In some societies intercourse is forbidden for any man or woman who is ill, and in a few cases all the relatives of a sick person are supposed to refrain from copulating. Among the Chewa, all the members of a family must remain sexually inactive when any one of them is sick. A Bena chief can proclaim a general prohibition against coitus when an epidemic is raging. On Bali intercourse is taboo for anyone who is either sick or deformed, and on Ponape wounded persons may not indulge in any sexual activity.

Various feasts, dances, and ceremonies are associated with a period of sexual continence in some societies. Hunting, fishing, and farming may be accompanied, preceded, or followed by temporary abstinence from sexual activities. Certain technological processes necessitate temporary avoidance of intercourse. The following examples illustrate the widespread tendency to refrain from coitus in connection with various occupational activities.

Among the Kiwai a man is forbidden intercourse before a hunting or harpooning expedition and before setting out on a journey, lest he be beset with bad luck. He must not copulate the night previous to working in his garden, on his way to the garden, or during an interval in his work there. Ila women are forbidden intercourse before brewing beer and before sowing crops. And men of the same society must be continent before starting on a journey, before setting out to fish or hunt, and while engaged in smelting iron. Among the

Jivaro, intercourse is taboo while making arrow poison or a blow-gun and after planting certain narcotic weeds.

In certain societies coitus is forbidden to some members of the community during wartime. Quite commonly[2] men are required to abstain from intercourse for some time before departing upon a military mission. In a smaller number of societies warriors are expected to abstain for several days after their return from battle. Returning from a head-hunting raid, the Lhota Naga hang up the heads, fingers, and toes of their victims and then sleep apart from their wives for six nights. In some cases wives who remain at home are specifically enjoined to be chaste while their husbands are at war. The general rationalization for continence at this time is that it will protect the husband and prevent his death in battle.

Frequency in the United States. The frequency with which married couples in our own society indulge in intercourse (when conditions permit) has been studied by several investigators. Dickinson interviewed 526 married pairs and obtained the information summarized in Figure 5. The most common frequency was two to

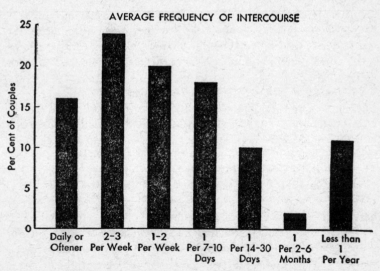

Fig. 5. Average frequency of marital intercourse in 526 American couples as reported to Dickinson.

[2] Ila, Keraki, Kiwai, Lamba, Lesu, Lhota, Omaha, Rengma, Taos, Trukese, Wappo, Yakut, Zulu.

three times per week. However, the age of the individuals involved
was not stated, and other evidence shows that this can be an important factor. It is possible that the rise in the last value shown (representing the lowest frequencies) reflects primarily the reports of older
people.

Kinsey, Pomeroy, and Martin found that the age of the husband
may strongly influence the frequency of marital coitus. Husbands
reported an average frequency of approximately four coital acts per
week when they were 15 to 20 years of age. At 30 years the figure
had dropped to about three, and at 40 to two times per week. Men
of 60 had an average of slightly less than one copulation with orgasm
per week. It is important to recognize that these are average figures
and that in any age group the individual variation is large.

The same investigators found that in every age group from 15 to
60 there are some men who engage in an average of ten or more
copulations per week, and that there are others of the same age
whose frequency of intercourse averages less than once per week.
The magnitude of individual differences tends to decrease with
advancing age. In other words, between the ages of 16 and 30 there
are some husbands whose average maximum frequency exceeds
twenty-five copulations per week. But the greatest frequency for
any 50-year-old man included in this study was an average of fourteen per week; and at 60 this maximal figure was reduced to three
acts per week.

Frequency in Other Societies.   The lowest average frequency of
intercourse in our sample of societies other than that of the United
States is reported for the Keraki, who generally copulate only once
a week. The Lesu average once or twice a week. Two or three times
a week is said to be typical among the Chiricahua and the Trukese.
The Hopi Indians copulate three or four times a week. Although the
Crow Indians think it weakening to have intercourse every night,
they find it difficult to do so less frequently. Among the Siriono of
eastern Bolivia, the natives usually engage in coitus once a day. As a
matter of fact, in most of the societies on which information is available, every adult normally engages in heterosexual intercourse once
daily or nightly during the periods when coitus is permitted.

There are societies in which intercourse is even more frequent,
particularly among the younger men and women. The Aranda of
Australia have intercourse as often as three or five times nightly,
sleeping between each sex act. The Ifugao of the Philippines admire

men who have intercourse several times a night. But to do this, the males find it necessary to abstain from sexual activity for the preceding day or two, and to sleep just before their engagement. Among the Thonga of Africa it is not unusual for a man to copulate with three or four of his wives in a single night. For Chagga men it is reported that intercourse ten times in a single night is not unusual. In instances of this sort, however, one must consider the possibility that the male orgasm does not occur with every act; the data unfortunately permit no definitive statements.

Because of the recognized effects of aging upon sexual capacity it is regrettable that ethnographic reports so often fail to allow for this factor, and refer simply to the copulatory frequency of the adult members of a society. In a few cases this factor does receive recognition. Gorer writes of the Lepcha:

In their youth and young manhood . . . Lepcha men would appear to be remarkably potent; trustworthy people said that when they were first married they would copulate with their wives five or six, and even eight or nine times in the course of the night, though they would then be tired the next day. . . . This potency diminishes around the age of thirty, but copulation once nightly is still the general rule for married couples. Tafoor claimed that in his youth he was almost indefatigable, but says that now he only sleeps with his wife once every three or four nights; this is the reason why he is relatively fat, for chastity induces fatness. It is believed that people accustomed to regular copulation will feel extremely uncomfortable for the first few days if for any reason their partner is removed; but it is considered that people over thirty should be able to support long periods of chastity. . . . (Gorer, 1938, pp. 329-330.)

A belief that very frequent sexual intercourse is weakening or debilitating exists in a few societies. In our sample this notion is confined to a few American Indian groups, the Trukese, and the Seniang of Malekula. The Seniang give the following advice to young men: A man with only one wife should copulate once a night for three successive nights and then rest for two nights. If a man has two wives and copulates twice nightly, he should do so only on two successive nights, then abstain during the third night. Despite such suggestions men frequently have intercourse two or three times each night, once with each wife. The oldsters who offer the advice maintain that it is entirely permissible for a man with white hair to copulate every night.

Frequency in Other Species. In subhuman animals the frequency of sexual relations depends to a large degree upon the physiological condition of the participants. The controlling effects of the female's ovarian cycle in some species and of the annual breeding-season changes in others are discussed at length in Chapters XI and XII. These matters will therefore receive no emphasis in the following pages; attention will be centered upon frequency of intercourse when both male and female are reproductively fertile and maximally responsive.

Observations of captive apes show that under special conditions some male chimpanzees can achieve two or three orgasms within one hour, but it appears that not more than three or four matings per day would be likely to occur for most males despite constant access to a co-operative partner. The female's capacity may be less limited, for R. M. Yerkes in his book on chimpanzees states that the estrous female will copulate repeatedly until her mate becomes satiated and exhausted.

Carpenter's studies of sexual behavior in free-ranging rhesus monkeys show that the female periodically passes through an estrous phase during which she is maximally receptive and stimulating to the male. The average duration of this stage is 9.2 days. For the majority of males three or four ejaculations per day seem to represent the greatest amount of copulatory activity, and after three or four days of sexual contact most males become unresponsive to the female. The female, in contrast, cohabits with several males in succession and may engage in as many as fifty to sixty completed copulations during her estrous period.

Carpenter also investigated the mating habits of the howler monkey. He found that when a male and an estrous female first enter into a temporary mateship, either individual may initiate coital relations. But after a few days of sexual performance, the male becomes lethargic and the female assumes a more and more aggressive role, repeatedly soliciting the male's attention and attempting to arouse him with gestures and vocalizations. She seems to be always ready for copulation, and the frequency of coitus is limited only by the reluctant response of the male. Even in a single day the occurrence of successive copulations is accompanied by a progressive decline in the readiness of the male to mate and an increase in provocative behavior by the female.

Bingham observed the sexual relations of a pair of "black apes." The species of the animals is not given, but they were not anthropoids. At the beginning of the observational period the male was able to copulate and ejaculate three times in the space of twenty minutes. But over a period of fourteen days his potency declined. Copulation became less frequent and less vigorous. Erection was lost after a single ejaculation, whereas formerly it had been maintained during the intercopulatory intervals. Bingham described no change in the attitude of the female.

In laboratory experiments it has been found that some male cats will regularly mate nine or ten times in an hour test. Other cats copulate four or five times and then cease to be responsive to the female. In both cases each copulation includes an ejaculation. The upper limit of the receptive female's responsiveness has not been tested, but it almost certainly exceeds that of the male. Under conditions of confinement male dogs rarely copulate more than once in an hour with a receptive bitch, provided the act is complete and sexual "locking" occurs (see Chapter II). Porcupines copulate repeatedly when the male is fresh, but within half an hour more or less the male is exhausted although the female remains eager for continued sexual contact.

Among many rodents ejaculation is produced by a series of very brief intromissions. Male rats, for example, mount the female, penetrate her, and dismount several times before orgasm takes place. Each ejaculation is followed by a period of inactivity and low sexual responsiveness in the male. In the course of fifteen minutes some rats achieve intromission as many as twenty or twenty-five times and have three or four ejaculations. If they are left with receptive females for three hours, as many as ten ejaculations may take place; but most individuals cease copulating before reaching this high a score, and in some cases three or four climaxes appear to represent the maximal amount of activity. In any case, the effects of a three-hour test are sufficiently debilitating to decrease greatly responsiveness in a second test conducted twenty-four hours later. During her period of estrus the female remains constantly receptive and is capable of exhausting temporarily a sequence of males.

The fact that in many mammals the copulatory capacity of the female exceeds that of the male may be due to the (presumed) absence in the female of any event comparable to the male's orgasm which temporarily depresses sexual ability (see Chapter II). Uncritical assessment of the zoological literature has led to the belief that male animals are sexually more vigorous than females. For example, male Alaskan seals maintain harems consisting of from four or five to as many as one hundred cows. Shortly after arriving at the breeding grounds the cow gives birth to the pup that was conceived the preceding year. Within a few days after parturition the female comes into estrus and is inseminated by the male. It is believed that the occurrence of impregnation brings her receptivity to a close. The cows do not arrive in a group; each day brings newcomers and therefore there are some receptive individuals available to the bull each day of the breeding season. For a period of six weeks the male goes without food and spends all of his time guarding and inseminating these females. A female may copulate only two or three times before she is impregnated. The male, in contrast, displays prodigious sexual potency, mating repeatedly with a succession of cows throughout the breeding period.

The comparison implied here does not provide an adequate indication of the female's capacity for coitus. If, as is believed, fertile copulation terminates her estrus, then no further sexual performance on her part is to be expected. The logical comparison would be between the vigor of the male and that of the female *while she is in heat*. The point will become more obvious if a few other species are considered.

Animal breeders often assert that the sexual drive of bulls exceeds that of cows and they attempt to support the contention by observing that a single bull is capable of inseminating a large number of females. But impregnating a female is not equivalent to "satisfying" her sexually. The estrous cow does not go out of heat as a result of fertile union; she will mate repeatedly with the bull throughout her heat period even though she has already conceived. In the course of a year female cats mate less frequently than males simply because they are in heat for only a few weeks of this time. But females that are artificially brought into estrus and kept receptive by hormone treatment will exhaust one male after another without showing any signs of lowered sexual desire.

SUMMARY

This survey of the circumstances under which coitus is likely to occur in different human societies and in various animal species has revealed several significant facts. Generally speaking, all animals tend to engage in sexual relations during the part of the day or night when they are most active in all other respects. Nocturnal species copulate at night and diurnal ones do so in the daytime. In many human societies coitus occurs most frequently at night, despite the fact that man is primarily a diurnal animal. This shift in preference probably reflects the effects of cultural conditioning. Human beings in general prefer to copulate under conditions of privacy, and to do so in the dark of night assists in the attainment of this goal. There is the additional possibility that through the effect of experience and learning, human couples come to find nighttime intercourse more satisfying.

The widespread human desire for concealment and perhaps the development of preference through satisfying experience help also to explain why intercourse customarily takes place out of doors in some societies and within the dwelling in others. If privacy is available inside the house people come to prefer to carry on their sexual activities indoors. If, however, such privacy cannot be obtained within the dwelling, sexual activities customarily occur elsewhere.

One circumstance influencing the occurrence of coitus is the recency with which it has previously occurred. As far as physiological capacity is concerned, it appears that during the prime of life most men and women would be capable of intercourse regularly once to three or four times daily, although it is extremely important to recognize that large individual differences exist. Even more significant is the fact that frequency of human sexual relations is rarely determined solely by the physiological condition of the participants.

In every human society there are social rules which forbid sexual activity to certain individuals at certain times, regardless of the desire or capacity for coital relations. Some of these restrictions are discussed in the present chapter. For example, men in some societies may not copulate before or after hunting or going to war. They are required to abstain from intercourse for a specified period before planting or harvesting crops. Women are even more circumscribed, particularly in view of the widespread restrictions during menstruation, pregnancy, and lactation which are described in Chapter XI.

As a result of the various social rules mentioned above, intercourse takes place rather infrequently in the majority of human societies. As far as marital relations are concerned, our own society is one of the most lenient. It is comparable to that of the Siriono and a few other peoples who demand sexual abstinence in adulthood only while the wife is menstruating and for a few weeks after she has borne a child. With the exception of the mourning period after the death of a spouse, coital behavior in our society is free from practically all the occasional restrictions that characterize most human societies.

The frequency of sexual relations among infrahuman animals is heavily dependent upon the breeding condition of the male and female. The control exerted by physiological rhythms is discussed at length in Chapters XI and XII. Therefore, we have here concerned ourselves with the frequency of coitus during those periods when both the male and the female are sexually ready for and capable of reproduction. Under these conditions it becomes apparent that for most species the capacity of the female markedly exceeds that of the male. This seems to be true for all infrahuman primates and for many lower mammals as well. We have suggested that this difference may be due in part to the apparent absence of sexual climax in females in subhuman species.

One obvious circumstance for the occurrence of sexual activity is the presence and availability of a suitable sexual partner. The next chapter deals with the ways in which males and females are sexually attracted to one another.

Chapter V

Attracting a Sex Partner

CHAPTERS II and III described the behavior which takes place after a male and female have come together and and are prepared to engage in sexual relations, and Chapter IV detailed the circumstances under which coitus is likely to occur. This chapter is devoted to a consideration of the factors that draw the two sexes together; it examines the ways in which males and females are attracted to one another. In other words, attention is now being focused upon those earlier phases of the heterosexual relationship that precede initiation of actual sexual contact.

THE IMPORTANCE OF PHYSICAL CHARACTERISTICS

Human Societies. Physical appearance plays an important role in the establishment of sexual partnerships among human beings. Among all peoples sexual attraction is based in part upon external bodily characteristics. In our own society the beautiful woman and handsome man are, other things being equal, considered sexually more attractive than ugly individuals. There is, of course, wide variation in taste, but in general terms most members of American society would probably agree that certain individuals are more attractive to the majority of the opposite sex than are others. For example, relative youthfulness in the female tends to arouse more masculine interest than does elderliness. Masculine-like women are in general considered less attractive than are those whose bodily structure is unmistakably feminine. Extreme corpulence, a poor com-

85

plexion, or baldness in either sex tends to lessen the individual's sexual attractiveness.

The cross-cultural evidence makes it clear that there are few if any universal standards of sexual attractiveness. Instead, the physical characteristics which are regarded as sexually stimulating vary appreciably from one society to another. A thin woman is regarded as more attractive than a plump one in some societies; the reverse is true in others. Furthermore, there are great differences between cultures with respect to the particular bodily organs or characters that are considered critical determiners of beauty. For some peoples, the shape and color of the eyes are extremely important factors contributing to sexual attractiveness; for others the formation of the ears seems to be of greater significance. One very interesting generalization is that in most societies the physical beauty of the female receives more explicit consideration than does the handsomeness of the male. The attractiveness of the man usually depends predominantly upon his skills and prowess rather than upon his physical appearance.

As far as general body build is concerned, the majority of societies whose preferences on this matter are recorded feel that a plump woman is more attractive than a slim one. In addition to being plump, the Chukchee, Hidatsa, Pukapukans, and Thonga believe that a beautiful woman should be relatively tall and powerfully built. There are, however, a few people who prefer slim women. The Dobuans, for instance, regard corpulence as disgusting and Tongan women diet to keep slim since they are thought to be particularly unattractive if their abdomens are large. Most of the societies in our sample prefer women who have a broad pelvis and wide hips. The Yakut are exceptional in that they specifically dislike a woman with these characteristics.

Some peoples single out the external genitals as important contributors to sexual attractiveness. It is probably significant that in all of these societies the genitals figure importantly as zones of stimulation in erotic foreplay. In some societies elongated labia majora are considered sexually attractive and it is often the practice to pull and otherwise manipulate the vulvar lips and sometimes the clitoris of the young girl in order to enhance her value as a sexual partner. Elongated labia majora among Nama women are considered a mark of beauty and are in many cases so prominent as to have been named "Hottentot Schurzen" by early white explorers. One interest ing side light is thrown upon this practice by Dickinson's observations to the effect that prolonged, habitual manipulation of the labia may result in an increased nerve supply to those regions. If this is the case it is conceivable that a woman with hypertrophied labia might develop a heightened vulvar sensitivity and therefore be more likely to react intensively to genital stimulation before and during intercourse. This responsiveness, in turn, could conceivably render such individuals particularly attractive as sexual partners.

In a few cultures the size and shape of the woman's breasts are important criteria of sexual attractiveness, the preferred shape ranging from small, upright breasts to long and pendulous ones. Head and body hair figures prominently in concepts of sexual beauty for the members of a large number of societies. Sometimes the nose, eyes, or ears receive special attention and many peoples consider the shape of the mouth to be particularly important.

The data available for a number of the societies in our sample on the characteristics considered to be marks of beauty are presented in Table 5.

The following excerpts give some further understanding of the variation in interest and taste in different societies:

The Masai ideal of [feminine] physical beauty calls for a well-built and slim body with lightly rounded forms. In contrast to the greater number of other negroes . . . a Masai beauty should not be fat. Limbs should be just sufficiently rounded not to seem angular. The other signs of beauty are: an oval face, white teeth, black gums, as light a facial complexion as possible, protruding buttocks (one cannot however speak of steatopygia), strong thighs, a deep navel. Lips should not obtrude either in shape or color so that small dark lips are considered beautiful. . . . With girls emphasis is placed on thin bones, small and delicate hands and feet, and upright semi-spherical breasts. (Merker, 1904, p. 123.)

[For the Wogeo] The petite has apparently less aesthetic appeal than the massive, for girls pointed out to me for commendation were all somewhat large . . . with broad hips and powerful limbs. The knock-knees with which most of them were disfigured were certainly deplored, and it was admitted that a narrower pelvis gave a better hang to a petticoat. "But knees aren't really important," I was told, "and a big woman is stronger than a little one."

. . . A young girl with pendulous breasts, "like a grandmother," is also held to be unfortunate—they should be firm with the nipples still facing outwards, not turning to the ground.

Dark men seem for the most part to prefer brunettes, and those who are themselves light select partners of the same hue. Europeans are most emphatically not envied for their blonde coloring, which is regarded as far too reminiscent of albinos. Condolences were offered to me on two occasions on account of my pallor, and Jaua was probably expressing the opinion of the majority when he said that if he were white he supposed

TABLE 5

Societies Showing Preference for Selected Female Traits

Plump body build   13
    Abelam, Chiricahua, Chukchee, Ganda, Hidatsa, Maricopa,
    Nama, Pukapukans, Ramkokamekra, Siriono, Tarahumara,
    Thonga, Wogeo.

Medium body build   5
    Apache, Hopi, Pima, Sanpoil, Thompson.

Slim body build   5
    Chenchu, Dobuans, Ila, Masai, Palaung, Tongans.

Broad pelvis and wide hips   6
    Chukchee, Hopi, Kwakiutl, Maricopa, Siriono, Wogeo.

Narrow pelvis and slim hips   1
    Yakut.

Small ankles   3
    Kwakiutl, Lenge, Tongans.

Shapely and fleshy calves   5
    Ila, Kwakiutl, Maori, Tongans, Wogeo.

Elongated labia majora   8
    Dahomeans, Kusaians, Marquesans, Nama, Ponapeans,
    Thonga, Trukese, Venda.

Large clitoris   1
    Easter Islanders.

Long and pendulous breasts   2
    Azande, Ganda.

Large breasts   9
    Alorese, Apache, Hopi, Kurtatchi, Lesu, Siriono, Thonga,
    Trukese, Wogeo.

Upright, hemispherical breasts   2
    Manus, Masai.

that he, too, would be ashamed and cover his body with as many clothes as possible. (Hogbin, 1946, p. 198.)

[Holmberg writes of the Siriono:] Besides being young, a desirable sex partner—especially a woman—should also be fat. She should have big hips, good sized but firm breasts, and a deposit of fat on her sexual organs. Fat women are referred to by the men with obvious pride as *eréN ekida* (fat vulva) and are thought to be much more satisfying sexually than thin women, who are summarily dismissed as being *ikáNgi* (bony). In fact, so desirable is corpulence as a sexual trait that I have frequently heard men make up songs about the merits of a fat vulva. . . .

In addition to the criteria already mentioned, certain other physical signs of erotic beauty are also recognized. A tall person is preferred to a short one; facial features should be regular; eyes should be large. Little attention is paid to the ears, the nose, or the lips, unless they are obviously deformed. Body hair is an undesirable trait and is therefore depilated, although a certain amount of pubic hair is believed to add zest to intercourse. A woman's vulva should be small and fat, while a man's penis should be as large as possible. (Holmberg, 1946, p. 181.)

[The following passage from Malinowski refers to the Trobrianders.] . . . It is a notable fact that their main erotic interest is focused on the human head and face. In the formulae of beauty magic, in the vocabulary of human attractions, as well as in the arsenal of ornament and decoration, the human face—eyes, mouth, nose, teeth, and hair—takes precedence. It must be observed that the head plays an important part in magic as an object for admiration, and not as the seat of the erotic emotions, for these are placed in the lower part of the belly. For the rest of the body, the breasts in the woman and build and size in the man are most important, with the colour and the quality of their skins. (Malinowski, 1929, pp. 295-296.)

In the majority of human societies certain physical attributes are considered sexually repulsive. In our own society ugliness, foul breath, uncleanliness, and excessive acne generally tend to render their possessor unattractive. A poor complexion is one feature that is considered sexually repulsive in a large number of societies. Pimples, ringworm, or other disfigurements of the face or body are considered particularly unattractive among the Dobuans, Kurtatchi, Tikopia, and Wogeo. Filthiness seems repulsive to most peoples, and in many societies cleanliness of the body is especially stressed as the *sine qua non* of sexual attraction. Among some peoples a dark skin is considered unattractive, but members of a few societies, such as the Pima, dislike light-skinned people. The Wogeo state that the darker-skinned natives of their population find lighter-skinned ones less attractive, and the latter prefer mates of their own complexion. The Chagga formerly disliked light-skinned persons, but since the coming of Europeans their standards in this respect have been reversed. Among the Dobuans albinos are classified as particularly repulsive.

Other Species. Man is the only animal capable of formulating abstract concepts of beauty, ugliness, or sexual attractiveness, but by their behavior animals of other species sometimes demonstrate an obvious preference for one type of sexual partner as compared with another. If an anthropologist were studying a native tribe whose language he could not understand and whose sexual mores were particularly free, he would be in a position similar to that of the comparative psychologist who investigates subhuman animals. By observing the types of men and women that were repeatedly chosen as sexual partners and those that were consistently avoided, he could formulate some ideas as to the tribe's standards of attractiveness or repulsiveness.

The majority of vertebrates breed only during restricted seasons of the year. And for a large number of these animals the advent of the mating season is marked by conspicuous alterations in physical appearance. Quite commonly the secondary sex characters (see Chapter X) become more prominent. Some fishes such as the jewel fish assume brilliant body colors when they are ready to spawn, and this new physical feature enhances an individual's sexual attractiveness, for mates that are given an opportunity to do so will choose the most highly colored partner available.

Charles Darwin propounded the theory that male birds whose nuptial coloration is brightest are chosen by females in preference to less gaudily colored mates. Subsequent experimentation has not entirely supported Darwin's theories in this respect, but it is nevertheless evident that the bright colors assumed during the mating season serve to attract the attention of potential sexual partners and may therefore be classified as having a sexually facilitative function.

In several species of subhuman primates the female's appearance changes dramatically when she comes into heat or estrus. Certain epidermal areas adjacent to the vulva are referred to as the "sex skin." In some apes and monkeys the sex skin is greatly swollen at the time that the female is fertile and most desirous of intercourse. In certain other primates the mass of this tissue does not change, but instead it becomes highly colored. It has been repeatedly demonstrated that male apes and monkeys are most powerfully attracted to females of their species at those times when the condition of the latters' sex skin indicates the occurrence of estrus. In this sense, therefore, a swollen or brightly colored sex skin may be classified as a sexually attractive trait.

In addition to the condition of their secondary sexual characters, the male chimpanzee is attracted to certain females on the basis of their general behavior, which in turn serves as an index to readiness for coitus. It is apparent that the male can tell from a distance of several yards whether or not a female is sexually receptive. He seems to rely upon her gross movements, postures and gestures, and probably upon her facial expression.

In apes as in human beings some males are much more selective than others. A few male chimpanzees copulate promptly and eagerly with any female that will receive them, whereas other individuals are very particular and will not accept a female until they have carefully examined her and are completely satisfied with her condition. Yerkes and Elder observed many instances in which a male refused a presenting (i.e., receptive) female while expectantly awaiting a preferred partner who at the moment was not visible.

Carpenter's studies of free-living macaque monkeys confirm the theory that physiological readiness to mate is the most important single factor determining a female's sexual attractiveness. When a female first comes into estrus she copulates only with males whose social status in the group is low. In the middle of her estrous period, when she is maximally receptive, the same female becomes the consort of the most dominant male in the group; and toward the end of the period as her attractiveness wanes she passes back into the company of less dominant individuals. The ruling male, having access to any female he desires, displays a preference for those that are most intensively receptive. Socially subordinate males have to be satisfied with less attractive consorts.

Reproductive condition is not, however, the only characteristic affecting the female monkey's erotic value as far as the male is concerned. In some cases, at least, other aspects of her physical appearance are important. Some males seem to develop definite preferences for females with a particular facial appearance. At any rate, mated pairs occasionally engage in activities which seem to be directed toward deliberate modification of the partner's physiognomy. A case in point has been reported by Tinklepaugh, who describes a male and female macaque that lived together for several years and were temporarily separated on two occasions.

. . . . When the two animals were separated for several weeks, the eyebrows and cheek tufts of the female grew sufficiently long to alter her appearance definitely. Both times when the pair were reunited the male immediately proceeded to pull out the hairs of the eyebrows of the female and to bite off others which were unusually long. One by one he pulled out practically all of the long hairs of the cheek tufts, greatly changing the female's appearance. During this hair-pulling activity, the male frequently leaned back and surveyed the female as if evaluating his results. (Tinklepaugh, 1931, pp. 430-431.)

The probability that factors other than sexual condition contribute to a female monkey's attractiveness is increased by the observations of Zuckerman. This investigator mentions one male macaque who lived with two adult females of his own species. He associated closely with one of the females throughout the two-year period of cohabitation, copulating frequently with her at all stages of her menstrual cycle. The male also mated with the second feminine cagemate, but only when she was in physiological estrus. At all other times he ignored her. This suggests that female macaques are maximally attractive during estrus and that at the same time other characteristics are involved which make some nonestrous females more suitable partners than others.

Females of subhuman primate species display a certain degree of discriminatory behavior which indicates that males differ in the degree of their sexual attractiveness. Yerkes states that for the majority of female chimpanzees the most desirable masculine sexual partner is one whose penis is long, who copulates for the longest periods of time and executes the greatest number of thrusts per copulation. It is Hamilton's belief that female baboons prefer males with a large copulatory organ.

Even more important than his anatomical characteristics is the behavioral attitude of the male. Male chimpanzees that are highly selective in their choice of a mate are less attractive to the female than others who show relatively little discrimination. In this same species the male's charm is lessened if he is excessively aggressive and dominant over the female. Quite the opposite form of attraction appears to operate in certain other primate species. Among baboons the male is always socially dominant over the female, and Zuckerman has concluded that pronounced dominance renders a male highly attractive. He points out that it is the most dominant male who possesses the largest number of females. Similarly in the

macaque monkey Carpenter found that highly receptive females
seek out and prefer to consort with the most dominant male in
the troop.

There are indications of sexual selectiveness in mammals below
the primates on the evolutionary scale, but objective and quantita-
tive data are too scarce to permit any detailed definition of the
differentiating characteristics. Marshall and Hammond (1943) state
that stallions which are in the habit of serving dark mares will sometimes refuse to breed with a white one. Jacks that are intended to
be used at stud in mule breeding are not permitted to copulate with
a jennet, for if they do so they are thenceforth less likely to serve a
mare. According to McKenzie and Berliner, sexually experienced
bulls occasionally display distinct preferences for cows that are of
a particular color. Some male dogs appear reluctant to mate with a
particular female even though she is fully receptive; but the same
male may eagerly attempt to copulate with a second female who
appears much less willing to engage in intercourse. In general, all
male mammals prefer a female that is fully in heat. The physiological
changes occurring in the female at this time are described in
Chapter XI.

METHODS OF INVITING INTERCOURSE

Exposure of the Genitals. Deliberate exposure by a woman of
her genitalia to a man's gaze is a common form of sexual invitation
in a few societies. The Lesu woman, for example, may attempt to
seduce a man by displaying her sexual organs. Young men of Tikopia
occasionally take the initiative by flipping up a girl's skirt so that her
genitals are exposed. Among the Dahomeans, women who belong to
the serpent cult wear a short skirt; and if one of them is desirous and
meets a man alone, she drops the skirt, thus exposing her genitals to
him. Blackwood describes the situation among the Kurtatchi as
follows:

A woman desiring sexual intercourse with a man who does not make
advances to her will, when opportunity arises, lie down in his presence
with her legs apart, a position otherwise regarded as indecent. . . . If a
woman exposes her genitals, even unwittingly, as in sleep, the situation
is liable to be taken advantage of by any man whose passions may thereby
be aroused. Both types of incident figure frequently in my collection of
tales, as well as in village gossip. The proper behaviour for a woman is
to sit or lie with her legs stretched out in front of her, keeping them close

together. This is still the rule, although every adult now wears a loin-cloth. (Blackwood, 1935, p. 125.)

The provocative gesture of exposing the genitals has become the subject of widespread social control in every human society. There are no peoples in our sample who generally allow women to expose their genitals under any but the most restricted circumstances. The wearing of clothing by women appears to have as one important function the prevention of accidental exposure under conditions that might provoke sexual advances by men. Other parts of the body, the breasts for example, may or may not be covered, but in societies where women wear any clothing whatsoever the genital region is always concealed. The Trobrianders furnish an example in point:

Modesty in the Trobriands requires only that the genitals and a small part of the adjacent areas should be covered, but the native has absolutely the same moral and psychological attitude towards any infringement of these demands as we have. It is bad, and shameful, and ludicrous in a degrading sense not to conceal, carefully and properly, those parts of the human body which should be covered by dress. Moreover there is a certain coquettish emphasis in the care and elegance with which women manipulate their fibre skirts whenever they fear that dress may fail in its duty, through wind or rapid movement. (Malinowski, 1929, p. 450.)

There are often different customs of dress for females of different ages. When this is the case it is always the young girl and sometimes the woman past menopause who go unclothed; the mature woman keeps her vulva covered. Even in societies where no clothing is worn, as for example among the Kwoma, there are rules of etiquette which prevent the exposure of the female genitals. A man observing a woman walking down the path toward him is obliged by custom to step aside and avoid looking at her while she passes.

The Azande believe that a man will come to harm if a woman provokingly exposes her genitalia to him. Kurtatchi women sit or lie with their legs close together, for even unintentional exposure of the sexual organs is likely to evoke sexual assault by any nearby man. Chagga women will not climb a tree for fear of exposing their genitalia, and girls are taught to sit with their legs pressed together. Among the Ila, no sitting position is specifically forbidden, but girls and women are very careful to keep the vulva covered and to be sure always that a garment is wrapped about their legs when they are sitting down in the presence of others. Palaung girls wear long skirts and are criticized if they pull them up to the knees.

Viewed in cross-cultural perspective the practice of concealing the woman's genital region with some type of clothing is far more common than is covering the masculine sex organs. There are a number of societies in which the woman customarily covers her pubic region with some form of clothing, whereas the man does not conceal his genitals. Although there are a few societies in which both sexes are usually nude, there are no peoples who insist upon the man covering his genitals and at the same time permit the woman to expose her genital region.

Exposure of the genitals by the receptive female seems to be an almost universal form of sexual invitation throughout the mammalian scale. Descriptions of the mating patterns characteristic of various subhuman primates were presented in Chapter II, and the ubiquitousness of feminine exposure was noted. In addition to using special gestures and vocalizations, the female ape or monkey characteristically invites intercourse by turning her back to the male and bending sharply forward at the hips, thus calling attention to her sexual parts. The effectiveness of this stimulus is greatly enhanced in several species by the pronounced swelling and bright coloration of the sex skin described earlier in this chapter.

Although the genitalia of most subprimate females are less prominent than those of apes and monkeys, the precopulatory behavior in such cases nevertheless involves bodily movements and postures that bring those parts of the feminine anatomy under the male's scrutiny. Cows that are fully receptive follow the bull about continuously, and repeatedly place themselves directly in front of his head with their genitals close to his nose. Receptive sows which are approached by the boar move the tail to one side and elevate the hind quarters. In response to touch on the genitals they press heavily backward. The estrous bitch behaves similarly when allowed access to a male dog. Female porcupines that are ready to mate try to back into males, shoving steadily against the partner's nose and mouth. Female rodents of several species dart away at the male's approach, and then stop, waiting until he comes up to them again. Because the male is following the female his line of approach is automatically from the rear and this increases the probability that the genitalia will be the first part of the female's body with which he comes into contact.

Employment of Odors. The widespread use of perfumes by women in our society is in many instances designed to increase their sexual attractiveness. In many societies sweet-smelling flowers are worn, as often by men as by women, either on the body or in the hair. In some peoples this behavior seems to be intended as an erotic stimulant. It is specifically stated that Cayapa men use sweet-scented herbs to attract women, and Western Apache girls wear aromatic plants to attract boys. Most peoples insist upon cleanliness as a means of ridding the body of foul and repulsive odors. In some societies a perfume is used specifically to cover up offensive body odors. The Wogeo, for example, use aromatic leaves to combat the odor of perspiration. Many peoples anoint the skin with oils which are usually scented. This is a general pattern followed by both sexes; in addition to providing a pleasant odor it functions to protect the skin and to preserve its pliant texture.

Odor is clearly an important sexual attractant among many mammals. The female's genital secretions, her urine, and probably several bodily excretions have a characteristic smell when she is in estrus. Male dogs discriminate between the urine of estrous and nonestrous bitches even though the females are not present. Male porcupines react sexually to sticks, stones, or dirt upon which an estrous female has urinated. The male picks such objects or materials up in his paws and sniffs at them repeatedly. A urine-soaked stick may be held in one forepaw while the male rides it as a child rides a broomstick. Monkeys and apes investigate the female's genitals with the nose and tongue and probably derive from such activity a very definite sexual stimulation.

Use of Musical Instruments, Song and Vocal Gestures. The practice of singing and playing musical instruments as an erotic overture has been highly developed in some societies. Love songs are sung to girls among the Chiricahua, Hopi, Lakher, Orokaiva, Samoans, and Sanpoil; and in the western Carolines men sing to their sex partners both before and after coitus. Male lovers among the Crow, Menomini, Oto, and Western Apache blow on flutes to charm and entice girls to meet with them. The Trukese, who formerly used nose flutes for this purpose, now seek to attract girls by playing the guitar or harmonica. The Lhota symbolize girls' names with simple tunes on the flute, and the young man seeking a girl's favors plays the tune indicating her name. Ifugao men and women use the lover's harp in preliminary sexual advances. To attract the attention of a girl, a man will whistle to her on Truk and in the Marianas. Among the Eastern Cherokee the young man sings an attraction song at midnight while he faces in the direction of his girl's house; she will dream of him, become lonesome for him, and, when they next meet, be drawn irresistibly to him.

The courting songs of human beings have their counterpart in the sexual calls of many animals. During the breeding season male frogs and toads utter special mating calls which in many cases appear to attract the fertile female and at the same time stimulate other males to increased excitement. Bull alligators bellow periodically throughout the reproductive period, and some lizards such as the gecko emit a chirping call to which females respond by approaching the calling individual. The well-known mating songs of birds appear to have two effects. They often serve to warn off potential rivals and in some instances they attract and stimulate the singer's mate.

The rutting calls of male mammals have been recognized for thousands of years. Sexually aroused male porcupines utter a piercing whine, and the bull moose and elephant signal their readiness to mate with characteristic vocalizations that are not produced by immature or out-of-season individuals.

Some infrahuman primates employ vocal gestures as one form of sexual invitation. The male or female howler monkey who desires to copulate approaches an individual of the opposite sex and makes rhythmic tongue movements that produce an audible sound. This reaction involves opening the mouth and repeatedly protruding the tongue while moving it rapidly up and down.

Male howler monkeys respond to the resultant sound over a distance of forty feet or more. That it constitutes intentional solicitation is indicated by the fact that the behavior is always directed toward a potential consort and is given only when the other individual is watching. Carpenter is convinced that the lingual gestures are specifically sexual and are engaged in because of strong motivation with reference to a particular member of the opposite sex. Characteristically the individual that is solicited in this fashion responds by producing the same tongue movements, and then the pair copulates.

Vocal sounds are erotically exciting to several other species of monkeys. The receptive female macaque approaches her mate with affinitive gestures, elevated eyebrows, projected muzzle, and a typical expression. At the same time she makes rhythmic mouth movements usually referred to as "smacking of the lips." Hamilton, Kempf, and Carpenter all describe this vocal reaction and consider it an almost invariable accompaniment of sexual arousal. Males indulge in the same behavior and appear to use it as one way of inviting or stimulating the female to engage in coition. Before and during homosexual matings male monkeys of this species engage in a great deal of lip smacking (see Chapter VII).

The male and female baboon solicit intercourse with a series of rapid dental "clicks" which are produced by placing the tongue against the upper front teeth and then pulling it away quickly. Bingham reproduced this sound in the presence of a male baboon and the animal promptly showed an erection, went to his mate, and attempted copulation. On other occasions this same male was observed uttering the clicking sound while pulling at the female's hind quarters in an attempt to force her into the copulatory position. Zuckerman states that lip smacking and the production of dental clicks form an essential part of all friendly and sexual activities on the part of baboons. The sounds serve as both a preliminary gesture and an accompaniment of intercourse. Copulating pairs often utter a series of deep grunts which appear to engender sexual excitement in any other baboon within hearing.

Presentation of Gifts. In a number of societies the giving of a small present in the form of food or some other material object accompanies any solicitation of sexual favors. Gifts of food usually accompany the man's request for intercourse among the Siriono, and coitus always brings the woman a present of goods, money, or jewelry among the Hopi. On Pukapuka sexual intimacies usually follow an exchange of gifts between two lovers. The Tikopia suitor slips some tobacco or an areca nut into the hand of his intended partner. This behavior is not a form of prostitution in which sexual intercourse is traded for a price. Instead it bears a close resemblance to such courting procedure in American society as when a lover brings his girl flowers or a box of candy.

The Yako boy who hopes to become the sex partner of a particular girl induces one of his agemates to take her a gift and to express his compliments on her beauty and grace. Among the Wogeo a boy makes the initial sexual advances through a friend who takes to the girl a present of tobacco or some other desirable material. In many of the societies in which gifts of food and other objects accompany the coitus pattern, there is a belief in a close relationship between these substances and sex. To cite but one example, the Tikopia speak of intercourse as the female genitals eating the male organ.

The system of employing presents to win a mate is not limited to human beings. "Courtship feeding" is a regular element in the sexual patterns of some birds. Male cuckoos and finches feed their mates while copulating. The male road runner captures a small lizard or some other kind of living prey and displays it before the female. She "begs" for the tidbit in stereotyped fashion, and copulation follows. Only then does the male deliver his prize to the female. Male terns present their mates with a small fish during courtship, just prior to mating. However, though they are intrinsically interesting, the sexual habits of birds throw very little light upon an evolutionary interpretation of human behavior. Much more significant would be evidence to the effect that subhuman mammals, particularly primates, regularly indulged in precoital behavior comparable to that just described for men and women.

In general no such evidence exists. It is known that the male ape or baboon behaves more generously toward his female when she is in estrus, and tends at such times to share his food with her. In fact some male chimpanzees insist that their mates take the first choice of food under such conditions—a tendency which usually is absent during other stages of the female's sexual cycle. In the main, however, attempts to win a sexual partner involve extremely simple and direct procedures.

Other Forms of Symbolic Invitation. For human beings speech is undoubtedly the most important single medium of sexual solicitation. People in all societies have verbal symbols representing sexual activities and the sex organs. Spoken invitations serve in many societies as the primary means of initiating the customary precoital activities and may even be directly followed by copulation. On Bali a man who is strongly attracted to a girl simply asks her directly to have intercourse, and it is not uncommon for a girl to make the same request of a man. In the west central Carolines the man invites a woman to copulate with him and she expresses consent by moving her hand over her face from the forehead down. Among the Lepcha sexual invitations are not elaborate, the man simply asking a girl or woman to copulate. But if she refuses, there may be some attempts on his part to persuade her. Lepcha women often ask men to copulate, although theoretically they are not supposed to solicit intercourse. On Jaluit in the Marshall Islands men make advances by rolling the eyes and pronouncing the name of the sexual organs. The Siriono man generally whispers his desire to the girl or woman of his choice and if she is willing they steal off into the bush.

In the societies which have developed some form of writing, love letters may serve as symbolic invitations to intercourse. For example, a Yukaghir girl seeks the advances of the young man of her fancy by sending him a letter written on birch bark, because according to native custom only a man may request intercourse in spoken words.

Symbolic objects may be employed to convey the wishes of a person to a desired sex partner and to serve as a preliminary invitation to coitus. As a symbol of their intentions Yungar men send a carved stick smeared on one end with yellow clay. For many peoples in the Pacific the so-called love-rod serves the dual purpose of secretly inviting the girl to copulate and identifying the male requesting intercourse. Each young man carries a distinctively carved stick about with him during the day so that he will be recognized as its owner. At night a man slips up outside of the house where the girl of his choice is sleeping and thrusts the stick through the wall, prodding her with it. By feeling the carving on the rod she can tell to whom it belongs and may accept or reject this invitation to copulate.

The free use of language symbols as stimuli to sexual activity has become considerably restricted in many human societies. Direct verbal references to sex generally are avoided in conversation, particularly in "mixed" company. In all the societies in our sample on which adequate information is available, people on most occasions refrain from talking about the sex act and the genitalia in the presence of members of the opposite sex. Even in societies such as the Lepcha, where direct verbal solicitation of intercourse is permitted, there is a general avoidance of sexual references in serious conversations between men and women.

Love Magic. The development of love magic has been particularly widespread in human societies. In nearly every society love potions or medicines, magical charms, or ritual acts are available for the man or woman who seeks the affection of a particular partner. The elaboration of magical means for indirectly stimulating a member of the opposite sex to future coital activity seems to be least developed among the people who customarily employ direct solicitation. The Lepcha, for example, though they know some love magic, rarely practice it. Usually, to ask a member of the opposite sex is sufficient to obtain sexual favor. And the Siriono, whose erotic approaches are very direct, have no concept of magical devices for obtaining a sexual partner.

Some idea of the varieties of love magic employed in these societies is conveyed by the following examples. Chewa boys wear a love charm consisting of two pieces of wood tied to the left arm or wrist. While the young man is talking to the girl he loves he tries to charm her by rubbing the wooden pieces with his right hand. On Bali it is believed that a girl will fall in love with a man who succeeds in feeding her a certain leaf inscribed with an image of a god who possesses a very large penis. Chukchee men pronounce love incantations to obtain a woman's favors. The Menomini wear a pouch suspended from the neck and containing a love powder which is composed of vermilion and mica laminae ground into a fine powder, together with some hair or nail clippings of the desired sweetheart. The Siwans believe that the most potent love charm a man can employ is to conceal some of his sperm in food that is to be eaten by the girl of his choice. According to the Trobrianders, all success in love results from magic. A bit of food or betel nut is charmed and given to the girl; or an aromatic herb is rubbed on her body, preferably on the breasts, or put on a flower for her to smell. In some societies the woman also employs love magic to attract a particular lover. But in cross-cultural perspective, generally speaking, love charms are much more often employed by men than by women.

DISTRIBUTION OF INITIATIVE IN SEXUAL INVITATIONS

According to the rules of etiquette in our society the initiative in sexual advances should always be taken by the man. As in the sex act proper, the male is expected to assume the more active role. The majority of the other societies for whom this information is available also believe that only men should take the initiative in seeking and arranging a sexual affair.[1] Among the Mbundu, for example, a girl must not show in any way that she loves a boy; and it is considered shameful if a girl makes the slightest sexual advance. However, in most of the societies with which this book deals, girls and women do actively seek sexual liaison with men, even though they may not

[1] Aymara, Balinese, Colorado, Dusun, Goajiro, Hopi, Kiwai, Kwakiutl, Lepcha, Marshallese, Mbundu, Miriam, Ojibwa, Pukapukans, Siriono, Trukese, Wogeo, Yako, Yukaghir, Zulu.

be supposed to do so. On Bali, girls commonly make overtures to boys or give encouragement to a shy suitor. At a ceremonial dance the Goajiro woman is permitted to trip a man; and if she succeeds he is duty-bound to have intercourse with her. In theory the Lepcha woman should never make direct sexual advances; but in point of fact nearly every boy has his first complete sexual experience with the wife of an "elder brother" or "uncle" and this occurs as a result of the woman's direct invitation.

A few societies make little or no distinction between the sexes in the matter of initiating sexual affairs. Among the Trobrianders, Lesu, and Kurtatchi either the boy or the girl is permitted by custom to take the first steps in soliciting intercourse. In these societies love-making is said to be as spontaneous on the part of one sex as of the other.

There are a few societies in which the girl generally begins all love affairs. Among the Kwoma the girl makes the first advances; the boy is afraid to do so because the girl's relatives might be angered. Should the boy solicit the favors of a girl who did not like him she might call out that he was raping her and he would run the risk of being severely punished. Maori women are considered more amorous than their men and they attempt to attract attention by slyly pinching or scratching the hand of the desired sex partner. Among the Mataco it is always the girl or woman who makes the first sexual advances.

There is a widespread belief that male animals of most species always assume complete command of the mating situation and inevitably play the more active role in precoital courtship. Nothing could be further from the truth. Distribution of initiative varies from species to species, but in the main the relationship is a recip-rocal one in which both partners are sexually aggressive and each contributes to the complete arousal of the other. The relative sexual readiness of the male and female frequently determines which indi-vidual will solicit and which will respond.

Yerkes and Elder studied mating behavior in chimpanzees and defined initiative as the tendency of one animal to enter the other's living cage as soon as the connecting door was raised. They found that when the female was in estrus and the sex skin was maximally swollen, she took the initiative in 85 per cent of all matings. At other stages of her sex cycle she approached the male only 65 per cent of the time. These findings are interpreted as follows: ". . . It is our strong impression that under generally favorable conditions of experimental mating, the female always tends to take the initiative by approaching the male and that this is almost invariably true if conditions are appropriate for mating and the consorts acquainted and congenial." (Yerkes and Elder, 1936, pp. 25-26.)

Exceptions to this generalization occur when the male is unusually aggressive and the female is not maximally receptive, or when the two animals are not congenial and the female accedes sexually to avoid injury. One further qualification that should be added is the observation that a few female chimpanzees appear to be so timid that they never initiate sexual relations even though they may be highly receptive. In most cases when a male is slow to respond to her initial invitation, the female chimpanzee becomes increasingly active and may indulge in a variety of provocative and stimulating activities which tend to arouse her partner's sexual interest. Carpenter reports that upon the few occasions when he witnessed coitus between wild gibbons, initiative was shown by both partners; and he adds that matings occurring in captivity are more often than not begun by definite invitation on the part of the female.

Bingham has observed that distribution of initiative in the mating of "black apes" changes as sexual relations are repeated several times. In the beginning it is the male who approaches and solicits the female, but after several completed matings he becomes lethargic and the female shows more and more active courtship responses. A comparable change occurs in the sexual relations of howler monkeys, according to Carpenter. When male and female howlers first form a consort relationship during the female's estrus, the male is plainly the aggressor. But as he becomes more and more nearly satiated there is a marked increase in the amount of provocative behavior shown by the female and she becomes the more active and desirous partner.

So far as we have been able to ascertain, there is no mammalian species in which sexual initiative rests solely with either the male or the female. During their period of receptivity female rodents, carnivores, and ungulates actively seek out the male. If he does not respond sexually the female is very likely to stimulate him physically, thus increasing his interest and eventually evoking coital attempts on his part.

SUMMARY

In this chapter we have described some of the factors which serve to draw the sexes together as a precursor to intercourse. Physical appearance plays a role of considerable importance among human beings, particularly in the attraction of men to women. However, in cross-cultural perspective there seem to be no universal standards of sexual attractiveness. Females of several subhuman primate species undergo characteristic changes in appearance when they are in estrus. The skin surrounding the sexual organs is greatly enlarged in some species and brightly colored in others. Male apes and monkeys definitely prefer feminine partners who show these bodily signs of sexual receptivity. As far as females are concerned, a male's general behavior and in some instances his social status within the group are more important than physical appearance. It is difficult to determine the importance of physical appearance in attraction between the sexes among the lower mammals, although this factor appears to have some influence, at least in some individuals among the infrahuman primates. Previous familiarity with a particular sex partner is a significant factor in subsequent attraction in all human societies and among many infrahuman animals.

Deliberate exposure of the genitalia as a method of enticing a male to copulate seems to be a general mammalian pattern of feminine behavior. In a few human societies this is a recognized form of sexual invitation. But most peoples consider exposure of the female genitalia highly improper. The wearing of clothing serves to prevent accidental exposure of the genital region under conditions that might provoke sexual advances. It is probably significant in this connection to note that in cross-cultural perspective the woman's genital region is concealed by customary garb far more universally than are the genitals of the man. Among the subhuman primates and practically all the lower mammals the most common method by which a receptive female solicits the sexual attention of a male is exposing her genitalia for his investigation.

Odor is an important attractive agent among most mammalian species. The role played by scents and perfumes in human societies is somewhat difficult to determine since scented oils and other substances that are in widespread use serve other functions as well. Further investigation of this matter will be necessary before the importance of odors in attracting human sex partners to each other can be determined. However, it seems clear, first, that some smells are considered offensive and it is advantageous to get rid of them or to cover them up by some more pleasant odor, and second, that the role of odors in attraction between the sexes is less significant among human beings than it is among many lower animals.

Characteristic human means of attracting a sex partner are those involving elaborate symbolism. Songs, verbal requests, love letters, and love magic are all widespread among people of many different societies. These elaborations find only rudimentary and primitive counterparts in the mating calls and simple vocal reactions of the lower animals. The fact that people everywhere are able to communicate with their fellows by means of language introduces a series of techniques for attracting a lover that cannot be expected to occur in animals without language. At the same time it is interesting to note that direct verbal solicitation to copulate is considered to be quite improper in many societies. Instead, the man or woman desiring a sex partner is required to express these wishes in roundabout fashion.

Whatever the methods of solicitation employed, the evidence indicates that initiative is more or less evenly distributed between the sexes in most mammalian species. From the cross-cultural evidence it seems clear that unless specific pressures are brought to bear against such behavior (as in our society), women initiate sexual advances as often as do men.

In considering the factors that tend to bring men and women together for sexual intercourse we have ignored the ways in which the choice of sex partners can be delimited by social control. The following chapter is devoted to an examination of how sex partners are selected within the context of a social group, and the nature of the partnerships which develop.

Chapter VI

Sexual Partnerships

IN CHAPTER V we discussed the factors that serve to bring males and females together and to engender in them the desire for coitus. These forces are not, however, the sole determiners of human sexual relations. The desire and willingness of two individuals to copulate may or may not be realized in action, depending upon a number of other equally important influences. No human society condones promiscuous or indiscriminate mating. Every culture contains regulations that direct and restrict the individual's selection of a sexual partner or partners. Every society has its own concepts as to the number and nature of permissible partnerships that may be formed. The present chapter is devoted to a discussion of the kinds of partnerships that are permitted and their relation to sexual behavior.

DEFINITIONS

Sexual partnerships may be of two general types: (1) mateships and (2) liaisons. We define mateships as relatively permanent unions based upon economic as well as sexual co-operation. Among human beings such unions are generally recognized as marriage and are regularized by customary legal or religious ceremonial. Liaisons are less stable partnerships in which the relationship is more exclusively sexual. Human liaisons are generally subdivided on the basis of their premarital or extramarital character.

A complete treatment of the subject of sexual partnerships would include consideration of child-rearing practices, of economic and other nonsexual aspects of such relationships, and of the ways in which the social structure of a group determines the types and forms of regulation that will occur. These aspects of the subject are peripheral to the central theme of the present volume and will therefore be disregarded, with a few exceptions. Readers interested in analyzing the social regulation of partnerships in greater detail are referred to G. P. Murdock's volume, *Social Structure* (1949).

MATESHIPS IN HUMAN BEINGS

Mateships may consist of (1) the union of one man and one woman ("monogamy"), (2) the union of one man and two or more women ("polygyny"), (3) the union of one woman and two or more men ("polyandry"), or (4) a combination of polygynous and polyandrous unions in which two or more men form a mateship with the same two or more women simultaneously. As employed in the literature such terms as monogamy, polygyny, and polyandry refer to forms of marriage. For our purposes, however, these terms will be used to classify types of mateships whether or not the union is socially recognized as formal marriage. For example, any society that permits a man to marry only one woman but nonetheless permits him to support as concubines other women with whom he forms a lasting sexual union is classified in this book as a society that approves of multiple mateship for the male.

Single-Mateship Societies. American society formally recognizes only one form of sexual partnership, namely, that of one man legally married to one woman. Except when the union is dissolved by annulment, divorce, or the death of one spouse, every man and every woman is expected to confine all sexual activity to relations with a single partner. Multiple mateships and premarital and extramarital liaisons are socially and legally forbidden.

In cross-cultural perspective this formal attitude toward sexual partnerships is exceedingly rare. To be sure, there are a great many societies in which the majority of the population form single mateships, but most of these groups permit any man to take more than one mate (either wife or concubine) if he can support them. Examination of societies in our sample reveals that formal restriction to single mateship characterizes 29 (less than 16 per cent) of the 185 groups on whom this information could be obtained. Furthermore, of these 29 societies, less than one-third wholly disapprove of both premarital and extramarital liaisons.

Sociologists have sometimes asserted that monogamous mateship represents a peak of societal evolution and that our own ideal form of marriage is a criterion of advanced civilization. Insistence upon monogamous unions is unquestionably a product of societal evolution, but it is not always correlated with other criteria of advanced cultural status. Some of the most "primitive" peoples are strictly monogamous in their ideals.

Multiple-Mateship Societies. In 84 per cent of the 185 societies in our sample men are permitted by custom to have more than one mate at a time if they can arrange to do so. In most of these societies the mating of a man with several women is legalized as polygynous marriage. Rarely, however, do the several wives of a given husband share equal social status. Usually the first woman a man marries is the principal wife, and the remaining secondary wives are accorded a relatively inferior status. In a small fraction of the societies that permit multiple mateships a man has but one legal wife; the remaining feminine mates are concubines attached peripherally to the nuclear family.

Although multiple mateships are permitted to men in most societies it does not follow that under these conditions every man takes more than one mate. The actual establishment of such unions is always limited by the sex ratio and by economic factors. Moreover, every society specifies the women who may be chosen as sexual partners and limits the groups from which a mate may be chosen. It therefore happens that in 76 (49 per cent) of the 154 societies that allow multiple mateships for men, single mateships are actually the rule. Even in societies where polygyny is greatly preferred and said to be general, it is probable that at any given time less than half of the adult males are in fact mated to more than one woman. It may happen, however, that every man who lives long enough will eventually have a large number of approved mates.

It is significant that in 22 (14 per cent) of the 154 societies that approve of multiple mateship for the male, the only permissible mates in addition to a man's first wife are her sisters. In a number of other societies this sororal polygyny, as it is called, is not insisted upon but is much the preferred form of multiple mateship. This fact is particularly interesting in view of the large number of societies that permit extra-mateship liaisons between siblings-in-law, a matter which will be discussed later in this chapter.

In a very few human societies both men and women are permitted to enter into multiple mateships. Even when they are theoretically allowed to do so, women seldom actually establish polyandrous unions. Still more rarely does it happen that two or more men are mated jointly to two or more women. The most frequent occurrence of this form of mateship is found among the Kaingang of Brazil. And even here Henry's statistical analysis of Kaingang genealogies shows that over a period of 100 years only 8 per cent of the mateships involved two or more men and two or more women; 14 per cent involved a single woman and several men; and 18 per cent involved one man and several women. In other words, although these people approve of permanent sexual unions involving several men and several women, in actual practice 60 per cent of all the unions formed during an entire century consisted of single mateships.

The union of one woman with two or more men as the preferred and accepted form of mateship appears to characterize only two of the societies in our sample, namely, the Toda of India and the Marquesans of Polynesia. Among the Toda each woman marries the younger brothers of her first husband. If he has no male siblings she may mate with some other man if one is available. Among the Marquesans, on the other hand, a woman rarely if ever mates with her husband's brother; instead she marries a man not closely related to her first mate.

MATESHIPS IN OTHER SPECIES

It is often difficult to determine the structure of mateships in wild animals; and although the task is easier when domestic species are concerned, there is reason to believe that the process of domestication has radically altered the original sexual patterns of at least some animals.

Subhuman Primates. Most species of anthropoid apes appear to form multiple mateships involving one male and several females. Yerkes and Yerkes reviewed the naturalistic literature on this subject and arrived at the conclusion that wild chimpanzees live in small groups consisting of one dominant male, several mature females, and several subadults and infants. The same adult male is thought to serve as sexual partner to all the females, even though the group may include a second male capable of breeding. According to Zuckerman, the same type of sexual mateship probably is characteristic of the gorilla.

Carpenter's careful field studies of the gibbon suggest that in this primate species a family consists of one adult male, one adult female and their immature offspring. The female drives away any other adult member of her own sex who attempts to enter the group, and the male similarly attacks strange males. Carpenter believes that as male and female offspring approach maturity, they either leave spontaneously or are expelled from the family by the like-sexed parent.

Mateships among monkeys vary from species to species. Wild baboons wander in troops of 25 to 100 or more individuals. A troop consists of several independent family groups each of which includes one dominant male, several adult females, their young, and sometimes one or more supernumerary bachelor males. Zuckerman studied one colony of captive baboons consisting of 25 males and 25 females. Five of the males possessed all the females; the remaining 20 males were unmated. One baboon had seven wives, whereas some others had only one. These individual differences are reminiscent of the human societies that permit multiple mateships, but in which a man takes only as many permanent partners as he can protect and support. Economic and social considerations loom large in the human picture, of course, and this introduces a major difference. However, the more primitive criteria of social dominance and physical prowess which determine the formation of plural mateships in baboons may be more closely related to human standards than is at first apparent.

From his own findings and those of other observers Zuckerman drew the following conclusions: "The literature provides sufficient evidence to enable one to make the generalization that the tendency of sub-human male primates is toward polygyny. Every adult male attempts to secure for himself as many females as possible. There is no selection. The most dominant males secure for themselves the largest number of wives, and maintain ownership until they are deposed." (Zuckerman, 1930, p. 725.) More recent studies indicate that this generalization does not apply to all monkey species. Carpenter's detailed description of sexual partnerships formed by free-living macaque monkeys shows that durable mateships are not formed in this species. Males and females rarely are closely associated except when the female is in estrus. Carpenter has also observed that howler monkeys fail to form lasting mateships.

Lower Mammals. Among subprimate mammals enduring mateships are seen in the wild relatives of the domestic dog. Adolph Murie's studies of the wolves of Mount McKinley National Park strongly suggest that although several adult males and females may inhabit the same den and run together as a hunting pack, each female is mated to a single male, and vice versa. As far as Murie was able to ascertain, these partnerships continue from one denning season to the next and rematings are rare unless one partner dies.

It is generally believed that the wild fox forms permanent monogamous mateships and this impression is confirmed by the findings of commercial fox breeders. Fox ranchers often find it advantageous to have their most valuable males sire as many litters as possible; and in order to achieve this result the male must be induced to copulate with several different vixens during the short annual breeding season. Males that have been allowed to form a sexual partnership with a particular female are unresponsive to other females and it therefore becomes necessary to train individuals to enter into multiple sexual relationships.

The customary procedure is to rear males in segregation and to place young adults with receptive females for a few hours at a time. Under these conditions some males learn to fertilize a new female each day or so. According to Enders, however, if a trained male is permitted to remain overnight with a vixen he is likely to be unresponsive to other females for the remainder of the season. It is of interest to note that the female fox is less discriminatory than the male. A vixen that is in full heat will accept any male who attempts to copulate with her.

Sexual Liaisons in Human Societies

Sexual liaisons refer to partnerships which are relatively impermanent and do not ordinarily involve economic or other nonsexual forms of co-operation. Liaisons that take place between two unmated individuals generally are referred to as premarital relationships. Premarital liaisons and the restrictions placed upon them are discussed in detail in Chapter X. After a man or woman has established a regular mateship there remain two opportunities for sexual liaisons: i.e., with some unmated person or with the mate of some other individual. These two types of liaisons involving at least one mated individual form the subject matter of this section.

Incestuous Liaisons. In all human societies every mated man or woman is limited by custom in the establishment of sexual liaisons. In a few societies like our own no liaisons are condoned, although this is not the rule for most peoples. However, even the most lenient codes involve certain basic restrictions. Among all peoples both partners in a mateship are forbidden to form sexual liaisons with their own offspring. This prohibition characterizes every human culture. This generalization excludes instances in which mothers or fathers are permitted to masturbate or in some other sexual manner to stimulate their very young children. A second exception is represented by the very rare cases in which a society expects a few individuals of special social rank to cohabit with their immediate descendants. The Azande of Africa, for example, insist that the highest chiefs enter into sexual partnerships with their own daughters. In no society, however, are such matings permitted to the general population.

Strict regulations against intercourse between brothers and sisters are nearly as universal as those prohibiting parent-offspring relations. Coitus between siblings does of course occur both in our society and in many others, but it is always condemned and is believed to be relatively uncommon. As far as social codes are concerned, it is possible to identify only one or two societies that permit or require sibling unions among certain individuals, and they are always of a specific social status. In all such instances the permissible unions are mateships rather than casual liaisons. Thus the royal families among the Incas and among the ancient Egyptians are reported to have been perpetuated for a brief time through brother-sister marriage.

The functional outcome of taboos against incest is a subject of considerable significance and has been discussed at length in Murdock's book, *Social Structure*. Suffice it to note here that prevention of liaisons between parents and offspring and between siblings tends to hold intrafamilial sexual rivalry and jealousy to a minimum. Therefore, regulations against incest serve to protect the integrity and effectiveness of the nuclear family group.

It is clear that social rules against intercourse between close relatives reflect cultural rather than physiological or biological tendencies. Close genetic relationship is no barrier to erotic attractiveness. Analysis of the fantasy and dream lives of members of our own and many other societies often reveals strong sexual attraction between parents and offspring as well as between siblings. In the vast majority of cases such incestuous tendencies are not recognized by the individual because of the powerfully inhibiting effects of early training.

All societies have extended incest prohibitions beyond the nuclear family unit. The range and direction of such ramification vary from society to society. In some cultures the prohibition extends only to secondary relatives (e.g., father's sister, mother's sister, sister's daughter, brother's daughter); in addition our society and some others include a few other relatives such as first cousins. But the majority of the societies in our sample (72 per cent of the 133 groups on whom this information is available) have much more extended incest prohibitions that include a far greater number of relatives. In some cultures the interpretation of incest is so broad as to exclude as potential sex partners half the available population. These facts will be especially important to bear in mind when considering the societies that at first appear to place relatively few restrictions on sexual liaisons outside of mateship.

Societies Approving Certain Liaisons. We stated above that all societies prohibit sexual liaisons in accordance with the prevailing incest regulations. However, unlike our own society, which will be given special consideration below, there are a number of peoples in our sample (39 per cent of 139 groups) that approve of some type of extra-mateship liaison. In a very few societies the customary incest prohibitions appear to be the only major barrier to sexual intercourse outside of mateship.[1] Men and women in these societies are free to engage in sexual liaisons and indeed are expected to do so provided the incest rules are observed.

Among the Toda of India, for example, mated men and women are generally allowed to form liaisons. A woman may have one or more recognized lovers as well as several husbands. There is no censure of adultery. In fact the Toda language includes no word for adultery. As far as these people are concerned, immorality attaches to the man who begrudges his wife to another. There is evidence, however, that men in Toda society do occasionally resent sharing a mate with a second man. The Toda are polyandrous and each

[1] Dieri, Gilyak, Hidatsa, Lesu, Masai, Toda, Yapese.

woman usually has more than one husband. But even within these
mateships there is sometimes friction between the husbands with
respect to sexual matters. It is interesting that this type of disagreement is much more pronounced in instances when the husbands
are not brothers. Expressed rivalry among siblings married to the
same woman is practically unknown.

With the few exceptions mentioned above, every society that
approves of extra-mateship liaisons specifies and delimits them in
one way or another. There are some peoples, for example, who
generally forbid extra-mateship liaisons except in the case of siblings-
in-law. This is true among the Siriono. These people do not disapprove of polygyny, although in actual fact it is rarely possible for
a man to support more than one wife. Among the Siriono a man
may have liaisons with his mate's sisters and with his brother's
wives and their sisters. Similarly, a woman has sexual access to her
husband's brothers and the husbands of her sisters. It will be recalled
in this connection that many polygynous societies expect a man to
marry the sisters of his wife. Of the two polyandrous groups in our
sample, the Toda prefer a woman to marry the brothers of her
husband and the Marquesans expect both men and women to have
intercourse with their siblings-in-law.

In some societies extra-mateship liaisons take the form of "wife
lending" or "wife exchange." Generally, the situation is one in which
a man is granted sexual access to the mate of another only on special
occasions. If the pattern is reciprocal an exchange of wives occurs.
Both wife lending and wife exchange may be involved in patterns
of hospitality. A visiting male guest may be invited to form a sexual
liaison with the mate of his host, and when the host is himself a
guest at the other man's home the favor is returned. It is noteworthy
that in most such instances permission of both spouses is necessary
before the liaison can occur legitimately. Moreover, in many such
societies if the men who thus share the same women are not genea-
logically related they establish some artificial kinship bond, such as
"blood brotherhood."

The Chukchee of Siberia furnish an interesting example of this
sort of permissiveness with respect to extra-mateship liaisons. Chukchee men often travel to distant communities and each married
man generally makes special arrangements with some man in each
of the communities he has occasion to visit. These arrangements are
such that wherever he goes he may engage in a sexual liaison with

his host's mate in return for permitting these men the same privileges when they visit his community.

Another type of permission in respect to extra-mateship liaisons appears in some societies in the form of ceremonial or festive license. Sexual liaisons may be generally prohibited, but on certain special occasions the prohibitions are lifted for a short time and everyone is expected to have sexual intercourse with someone other than the spouse. The occasions for sexual license usually appear to have religious significance and may range from harvest festivals to mortuary feasts.

Societies Disapproving Liaisons. Sixty-one per cent of the 139 societies in our sample for whom evidence is available forbid a mated woman to engage in extra-mateship liaisons.[2] In some societies the mated man is similarly restricted, although the great majority of these peoples are much more concerned with the behavior of the mated woman than with that of the mated man. Nevertheless, in most of these societies the man who seduces a mated woman is punished. In addition, many of the peoples in this category expect unmated girls to be chaste. The result is that although certain liaisons are theoretically permitted them, men may be unable to find any socially approved sex partners outside of mateship. Even in the few societies (14 out of 85) in which a mated man may technically be free to have sexual intercourse with unmated girls and in which the girls are not expected to be chaste, he must compete with younger, unmated men for a girl's favor. Furthermore, in those societies that punish only the mated woman for her extra-mateship liaisons, any man who wishes to have sexual relations with her must first overcome her fear of being caught. These various facts force us to the conclusion that although in theory many societies accept a double standard of restrictions on extra-mateship liaisons, it is only in a few cases that the mated man can take advantage of his theoretical liberties.

Although 85 societies are here classified as restrictive, in at least

[2] Abipone, Ainu, Aleut, Alorese, Apache, Ashanti, Aymara, Azande, Bena, Chagga, Chewa, Chiricahua, Colorado, Creek, Crow, Dahomeans, Dobuans, Easter Islanders, Fox, Ganda, Gilbertese, Haitians, Ifugao, Jivaro, Jukun, Kansa, Kazak, Khasi, Klamath, Kurd, Kurtatchi, Kutenai, Kwakiutl, Lakher, Lamba, Lango, Macusi, Mandan, Maori, Maricopa, Mataco, Mbundu, Menomini, Mongols, Nauruans, Omaha, Oto, Pedi, Penobscot, Ponca, Quinault, Rengma, Riffians, Rossel, Rucuyen, Rwala, Samoans, Samoyed, Sema, Semang, Seniang, Siwans, Swazi, Taos, Tehuelche, Thompson, Thonga, Tinguian, Tiv, Tlingit, Tokelauans, Tolowa, Tswana, Tubatulabal, Tupinamba, Vedda, Venda, Walapai, Wappo, Witoto, Wogeo, Xosa, Yakut, Zulu.

17 of them extra-mateship liaisons appear to be extremely common and are not seriously punished.[3] For many of these peoples disapproval of liaisons outside of mateship becomes serious only when an affair is conducted in a flagrant manner. The Bena of Africa furnish a typical example. In this culture mateship is supposed to carry with it exclusive rights to sexual intercourse. But in actual practice mated individuals very frequently enter into liaisons with other members of the community. For both sexes undetected extramarital seduction is the spice of life. If one mate does apprehend the other in an affair there is likely to be a furious outburst of temper in which the offending partner bears the brunt of a fierce attack. But the tantrum is soon over and both partners renew the game, with the recently caught one determined to be less careless on the next occasion.

It is important to note, however, that in most of the societies which forbid extra-mateship liaisons the punishments meted out to offenders are more severe.[4] This is not to say that such liaisons do not occur. On the contrary, there is evidence to show that some men and women in all societies do occasionally engage in extramateship liaisons. But if they are caught, the punishment is harsh, and detected violations are infrequent.

American Society. According to the ideals of American culture, all sexual liaisons are forbidden. That they are nevertheless indulged in, particularly by married men, is well known. Landis and his collaborators report that 14 per cent of the 85 women they interviewed admitted the occurrence of extramarital relations. Twenty-four of 100 American husbands studied by Hamilton confessed at least one extramarital affair. In their interviews with more than 6000 American males Kinsey, Pomeroy, and Martin discovered that approximately 27 to 37 per cent of the married men admitted having had intercourse with women other than their wives. Since many men are reluctant to confess this kind of behavior, Kinsey and his asso-

[3] Bena, Colorado, Easter Islanders, Fox, Kurtatchi, Kwakiutl, Mandan, Mbundu, Mongols, Osset, Rucuyen, Samoans, Samoyed, Siwans, Tubatulabal, Wogeo, Yakut.

[4] Abipone, Ainu, Aleut, Alorese, Apache, Aymara, Azande, Chagga, Chewa, Chiricahua, Creek, Crow, Dahomeans, Ganda, Haitians, Ifugao, Jivaro, Jukun, Kansa, Kazak, Khasi, Klamath, Kurd, Kutenai, Lakher, Lamba, Lango, Macusi, Maori, Maricopa, Mataco, Menomini, Nauruans, Omaha, Oto, Pedi, Penobscot, Ponca, Quinault, Rengma, Riffians, Rwala, Sema, Semang, Seniang, Swazi, Taos, Tehuelche, Thompson, Thonga, Tinguian, Tiv, Tlingit, Tokelauans, Tolowa, Tswana, Tupinamba, Venda, Walapai, Wappo, Witoto, Xosa, Zulu (63). Punishment inferred: Ashanti, Dobuans, Gilbertese, Rossel, Vedda (5).

ciates feel that their figures are minimal and that probably 50 per cent of American husbands are unfaithful at one time or another.

Nearly three-quarters of the men interviewed in the Kinsey study expressed a wish for extramarital relations and the authors suggest that this reflects a basic masculine desire for variety in sexual partners. They state that "the human male would be promiscuous . . . throughout the whole of his life if there were no social restrictions." (Kinsey *et al.*, 1948, p. 589.) It is of interest that Kinsey found fewer American wives who said that they were interested in sexual variety. This result agrees with those of other investigators including Terman who asked 769 husbands and 770 wives whether they had ever wanted to engage in sexual relations with anyone except their spouses. The results represented in Figure 6 show that more husbands are likely to state that they consider the possibility of extramarital intercourse attractive.

Interpretation of this apparent variation between American husbands and wives must be made with caution. In the light of the cross-cultural evidence which we have presented it seems at least

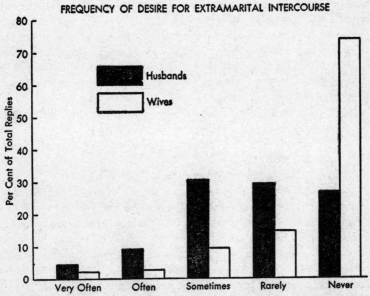

FIG. 6. Frequency of desire for extramarital intercourse as reported to Terman by 769 American husbands and 770 American wives.

possible that the difference reflects primarily the effects of a life-time of training under an implicit double standard. It has not been demonstrated that human females are necessarily less inclined to-ward promiscuity than are males. What the evidence does reveal is that in a great many societies the woman's tendencies to respond to a variety of sexual partners are much more sharply restricted by custom than are comparable tendencies in the man. And most important is the additional fact that in those societies which have no double standard in sexual matters and in which a variety of liaisons are permitted, the women avail themselves as eagerly of their opportunity as do the men.

SEXUAL LIAISONS IN OTHER SPECIES

As explained below, there is some reason to believe that in some subhuman animals incestuous liaisons are partially prevented as a result of the domination of all adult females by a single, full-grown male. This, however, appears to reflect a form of social control and has nothing to do with any lack of sexual attraction between closely related males and females. There is no reliable evidence to indicate the frequency of parent-offspring intercourse or of sibling matings among wild animals that fail to form more or less regular mateships. As far as domesticated species are concerned, there is no serious obstacle to breeding mother to son, father to daughter, or brother to sister. The only exception of which we are aware occurred in connection with Hodgson's attempt to establish several closely in-bred lines of swine. In a few strains some of the second- and third-generation boars were reluctant to serve their female littermates although they readily copulated with unrelated gilts. Despite this one instance it is safe to state that in general domestic and probably wild animals will copulate as readily with their own parents, off-spring, or siblings as with other potential sex partners.

Subhuman Primates. Among the animal species in which regu-lar mateships are formed there appear to be some barriers to extra-mateship liaisons. For example, when a family group exists it is not unlikely that mother-son copulation is partially inhibited by the aggressive behavior of a dominant male. Sokolsky has described a group of captive chimpanzees consisting of one fully adult male, several mature and immature females, and other adolescent males. The mature male copulated freely with all the females, but if he observed a younger male in the act of mounting a female the dominant individual promptly interrupted the relationship by biting and striking the smaller male. The old male's behavior had nothing to do with the fact that the younger males were sons of some of the mature females. It was simply a reaction against any sexual rival. Furthermore, despite the despot's vigilance he was not completely successful, for the younger males occasionally succeeded in copulating with the females while he was asleep. In this case it was obvious that the females were quite willing to receive males other than their mate when they could safely do so.

As explained earlier in this chapter, the typical gibbon family is believed to include only one adult male and female. It is Carpenter's theory that the female expells from the group any daughter who attains maturity. And the male responds similarly to maturing male offspring. If this interpretation is correct, the "monogamy" of the gibbon is a product of the sexual jealousies of the parents, each preventing the other from forming a sexual relationship with offspring of the union.

Zuckerman's description of sexual behavior in wild and captive baboons shows that the male overlord of a harem constantly guards his females against sexual relations with another adult male. Occasionally a bachelor attempts to steal one of the females from a particular overlord, and the usual result is a violent battle that may continue for several days. During the conflict the female remains completely passive. The seducer stands over his prize, copulating with her when allowed to do so and warding off other males who attempt to pull her away. Very frequently the female is killed, but the fight continues to rage over her dead body. When a former bachelor succeeds in keeping a female whom he has stolen, it is a sure sign that the dominance of her original overlord is waning within the colony. If a male possesses only one mate and she is successfully seduced, he reverts to the social position of bachelorhood.

Bachelor baboons rarely attempt to seduce females that belong to strongly dominant overlords, but the females themselves are quite prepared to engage in clandestine relationships when their mate is not looking. Zuckerman recounts one case in which a female was left alone for 40 seconds while her regular partner was chasing another baboon. In this short time the female presented to and was penetrated by two unmated males. It appears that in the baboon as in the chimpanzee restriction of a female's sexual partnership to a single male depends on masculine domination rather than on feminine reluctance to accept additional partners.

Female baboons who are detected in the act of copulating with bachelors often manage to avoid punishment. While her mate's head is turned a female may make sexual overtures to another baboon, and if he responds she receives him eagerly. However, if the overlord gives evidence of noting the violation, the female breaks away and runs to her mate, presenting to him sexually and simultaneously threatening her erstwhile suitor with aggressive grimaces and gestures. Very frequently the overlord reacts by vigorously attacking the intruding male, whose only offense was to accept the female's invitation to copulate.

There are some species of monkeys whose sexual partnerships

TABLE 6

Number of Different Masculine Partners Accepted by Female
Macaque Monkeys During Estrus (from Carpenter, 1942, p. 138)

NUMBER OF MALE PARTNERS IN THE SAME ESTROUS PERIOD	PERCENTAGE OF FEMALE POPULATION HAVING THIS NUMBER OF PARTNERS
4 or more	51.2
3	11.0
2	17.8
1	20.0

are clearly structured but can be classified neither as lasting mateships nor as brief liaisons. Carpenter's detailed description of sexual behavior in free-living macaque monkeys presents a case in point. There are no permanent mateships in this species and males and females are closely associated only when the female is in estrus. However, during her monthly period of receptivity, which lasts for approximately nine days, the female macaque engages in a succession of what Carpenter terms "consort relationships." Each such partnership is restricted to one couple while it lasts; but in most cases a male is sexually satiated after a few days of frequent copulation, and when this occurs the female shifts to a new and more potent masculine partner.

Carpenter's daily observations of one band of macaques yielded the data presented in Table 6, which indicates the number of successive partnerships entered into by receptive females in one period of estrus. Although estrous females customarily pass to a new masculine partner when the current one becomes sexually satiated, the exchange is not always effected amicably. Despite the fact that they are temporarily unable to satisfy the female's sexual appetite, male macaques often attempt, albeit unsuccessfully, to prevent her from engaging in sexual relations with another masculine partner.

Regular sexual partnerships are sometimes formed between captive male and female primates that belong to different species. Hamilton mentions such a liaison between a female baboon, Grace, and an adult male macaque, Timmy. On occasion Grace invited younger monkeys to copulate with her. But if Timmy approached while such a union was in progress Grace dislodged the smaller monkey and barked angrily at him. This often stimulated her mate to attack the adulterer. This monkey-baboon partnership was interrupted on occasion when Hamilton put one animal or the other in with a new mate. In one instance Grace was introduced into an adjacent cage that contained a second male macaque named Skirrel. The new pair copulated promptly and Timmy, who could see the activity, screamed and shook at the wire netting separating the two cages. Ordinarily, Skirrel would have responded in kind, for the two males were not friendly; but while he was copulating with Grace, Skirrel completely disregarded his excited neighbor. Hamilton describes the subsequent developments in the following quotation: "Timmy continued to rage at Skirrel until the latter had ceased copulation and had assumed a semi-recumbent position on the shelf. Then Timmy went about a foot from the netting, . . . smacking his lips as if to invite [homosexual] copulation with Skirrel,—Grace had descended to the floor in quest of food. As soon as Skirrel approached the netting Timmy whirled and thrust his forefinger into Skirrel's eye." (Hamilton, 1914, pp. 303-304.) Although he strenuously objected when Grace copulated with another male, Timmy showed no hesitation about entering into sexual relations with a second female. And when this occurred his original mate lured her rival to the screen partition and attempted to assault her.

Lower Mammals. As stated earlier in this chapter, there are relatively few mammalian species below the primates whose sexual partnerships can be classified as mateships. However, in those animals that do form relatively permanent associations the picture usually is one in which a single male possesses several females. Under such circumstances it is customary for the male to prevent, whenever possible, any mating between one of his females and a second male. This is true, for example, of the bull fur seal, who actively attacks any intruder that attempts coitus with any cow in his harem. There is no indication of comparable discrimination on the part of the cow.

Little is known with regard to the frequency of extra-mateship liaisons in the species in which each male has but a single female partner. It is known, however, that the female fox will mate with males other than her mate, although he is unresponsive to other vixens. Such evidence as is available suggests that with subprimate mammals, as with primates, the existence of regular sexual partnerships depends primarily upon the male's ability to dominate his feminine mate or mates and to prevent infringement on his rights. We see no indication that females of the same species tend voluntarily to restrict the number of their sexual partners; feminine fidelity, when it occurs, appears to reflect masculine domination.

Sexual partnerships in most lower mammals are temporary liaisons rather than enduring mateships. These liaisons seem to be of two major types: The first is a relationship which permits relatively promiscuous sexual relations between individuals that have lived together for some preliminary period, but prevents copulation between strangers; the second is a relationship in which promiscuous mating occurs whenever males and females are fertile and capable of erotic arousal. Some rodents such as the Norway rat or the common house mouse copulate indiscriminately at any time that a female is in heat and a male is potent. In some other species, however, sexual relations do not occur between strangers. The male British meadow mouse attacks any new female even though she is in estrus; and approximately two weeks must elapse before he will respond to her sexually. Chinchillas that have been mated for a long period are difficult to remate with other individuals, and fatal fighting often follows any attempt to establish a new partnership. Male porcupines readily copulate with females that have been living in adjacent cages, but do not mount individuals with whom they are unfamiliar.

SUMMARY

In this chapter we have surveyed the evidence concerning partnerships involving heterosexual intercourse in different human societies and various animal species. From the data available it appears that more or less stable mateships are formed in all societies.

among several species of subhuman primates, and in some lower animals. The most prevalent pattern of mateship among all primates, including man, is a multiple one in which two or more females are attached to a single male. However, in human societies at least, the majority of males at any given time have but a single mate. It follows that most people are in fact monogamous, although the majority of societies permit a man to support more than one sex partner if he can contrive to do so.

Once established, mateship imposes certain restrictions upon the sexual behavior of the members of the partnership. In human societies a universal regulation forbids mated men or women to have intercourse with their own offspring. This prohibition is extended to the relationship between brother and sister, for with very few exceptions intercourse between siblings is forbidden in all human societies. These incest regulations do not reflect an inborn tendency of human beings to avoid sexual relations with their offspring or siblings. Instead it appears that the opposite is the case; the tendency to effect sexual relations within the family is so strong that it occasionally occurs even in the face of severe punishment. Regulations against incest are believed to reflect the result of social learning. They seem to have arisen as a defense against the intrafamilial sexual rivalry and jealousy which would develop if they were not in force. Although there are no incest regulations in the formal sense among subhuman primates, there is evidence that among those animal species in which regular mateships are formed, sexual jealousies are aroused if the dominant male observes another individual attempting to copulate with any of the females in his group.

The data suggest that incest regulations should be considered within the wider frame of reference provided by a general tendency on the part of men to resent sexual relations between their mates and any other sex partner. In a great many human societies extramateship liaisons, particularly on the part of women, are reduced to a minimum by a combination of rules against adulterous unions and extensions of incest regulations to other relatives. Mateships appear to establish a relationship such that extra-mateship liaisons, particularly on the part of the female, are brought to a minimum by social regulation, thus reducing the opportunity for intense sexual rivalry to develop within the community.

At the same time there appears to be a strong tendency for both men and women to seek sexual liaisons outside of mateship. Even in societies in which all liaisons are considered adulterous and are subject to severe penalties, they do occasionally occur. And a number of societies make some provision for legitimate extra-mateship liaisons. Most of these societies, however, carefully restrict such liaisons, either by confining them to relatively rare occasions of ceremonial license or by specifying the persons with whom such unions may take place. Of particular interest is the large proportion of these societies which permit extra-mateship liaisons only between siblings-in-law. Friction between brothers and between sisters sharing the same sex object appears to be less intense than when unrelated persons are involved. Furthermore, where "wife lending" or "wife exchange" is permitted, the men involved are often brothers, or friends whose relationship is often an artificial "blood brotherhood."

Up to this point we have been concerned with the heterosexual behavior of adults and the sexual partnerships which coitus involves. This is clearly the most important aspect of sexual behavior as viewed in cross-cultural and cross-species perspective. But coitus is not the only adult sexual activity. Various other forms of sexual behavior which occur in human beings and other animals must be considered in order to round out our understanding of the full scope of adult sexuality. Therefore in the following chapter we turn our attention to the sexual relations between individuals of the same sex, behavior which is commonly termed homosexual.

Chapter VII

Homosexual Behavior

IN THE preceding chapters we have dealt exclusively with sexual relations between males and females. It is well known, however, that men may engage in sexual activities with other men, and women with other women. Comparable behavior occurs in many animal species. In the present chapter we shall consider homosexual alliances, their frequency, the forms they take, and the attitudes of various societies toward them.

Goethe wrote that homosexuality is as old as humanity itself and can therefore be considered natural, and human history lends his statement the ring of truth. It is generally known that at particular periods in certain civilizations homosexual love affairs were socially approved. This was true, for example, among the early Greeks; but for reasons given in Chapter I the historical aspects of the subject are not included in this discussion.

THE UNITED STATES

Our own society disapproves of any form of homosexual behavior for males and females of all ages. In this it differs from the majority of human societies. Some peoples resemble us in this respect, but a larger number condone or even encourage homosexuality for at least some members of the population. Despite social and legal barriers to such behavior, homosexual activities do occur among some American men and women.

American Men. As a result of their interviews with more than

125

5000 American men, Kinsey, Pomeroy, and Martin concluded that 37 per cent of the postpuberal males in our society have had at least one homosexual contact which resulted in orgasm. This figure rises to 50 per cent if one includes only those men who do not marry before the age of thirty-five. Four per cent of the adult white males in this country are probably exclusively homosexual, having indulged in no heterosexual contacts from the time of adolescence. The average frequencies of orgasm achieved in homosexual contact are lower than those recorded for heterosexual coitus. Considering only those men who have engaged in some homosexual activity, Kinsey and his co-workers calculate that homosexual unions afford an average of 0.8 orgasm per week for adolescent males, 1.3 for individuals in the twenty-five-year range, and 1.7 for men of thirty-five.

The development of homosexual behavior in American males usually begins with exhibition of the genitalia to another member of the same sex. This generally is followed by manual manipulation of the partner's genitals, and somewhat later anal and oral contacts may be indulged in. Two-thirds of the adolescent American boys who engage in any homosexual behavior practice mutual handling of the penis. Only 16 per cent of the entire group use anal and interfemoral copulation. Kinsey and his co-authors estimate that approximately 30 per cent of the adult males in this country have at one time or another been brought to orgasm as a result of oral stimulation of the penis by another member of their own sex.

G. W. Henry interviewed a highly selected group of American men who had extensive, and in some cases exclusively, homosexual histories. The most common methods of stimulation proved to be mutual manual masturbation, oral-genital relations, and pederasty. A few men reported erotic responsiveness to stimulation of the nipple.

American Women. The attitude of our society toward feminine homosexuality might almost be characterized as one of disregard. The legal codes of many states provide severe penalties for men convicted of homosexual practices, but very few states have similar laws pertaining to women. Katharine Davis interprets this discrepancy as a reflection of the fact that intimacies between women tend to be "taken for granted." She adds that feminine inversion differs from masculine homosexuality in being more closely associated with sentiments and emotions that transcend a purely physical attraction.

Twenty-six out of 100 American women studied by Hamilton admitted having had "intense emotional relations" with others of their own sex, but the wording of this statement does not assure the occurrence of physical, sexual interaction. On the basis of questionnaires received from 1200 unmarried women, Davis concluded that more than one-half of her subjects (51.2 per cent) had experienced "intense emotional relations" with other women; and in addition, approximately one-fifth of the total number stated that the relations had included physical expression such as mutual masturbation or genital contact. An additional 78 cases in Davis' group replied that, although the physical expression of the relationship had not gone beyond hugging and kissing, the experience had been "recognized at the time as sexual in character." These two groups combined give a total of 26 per cent of the 1200 women with some specifically homosexual experience. Comparing this 26 per cent group with the remainder, Davis found several differences in their histories.

Many of the homosexually-inclined women reported that they had experienced their first recognizable sexual feelings during or after the college years, whereas with other individuals this experience usually came during late adolescence or shortly thereafter. Failure to establish heterosexual attachments at the expected age may leave the way clear for the subsequent formation of homosexual habits. Many women had some homosexual experiences before the end of adolescence, but those who went to college were less likely to discontinue such practices than were other individuals whose education stopped after high school. Homosexuality was more prevalent among unmarried than married women and more common in employed women than in those who did not have jobs. In interpreting these conclusions it is necessary to hold in mind the fact that Davis' group was a selected one and cannot be regarded as representative of the population as a whole.

Landis and his colleagues have gathered data concerning what they term *homoeroticism*, "the tendency for persons of one sex to have strong libidinal attachment to members of their own sex." The most common form of homoeroticism is seen in the "crushes" that are frequent during early adolescence (12 to 15 years). All but 22 of the 295 women interviewed by Landis reported having had such experiences. Concerning one group of women who were studied more intensively, Landis and his collaborators write as follows:

Homoeroticism and homosexuality are so complicated by cultural taboo, restriction, and disapproval that no simple psychological and biological interpretation of this variety of sexuality is possible. We have substantial evidence to the effect that crushes between adolescent girls constitute part of the normal course of development. In about 33 cases out of 34 these crushes were outgrown, but the thirty-fourth case remained fixed at this level of sexuality and became overtly homosexual. (Landis *et al.,* 1940, p. 56.)

These authors believe that development of overt homosexuality occurs most often in women who fail to free themselves from family ties, who cannot establish a normal degree of independence from their parents, and who have difficulty in achieving normal orientation to boys and young men. They point out the very important fact that homoeroticism exists in different individuals in different degrees. The population they studied appeared to be distributed along a continuum rather than being divisible into dichotomous groups.

Henry interviewed approximately forty American women who were chosen on the basis of long-term, active homosexual habits. Most of them were bisexual, enjoying heterosexual intercourse in addition to homosexual relations; but the majority preferred contact with another woman and some had never experienced satisfaction in any other kind of sexual relationship. Thirty-one of the thirty-four women reporting on the issue described their sexual reactions with other women as satisfactory. Only one individual had never had climax, and a second woman had experienced it but once. The remainder of the entire group (95 per cent) regularly achieved orgasm during homosexual activity. This is a much higher proportion than has been found among women in any married group indulging in heterosexual intercourse or in individuals practicing solitary masturbation.

Thirty-four of the women interviewed by Henry offered information concerning the stimulation employed during homosexual relations. In most cases several techniques were used. Hugging and kissing almost always occurred. Stimulation of the clitoris by the tongue or lips of the partner was practiced in 91 per cent of the cases. Mutual manual masturbation was employed by 41 per cent of the homosexual couples interviewed, and caressing of the breasts occurred in 24 per cent of the relationships. Self-masturbation and close rubbing together of the bodies were commonly practiced methods of stimulation in approximately 15 per cent of couples.

Only 3 per cent of the women employed the finger or some other penis substitute to stimulate the interior of the vagina. In Chapter II we emphasized the importance of clitoral stimulation for feminine orgasm during heterosexual coitus. Despite the small number of women studied, it is probably significant that the clitoris was reported to be by far the most frequently stimulated region during homosexual relations.

OTHER SOCIETIES THAT DISAPPROVE OF HOMOSEXUALITY

In twenty-eight[1] of the seventy-six societies for which information is available, homosexual activities on the part of adults are reported to be totally absent, rare, or carried on only in secrecy. It is to be expected, however, that the estimate would run considerably below actual incidence, since this form of sexual expression is condemned in these societies. In some societies it is clear that tendencies toward homosexual behavior are powerfully inhibited during childhood. Cuna children are prohibited from indulging in homosexual play. If Trukese boys masturbate in the presence of other members of their sex they are whipped. Chiricahua children who are observed to engage in any hetero- or homosexual play are severely punished, and the Sanpoil thrash soundly any child who exhibits behavior that is at all suggestive of homosexual tendencies.

Among all the societies in which adult homosexual activities are said to be very rare, definite and specific social pressure is directed against such behavior. The penalties range from the lighter sanction of ridicule to the severe threat of death. The Mbundu make fun of all homosexual practice, although it is said to occur secretly among both men and women. Homosexual play among Alorese children is frowned upon although it may not be punished, but adult homosexuality is strongly discouraged. One ethnographer has described an eighteen-year-old Goajiro boy who insisted upon dressing like a girl and working with the women. This individual was tolerated by the women, but men treated him with derision. Overt homosexuality was not observed among the Goajiro. Homosexuality in both sexes occurs in Haiti, particularly in urban areas, but it is socially condemned. Masculine and feminine inversions are known to take place in rare instances among the Manus. The only form of homo-

---

[1] Alorese, Balinese, Chiricahua, Cuna, Goajiro, Haitians, Ifugao, Klamath, Kurtatchi, Kwakiutl, Kwoma, Lakher, Lepcha, Manus, Marshallese, Mbundu, Ojibwa, Pima, Ramkokamekra, Rwala, Sanpoil, Sinkaietk, Siriono, Tikopia, Tongans, Trobrianders, Trukese, Tswana (males only), Yaruro.

sexuality known to exist in Bali is that connected with prostitution. The Kwoma consider homosexual sodomy (anal intercourse) unnatural and revolting. The Rwala Bedouins are so strongly opposed to homosexuality that they sentence male or female offenders to death.

Homosexual behavior is reported to be very rare among the Siriono. This is of particular interest because these people have no known social sanctions that would prevent such practices. As a matter of fact, in this culture the sexual relationships are particularly free. The Siriono thus appear to be an exception to the general statement made above that all societies in which homosexual activities are rare direct specific social pressure against such behavior. The major anxieties in this culture center about food rather than sexual behavior. Holmberg, who lived with a band consisting of about 100 Siriono natives, found no instances of overt homosexual behavior. One bachelor appeared to show some homosexual tendencies, but he was never seen to make overt sexual advances toward other men.

SOCIETIES THAT APPROVE OF SOME FORMS OF HOMOSEXUALITY

In 49 (64 per cent) of the 76 societies other than our own for which information is available,[2] homosexual activities of one sort or another are considered normal and socially acceptable for certain members of the community. The most common form of institutionalized homosexuality is that of the *berdache* or *transvestite*. The berdache is a male who dresses like a woman, performs women's tasks, and adopts some aspects of the feminine role in sexual behavior with male partners. Less frequently a woman dresses like a man and seeks to adopt the male sex role.

Approved Forms for Men. In some societies the man who assumes the feminine role is regarded by other members of the community as a powerful shaman. Among the Siberian Chukchee such an individual puts on women's clothing, assumes feminine mannerisms, and may become the "wife" of another man. The pair copulate per anum, the shaman always playing the feminine role. In addition

---

[2] Aranda, Aymara, Azande, Chamorro, Chukchee, Creek, Crow, Dahomeans, Easter Islanders, Hidatsa, Hopi, Ila, Keraki, Kiwai, Koniag, Koryak, Lango, Mandan, Maricopa, Menomini, Nama, Naskapi, Natchez, Navaho, Omaha, Oto, Palauans, Papago, Ponca, Pukapukans, Quinault, Reddi, Samoans, Seminole, Siwans, Tanala, Thonga, Tinguian, Tswana (females only), Tubatulabal, Tupinamba, Witoto, Wogeo, Wolof, Yakut, Yuma, Yungar, Yurok, Zuñii.

to the shaman "wife," the husband usually has another wife with whom he indulges in heterosexual coitus. The shaman in turn may support a feminine mistress; children are often born of such unions. The shaman enjoys considerable prestige and has a position of power in the community. He is believed to have been involuntarily transformed by supernatural power and some men fear being thus changed even though the procedure might enhance their social standing.

Among the Koniag, some male children are reared from infancy to occupy the female role. They learn women's crafts, wear women's ornaments, and become skilled in wifely duties. When he is mature such a male becomes a wife of one of the more important members of the community. He is usually credited with magical powers and accorded a great deal of respect.

A number of Lango men dress as women, simulate menstruation, and become one of the wives of other males. They are believed to be impotent and to have been afflicted by some supernatural agency. The feminine co-wives welcome these male-women into the family, but their prestige is not high. They suffer in particular from the fact that they are barred from owning property. An analogous situation prevails among the Tanala of Madagascar. Here a few men, called *sarombavy*, adopt the feminine role, and the natives aver that such individuals show feminine tendencies in early childhood. According to Ralph Linton, being a *sarombavy* is a refuge for impotent men, and they are usually younger sons. Not despised in any way, such men may become one of the wives of another man. The attitude toward them is neutral; they are neither ridiculed nor praised.

Male homosexual behavior in other societies most frequently involves anal intercourse.[3] In many cases this behavior occurs within the framework of courtship and marriage, the man who takes the part of the female being recognized as a berdache and treated as a woman. In other words, a genuine mateship is involved. In a few societies, however, this kind of sexual behavior, instead of being confined to a relatively small number of individuals, is practiced by a large part of the population, and the relationship is more appropriately classified as a liaison (see Chapter VI).

Among the Siwans of Africa, for example, all men and boys engage in anal intercourse. They adopt the feminine role only in

[3] Chamorro, Chukchee, Creek, Keraki, Koniag, Naskapi, Omaha, Palauans, Siwans, Thonga, Tupinamba, Wogeo, Yungar.

strictly sexual situations and males are singled out as peculiar if they do not indulge in these homosexual activities.[4] Prominent Siwan men lend their sons to each other, and they talk about their masculine love affairs as openly as they discuss their love of women. Both married and unmarried males are expected to have both homosexual and heterosexual affairs. Among many of the aborigines of Australia this type of coitus is a recognized custom between unmarried men and uninitiated boys. Strehlow writes of the Aranda as follows: ". . . Pederasty is a recognized custom. . . . Commonly a man, who is fully initiated but not yet married, takes a boy ten or twelve years old, who lives with him as a wife for several years, until the older man marries. The boy is neither circumcized nor subincized, though he may have ceased to be regarded as a boy and is considered a young man. The boy must belong to the proper marriage class from which the man might take a wife." (Strehlow, 1915, p. 98.)

Keraki bachelors of New Guinea universally practice sodomy, and in the course of his puberty rites each boy is initiated into anal intercourse by the older males. After his first year of playing the passive role he spends the rest of his bachelorhood sodomizing the newly initiated. This practice is believed by the natives to be necessary for the growing boy. They are convinced that boys can become pregnant as a result of sodomy, and a lime-eating ceremony is performed periodically to prevent such conception. Though fully sanctioned by the males, these initiatory practices are supposed to be kept secret from the women. The Kiwai have a similar custom; sodomy is practiced in connection with initiation to make young men strong.

More rarely reported than sodomy are mutual masturbation and oral-genital contacts between males. Manual stimulation of the genitals of one young boy by another is described only among the Hopi; childhood sex play apparently consists far more frequently of attempts to copulate with another member of the same sex. For the Wogeo, however, homosexual relations between adult males seem confined to mutual manual manipulation of the sexual organs. In Africa, Dahomean and Nama men practice mutual masturbation as the only form of homosexual behavior. Tikopia men manipulate

[4] The fact that the majority of males in some societies engage in homosexual relations has a direct bearing upon certain interpretations of such behavior that are current in our own society. Some clinicians assert that the homosexual individual is characterized by an abnormal glandular balance. This or any other exclusively physiological explanation for homosexuality seems to be contradicted by the cross-cultural evidence. The matter is treated at greater length in Chapter XII.

their own genitals in the presence of other members of the same sex, although mutual masturbation apparently never occurs.

Sodomy apparently is absent among the Crow Indians, although oral-genital contacts are fairly frequent. A few Crow men adopt women's dress and mannerisms, and live alone. Adolescent boys and occasionally older men visit these *bate*, as they are called. The *bate* stimulates the boy's genitals orally. One informant stated that there were four such men in his community and that seventeen of his adolescent friends visited them occasionally.

Approved Forms for Women. It appears highly probable that human females are less likely than males to engage in homosexual relations. At any rate, in most other societies, as in our own, feminine homosexuality is accorded much less attention than is comparable behavior among males. In fact, specific information concerning homosexual women is available for only 17 of the peoples included in our sample.[5] And in only a few of these cases is there evidence concerning the nature of the homosexual practices involved. Among the Australian Aranda, women characteristically stimulate each other's clitoris. Roheim writes:"Morica describes the mutual onanism of two women. She calls it . . . tickling the clitoris with the finger. After having excited each other for some time like this, one of them will lie on top of the other like a man, and then rub the two *chelia* together. While they do this tickling of the clitoris, one of them will say to the other, 'a man will come with a big penis and cohabit with you.'" (Roheim, 1933, p. 238.)

Frequently some substitute for a penis is employed, as it also may be in solitary masturbation. The Chukchee women of Siberia use an artificial penis made from the large calf muscle of the reindeer, but its mode of use is not described. In Africa, Mbundu and Nama women use an artificial penis in mutual masturbation. Women among the Azande, particularly wives of important men, use a wooden phallus, or occasionally a banana, manioc, or sweet potato which is tied around the waist of one of the women who simulates copulation with her partner. Among the Dahomeans, the common practice of homosexuality on the part of women is believed to be a cause of frigidity in marriage. Interestingly, the Haitians put it just the other way; the frigid woman who cannot please her husband seeks another woman as a sex partner.

[5] Aranda, Aymara, Azande, Chiricahua, Chukchee, Crow, Dahomeans, Haitians, Manus, Mbundu, Nama, Ojibwa, Quinault, Samoans, Sanpoil, Tswana, Yuma.

ANATOMICAL INTERSEXUALITY

A few men and women in all societies exhibit a condition known in the vernacular as hermaphroditism. More properly termed "intersexes," most of these individuals are characterized by the possession of external genitalia of an intermediate type. The technical anatomical details are not important for present purposes. It suffices to state that although the reproductive organs of the opposite sex are never duplicated perfectly, the genitalia may be sufficiently modified from the normal condition as to confuse ignorant adults concerning the true sex of the infant. Under such conditions it occasionally happens that an individual with ovaries is reared as a boy, or more commonly one with testes is brought up as a girl.

Ellis surveyed a large number of such cases and found that in general the individual preferred the sex role to which he or she had been reared even though it was in opposition to the reproductive physiology. For example, women whose genitals were not of the normal female type and who had therefore been reared as boys often stated that they would rather live a masculine life and assume the role of "husband" in relation to some other woman instead of reverting to their true genetic role. And men with genitalia superficially similar to those of the female preferred in most instances to retain the social and sexual position of a woman. Taken in combination with the evidence from other societies on transvestites, observations of this nature emphasize the tremendous importance of early experience and social conditioning upon human sexuality.

HOMOSEXUAL BEHAVIOR IN SUBHUMAN PRIMATES

Inversion of the sexual role is common among animals of several species other than *Homo sapiens*, and it is particularly frequent in infrahuman primates.

Males. The most detailed account of this type of behavior in male monkeys has been published by Kempf, from whose article the following quotation is taken:

If the exposure of the visual, olfactory and tactile receptors generated more sexual affect it was manifested in the more vigorous play of the aggressor and more animated smacking of the lips. Its intensification was often further expressed by the soft voice sounds. This usually aroused like responses in the sexual object [the second male] and the play continued until the summation of affect . . . had generated a very active sexual craving. Insertion of the penis into the anus was finally made, followed by

rapid strokes and kissing of the lips until mild general convulsive movements resulted. . . . The transitory functional paralysis attending a complete orgasm seems to be the ultimate reaction sought for as the erotogenic
play advances from one stage to another, and after a period of rest the
play begins all over again. (Kempf, 1917, pp. 134-135.)

In addition to the foregoing generalized description based upon
numerous homosexual matings, Kempf mentions several other behavioral items that occur occasionally. Sometimes the male that is
playing the feminine role reaches backward and handles the penis of
his homosexual partner. In other instances the "receptive" monkey
masturbates while a more dominant individual is copulating with
him.

G. V. Hamilton also observed homosexual relations between male
monkeys. He reports the occurrence of anal intercourse, and so far
as one can tell, the details are similar to those listed by Kempf.
Hamilton describes a homosexual friendship between an adult
and an immature male macaque which was accompanied by frequent sodomy, mutual embracing, and social protection of the
young animal by his full-grown partner. When the pair was separated
the adult male mated readily with available females; and when the
smaller male was reintroduced into the enclosure, the homosexual
partnership was resumed, although heterosexual coitus on the part
of the grown animal was not appreciably reduced.

Carpenter reports the occurrence of homosexual mounting by
free-living male macaques, but Kempf and Hamilton are the only
writers who have observed complete anal intercourse between
males. Their findings are of sufficient theoretical importance to demand repetition and confirmation. There is ample evidence to show
that males of many mammalian species will mount and attempt to
copulate with others of their own sex, but the occurrence of phallic
insertion has not been described for any other animal except man,
so far as we have been able to ascertain.

Young male chimpanzees occasionally handle the penis of a second
individual, and Bingham noted several instances in which one immature male of this species assumed the feminine position for copulation
while another preadolescent animal of the same sex stood over him
briefly in the coital position. There is no mention of thrusting or
attempts at insertion. According to Zuckerman, homosexual behavior frequently occurs in the baboon family group. All the members may be involved. The responses include mutual grooming,
genital examination, and sexual mounting. Adult males of this species

living in the native state sometimes present sexually to one another and mounting may follow.

Bachelor baboons who have restricted opportunities for contact with females sometimes strike up homosexual friendships, and for a time a masculine pair remains constantly together. Immature males often join full-grown bachelors and engage in sexual activity. Prepuberal and adolescent males show a wide range of sex responses. They display the feminine sexual presentation, masturbate, and mount one another. They also mount and are mounted by adult members of their own sex. And they engage in manual, oral, and olfactory genital examination with other males of their own age.

The question arises as to whether masculine homosexuality in infrahuman primates is solely a substitute for heterosexual coitus. That this cannot be considered a complete explanation is suggested by Hamilton's evidence to the effect that some adult male monkeys carry on homosexual alliances concurrently with heterosexual activities. Furthermore, Zuckerman says that adult male baboons may mount others of their own sex just before or just after copulating with a receptive female. In general, all mature male monkeys and apes show a distinct preference for heterosexual as opposed to homosexual partnerships, although in many cases this is not exclusive.

Hamilton states that homosexual behavior is more common in immature than in adult male primates. He believes that with the attainment of full reproductive capacity the male becomes more and more susceptible to the attractions of the opposite sex, and hence tends to direct more of his activities into heterosexual channels. Kempf postulates the existence of a developmental phase during which male monkeys definitely prefer homosexual contacts. Homosexual interests are supposed to precede and, temporarily, to dominate tendencies toward heterosexuality. Zuckerman, in contrast, simply concludes that immature primates have no preference as far as the sex of a partner is concerned and will attempt to mate indiscriminately with either males or females.

Several writers have suggested that the homosexual relationship is strongly affected by the relative social dominance of the individuals involved. According to Kempf, comparative inferiority, physical weakness, and biological impotence are implicitly acknowledged by any male that allows himself to be used as a sexual object by another member of his sex. There are, however, many advantages to be gained by a smaller and younger male who submits to a more dominant partner. Aggressive adults tend to protect their homosexual favorites from assault by other monkeys, and the favorites soon learn to seek this protection. In such a relationship the socially inferior partner often adopts the sexual presentation when his dominant partner starts to take food away from him and the procedure is often effective.

Other authorities feel that the occurrence of homosexual activity is more or less accidental, and that the dominance relationship is of primary importance. Zuckerman considers mounting, particularly among immature primates, as fundamentally controlled by social dominance, with the sex of the mounted individual being of secondary importance. According to Maslow, the sexual behavior of a dominant animal is always masculine, and masculinity may be *independent of the genetic sex of the individual.* Subordinate individuals, in contrast, customarily show feminine mating behavior regardless of their biological sex. With the exception of the female who is in heat, dominant members of a group are said rarely to assume the feminine position for intercourse. Maslow points out further that primates which are subordinate may show the sexual presentation repeatedly without the dominant animal making any attempt to cover them. Nevertheless, this gesture is frequently followed by permission on the part of the dominant partner for the subordinate to take food or to carry out some other activity that it would not ordinarily be allowed to perform.

Identification of "first causes" would be difficult if not impossible until the evidence is more plentiful. For purposes of the present discussion it is appropriate to disregard questions as to the existence of a specifically homosexual developmental stage and of the social patterning of this form of behavior between adult males. The significant fact would seem to be that, regardless of its origins and of its functions as an indicator of social dominance, homosexual behavior does occur. Furthermore, in some cases at least, it is preceded and accompanied by signs of erotic arousal and, perhaps, even of satisfaction.

Females. It is well known that female primates of subhuman species sometimes display coital responses similar to those of the male. It is beyond question, however, that homosexual arousal is much less frequent in females than in males. Usually, when one female stands over another in the copulatory position there are no signs of sexual excitement, bodily contact is minimal, and the act is terminated quickly.

Bingham, in his studies of prepuberal chimpanzees, observed

several occasions upon which one female showed marked interest
in the genitalia of another member of her own sex. In one instance
the partner's labia were taken between the teeth and manipulated
gently. It should be added, however, that this may have represented
nothing more than investigatory behavior or a form of grooming. At
other times one young female bent over another that was stooping
in the coital position. The covering position was like that of a male,
but there were no copulatory thrusts and we are disinclined to
classify such responses as indicative of sexual excitement. Zuckerman states that, although mounting of one female baboon by another is common, "true feminine homosexuality" is rare. The same
writer adds that comparable behavior often occurs in other species
of monkeys, and probably constitutes an expression of dominance
rather than sexual desire. Hamilton also believes that female monkeys are infrequently aroused sexually by other females.

There are some exceptions to the foregoing generalizations. An
example can be quoted from Bingham's monograph. The following
description refers to interaction between two adult female chimpanzees. One of the animals, Sita, had been masturbating and then,
suddenly, she approached her cagemate and initiated homosexual
relations:

[Sita] turned directly to Malapulga, and grasped her legs in an embrace.
. . . During an interval of two or three minutes Sita repeated these embraces several times. Malapulga appeared indifferent in the beginning, but
after Sita's repeated approaches her responsiveness was obviously awak-
ened. Among various activities strongly suggesting sexual interest there
was one adjustment which stood out. They turned their faces in opposite
directions, and standing on all fours pushed their buttocks together. There
was considerable pushing and sliding during the short interval they stood
in this position. Sita's immediately preceding sex behavior, quite unmistak-
able, coupled with these later genital contacts, convince me that her embracing of Malapulga was a factor in the sexual behavior. (Bingham, 1928,
p. 124.)

Hamilton records a single instance of homosexual relations in
female monkeys which he believes involved "true desire." This was
a case in which a mother and her grown daughter had been separated
for some time and were then reunited. The two animals rushed together and the younger individual promptly assumed the presentation posture. Her mother immediately mounted with vigorous
copulatory thrusts, making the lip-smacking sounds that accompany
normal coitus.

Homosexual Behavior in Lower Mammals

Males. Male mammals of many species below the primates will, under certain circumstances, attempt to mate with members of their own sex. However, the conditions under which these reactions occur suggest that the explanation varies from one situation to another. Behavioral evidence pertaining to cetaceans is exceedingly scant, but McBride and Hebb have published a preliminary report indicating that the psychological status of some aquatic mammals may be considerably above that of such terrestrial species as dogs, cats, cows, horses, and the like. In connection with other observations, these workers noted that adult male porpoises repeatedly attempt intromission with younger, less dominant members of their own sex. The large animal swims upside down beneath the intended partner. It is also stated that males which have been courted by a receptive female may avoid her and promptly attempt copulation with another male.

Two male porpoises that were studied for several months formed a close attachment to each other. One member of the pair was removed from the tank for three weeks. The reactions of the two males upon their reunion are described in the following quotation:

No doubt could exist that the two recognized each other, and for several hours they swam side by side rushing frenziedly through the water, and on several occasions they leaped completely out of the water. For several days, the two males were inseparable and neither paid any attention to the female. This was in courting season, and at other times the two males seemed bent only on preventing the other's copulation with the female. (McBride and Hebb, 1948, p. 121.)

The attempt of one male mammal to copulate with another may in many cases reflect nothing more than failure to identify the sex of the intended partner. A genuine homosexual attraction cannot always safely be inferred. A fairly common situation in which one male will attempt to mate with another arises when several males are placed together with receptive females. For example, male rats that have been intensely aroused by heterosexual intercourse tend to mount any other rat that is available, and under these conditions one male may grasp another and execute copulatory movements. A male rat that has penetrated a female several times in the preceding few minutes but has not yet reached the point of ejaculation may, if the female is removed, mount another male and ejaculate upon his back.

Anal penetration has never been observed in such cases and the second male is clearly an inferior substitute sexual object.

This type of behavior illustrates an important generalization. For all animals, including our own species, the range of potential partners capable of evoking sexual arousal depends in part upon the "degree of need" or "strength of drive" existing at any given time. "Degree of need" is inferred rather than observed directly. It is likely to increase with prolonged deprivation of sexual outlet and to be relatively slight for some time after satisfactory sexual contact. The sexually satiated male animal is unlikely to respond to any stimulus save that provided by a maximally receptive and co-operative female. But after a long period without any sexual exercise, the same individual may vigorously attempt to mate with a non-receptive female, another male, or even an animal of a foreign species. Furthermore, the "degree of need" is particularly strong in the male that has been intensely aroused by contact with a female but has not yet achieved orgasm. It is under these circumstances that an animal is most likely to mount a second male repeatedly, and in a few cases to reach orgasm as a result of the accompanying stimulation.

This sequence of events is quite different from that involved in the masculine homosexuality of monkeys. In the latter case homosexual copulation appears to be an alternative but not an exclusively compensatory form of sexual expression, since it continues to occur even when heterosexual contacts are available. The difference is due to two factors. First, primates are particularly susceptible to the effects of experience, and as a consequence of prepuberal homosexual play the male can learn that sexual satisfaction is derivable from coitus with other males. Second, and equally important, is the fact that during homosexual intercourse the submissive male monkey actively plays a feminine role. In contrast, male rats, rabbits, guinea pigs, cattle, sheep, cats, and dogs that are mounted by others of their own sex almost never show any "receptive" responses. Instead they attempt to escape from the other male and if this is impossible they may retaliate aggressively.

There are, however, rare instances in which male animals of certain lower mammalian species have been known to display mating behavior like that of the receptive female. Two observers (C. P. Stone and F. A. Beach) have independently discovered a few male rats that reacted to the sexual advances of other males with the display of coital reactions typical of the estrous female. When this occurs other males become much more active in their pursuit of the temporarily reversed individual. Two comments are pertinent at this point. First, male rats that are given a choice of mating with females or with "reversed" males usually select the feminine partner. Second, those few masculine individuals that occasionally exhibit feminine copulatory reactions are not "feminized" in the usual sense of the term. They inevitably prove to be vigorous copulators when placed with a receptive female. As a matter of fact, males of this type may respond in feminine fashion to the advances of another male and then within a few seconds switch to the masculine pattern and copulate with the female. The adjective "bisexual" has been applied to behavior of this type, but the data actually demonstrate reversible inversion of the usual sexual role. Kinsey, Pomeroy, and Martin correctly point out that "inversion of sexual behavior" would be a more accurate description of the phenomenon.

The physiological basis for inversion of mating reactions in males of lower mammalian species is not completely understood but it does not appear to involve hormonal abnormalities. One male rat showing this form of sexual activity was castrated and the feminine responses disappeared within a few days after operation. Masculine coital performance declined gradually, and after it had reached a base level a male hormone was administered by daily injections. The effect of the androgen treatment was to restore *both* male and female mating patterns. Subsequent administration of ovarian hormones evoked some feminine behavior, but the responses were less intense than those appearing under the influence of the male hormone. These findings suggest that the original capacity for both masculine and feminine behavior depends upon hormonal secretions from the testis. Apparently ovarian hormones are not essential to female behavior in such instances. This interpretation is supported by the fact that both types of reaction reappeared when androgen was administered. The injection of female hormones will evoke the receptive response but they are less effective than androgen.

Females. Mounting of one female by another is not confined to the primates. It is, in fact, common among many subprimate mammals including lions, domestic cats, dogs, sheep, cattle, horses, pigs, rabbits, guinea pigs, hamsters, rats, and mice. There are several indications that the appearance of malelike behavior in females is closely related to a condition of sexual arousal. For example, female rabbits normally do not ovulate unless they have copulated with a buck. But when one estrous doe mounts another and executes vigorous copulatory thrusts, the *mounting animal* may ovulate afterward. Furthermore, this type of behavior is, for many species, closely associated with estrus, the time at which the female is sexually receptive.

Stock breeders have long been aware of this fact and have taken the occurrence of masculine behavior as a reliable sign of receptivity on the part of the female showing the temporary sexual inversion. Sows that are ready to breed are often said to "go boaring," mares in heat are said to "horse," and cows to "bull." Laboratory investigations of female guinea pigs demonstrate that mounting behavior shown toward other females is a regular precursor or accompaniment of the estrous condition. This form of behavior is induced in spayed females by injections of the same ovarian hormones that produce feminine receptivity. A female hormone is not essential to mounting behavior in all species, however, for spayed rats and dogs are known to display such behavior without any endocrine treatment.

It is difficult to decide whether behavior of this type indicates sexual attraction exerted by one female toward another, or if it represents the expression of a high level of arousal in the mounting individual, the sex of the mounted animal being of little importance. Arguments in favor of the latter hypothesis can be adduced from the fact that for most species masculine responses most often occur when a female is in heat and, furthermore, that under such conditions the female will mount males as well as females. For some lower mammals, however, the sexual condition of the stimulus female is important. Female rats, for example, are most likely to display mounting reactions in response to another female that is in estrus. Apparently, in this case the stimuli presented by a receptive female are maximally effective in eliciting masculine reactions on the part of a second individual regardless of whether the latter is a male or a female.

The female mammal that is mounted by another member of her own sex usually responds as she would to a male, displaying the signs of sexual excitement. It is important to note that in the species mentioned here inversion of mating behavior is not aberrant; instead it constitutes one aspect of the female's normal sexual repertoire. Feminine and masculine reactions may and often do occur in the same female in rapid succession.

One other type of sexual inversion deserves mention although it does not belong under the general rubric of homosexuality. This is the relationship that occurs when a male and female engage in coital performance, but each one takes the role of the opposite sex. Hamilton has described an encounter between two monkeys which illustrates such double inversion. A large female approached a younger and smaller male and, apparently because of her aggressive bearing, the male assumed the feminine coital posture. The female mounted the male in masculine fashion, but dismounted almost at once and offered herself to the male who promptly copulated in the normal manner. It is not at all uncommon to observe the temporary display of masculine behavior on the part of receptive females confronted with sexually sluggish males. Female dogs, rats, and other animals in heat may mount the male repeatedly if he is slow to assume the initiative in the sexual relationship. Often this stimulation suffices to evoke more vigorous behavior on the male's part.

SUMMARY

The cross-cultural and cross-species comparisons presented in this chapter combine to suggest that a biological tendency for inversion of sexual behavior is inherent in most if not all mammals including the human species. At the same time we have seen that homosexual behavior is never the predominant type of sexual activity for adults in any society or in any animal species.

Some homosexual behavior occurs in a great many human societies. It tends to be more common in adolescence than in adulthood and appears to be practiced more frequently by men than by women. This is also true of the other animal species with which this chapter deals, and particularly so in the infrahuman primates.

The basic mammalian capacity for sexual inversion tends to be obscured in societies like our own which forbid such behavior and classify it as unnatural. Among these peoples social forces that impinge upon the developing personality from earliest childhood tend to inhibit and discourage homosexual arousal and behavior, and to condition the individual exclusively to heterosexual stimuli. Even in societies which severely restrict homosexual tendencies, however, some individuals do exhibit homosexual behavior. In our own society, for example, homosexual behavior is more common than the cultural ideals and rules seem to indicate. Within the societies which, unlike our own, provide socially acceptable homosexual roles, a number of individuals, predominantly men, choose to exhibit some measure of homosexual behavior.

Chapter VIII

Relations Between Different Species

THE type of sexual behavior with which this chapter deals is ordinarily termed "bestiality." The word refers to relations between a human being and an animal of some lower species. We propose to examine the kinds of such relations that occur, the frequency with which they take place, and the attitudes of different peoples toward the subject. In addition we will concern ourselves with the occurrence of similar behavior between males and females of different subhuman species.

Bestiality has been condemned by one society after another since the earliest times. The Hittite code, the Old Testament, and the Talmud all contained specific prohibitions against this sort of activity and the death penalty was imposed on transgressors. Medieval courts sentenced to death any human being proven guilty of animal intercourse, and in some cases both participants in the relationship were executed. The animals' complicity was determined by legal means.

This method of punishing transgressors died out slowly in Europe as well as in the United States. E. P. Evans states that at Vanvres in 1750 one Jacques Ferron was hung for copulating with a she-ass. The animal was acquitted on the grounds that she was a victim of violence and had not participated of her own free will. The prior of the local convent and several citizens of the town signed a certificate stating that they had known said she-ass for four years, and that she had always shown herself to be virtuous both at home and abroad and had never given occasion of scandal to anyone. This document was produced at the trial and is said to have exerted a decisive influence upon the judgment of the court. Cotton Mather records the case of a citizen of New Haven who, on June 6, 1662, was sentenced to death for having engaged in sexual relations with animals. Before his execution the guilty man was compelled to witness the slaying of a cow, two heifers, three sheep, and two sows with which he had been convicted of copulating.

As Evans points out, it is paradoxical that Christian lawgivers who adopted the Jewish code against intercourse with beasts should have enlarged it to include the Jews themselves. Cohabitation of a Christian with a Jewess was held to be equivalent to "buggery" with animals. Some authorities included Turks and Saracens in the same category, "inasmuch as such persons in the eyes of the law and our holy faith differ in no wise from beasts." (Evans, 1906, p. 153.) Men and women convicted of copulating with a human being who was not a Christian were put to death, together with their partners.

AMERICAN SOCIETY

Kinsey, Pomeroy, and Martin estimate that approximately 8 per cent of the present masculine population in the United States have engaged in sexual contact with animals at one time or another. This type of activity accounts for a smaller portion of the total sexual behavior than does homosexuality, intercourse with prostitutes, or even nocturnal emissions. The figure is particularly low in the case of city-bred males who have little opportunity for animal contacts. From 40 to 50 per cent of the boys reared on farms participate in sexual activity with other species and 17 per cent of this group achieve orgasm during the relationship.

This form of sexual expression is most frequent in adolescence and rare after the twentieth year, although it may continue to provide a significant source of outlet for a very small number of adult males. In certain instances a boy or man may become strongly attached to a particular animal and develop emotional ties resembling the sexual bonds usually formed between two human beings. Conversely, an individual animal that is repeatedly associated in sexual alliance with a human being may become strongly attached to that person. Kinsey and his collaborators state that male dogs which are masturbated regularly sometimes transfer their sexual responsiveness to the person who stimulates them and cease to react to receptive females of their own species.

In American society vaginal coitus is the most common form of interrelation between human beings and other animals. Alternative avenues of interaction include oral-genital contact (usually involving a nursing animal such as a young calf), anal intercourse, masturbation of the boy or man by friction against the animal's body, fellation of a male animal by the human partner, and masturbation of male animals by human beings.

OTHER SOCIETIES

There are some societies[1] for whom the only reference to bestiality is contained in their folklore. Most of the folk tales have an obvious moralistic aim: Animal contacts may have been practiced in the old days but they generally met with some form of punishment. Wogeo legends mention women having intercourse with dogs, but this is reputedly unknown in real life. A folk tale of the Bena in Africa relates that a man had a bitch which he made his wife but, of course, he did not let anyone know, for if he were discovered copulating with a dog he would have been killed. The bitch finally gave birth to a boy, who was told that he could not eat dog or he would become very ill.

The Lakher have a legend which tells of a priestess who had sexual intercourse with a python. And a myth of the Taos describes a woman who copulated with a snake. The woman was thought to have been made pregnant, but at birth both mother and child died. The Kiwai Papuans tell several tales about bestiality. Usually it is a man who is described as having intercourse with a sow, a bitch, or a female turtle; and in each case the animal is said to have given birth to a human child. The Kiwai attach no disapproval to such behavior as far as their folk tales are concerned, and it is related that long ago children resulting from such unions were accepted by the society.

In some societies[2] other than our own, animal contacts are condemned and harsh punishment is meted out to any offender. Balinese men occasionally have sexual relations with animals, but the natives regard this as a dreadful crime against the spiritual health of the

---

[1] Bena, Dahomeans, Kiwai, Lakher, Penobscot, Taos, Wogeo.
[2] Balinese, Gilyak, Lango, Marshallese, Nama, Rwala.

community. At one time the guilty individual and the animal were drowned in the sea. Today the animal is killed and the man exiled or put in jail. The Balinese explain such behavior as a consequence of bewitchment which confuses the man's vision so that the animal appears to him like a beautiful woman.

Among the Lango of Africa animal contacts are very rare, and, if discovered, both participants are put to death. In South Africa, Nama Hottentot males occasionally indulge in intercourse with animals but in so doing they run the threat of severe punishment. Gilyak people believe that a man who commits bestiality will be changed into a beast. On Jaluit in the Marshall Islands intercourse with animals is strictly forbidden and appears to be extremely rare. The Rwala Bedouins punish bestiality with death and the threat seems sufficient to prevent such behavior completely.

Extreme condemnation of animal intercourse, such as that which prevails in the societies that have just been described, is far from universal. In about the same number of societies[3] animal contacts are considered simply unnatural, silly, or disgusting, and definitely inferior to other forms of sexual activity. Kurtatchi men and women occasionally have sexual relations with dogs, but this is regarded as the last resort in the absence of a more appropriate sex partner. These people have a number of folk tales about animal contacts which provoke great amusement. But the relating of the actual sexual incident is accompanied by an expression of shame and disgust. The Trukese consider animal contacts an inadequate source of satisfaction, but instances apparently occur. Some women put coconut meat in their vaginas and then entice a dog to lick it out. This practice is grounds for divorce if a husband detects his wife in the act. Trukese men at one time used dogs as sexual objects. Among the Tswana of Africa, young boys assigned to the cattle posts frequently engage in intercourse with the animals. But this practice is regarded as silly by the older boys and they may beat any youthful comrade who is caught in the act. Young Riffian boys sodomize she-asses in the hope of developing themselves sexually and of making the penis grow. If it occurred in grown men, however, such behavior would be ridiculed.

There is a final category consisting of a few societies[4] in which

[3] Kurtatchi, Lesu, Palauans, Riffians (men), Trobrianders, Trukese, Tswana.
[4] Copper Eskimo, Kusaians, Masai, Riffians (boys). Inferred: Fez.

animal contacts are practiced and do not meet with condemnation. Among the Copper Eskimo intercourse between men and live or dead animals is not infrequent and is not prohibited. These people tell an interesting story recorded by Rasmussen as follows: "There was once a woman who would not have a husband. Her family let dogs copulate with her. They took her out to an island, where the dogs then made her pregnant. After that she give birth to white men. Before that there had been no white men." (Rasmussen, 1932, p. 240.)

Bestiality is fairly common among the Hopi Indians. Men are reported to have intercourse with burros, dogs, horses, sheep, and even chickens. Kusaian men occasionally use cattle as sexual objects and among the Masai it is customary for older boys to have sex relations with she-asses. Although there is no other reference to bestiality among the Fez, the natives practice certain magical rites which are said to make a man so strong that in one night he can "deflower seventy-two virgin cows."

INTERSPECIES MATING IN SUBHUMAN ANIMALS

All the behavior described thus far has involved interaction between human beings and other animals in which the human partner took the initiative and controlled the relationship. This is not always the case. There are recorded instances in which subhuman animals have made distinctly sexual advances toward men or women. There is, furthermore, ample evidence to indicate the occasional occurrence of sexual relations between male and female animals belonging to different infrahuman species.

Yerkes describes behavior of this type shown by an immature female gorilla named Congo. The ape made sexual responses to male and female dogs, showing a distinct preference for the male. She also reacted sexually to human males and, if permitted to do so, sometimes grasped a man's hand and pulled it into contact with her genitalia, making masturbatory movements. On other occasions Congo assumed the coital position and presented her genitals to human visitors. The following quotation from Yerkes' monograph *The Mind of the Gorilla* illustrates a clear-cut case of sexual solicitation:

Congo came close to me . . . [and] throwing herself on her back she pressed her external genitalia against my feet and repeatedly and de-

terminedly tried to pull me upon her, precisely as in the previous winter
she had been observed to react to the male dog. In this activity she was
markedly and vigorously aggressive, and it required considerable adroit-
ness and strength of resistance on my part to withstand her attack.
Thwarted in her first attempt, she arose, and standing in natural position
on all fours, immediately made what presumably is the usual or normal
sex presentation of the female gorilla. As previously, the genitalia were
directed toward me and she made persistent efforts to achieve contact.
It was during this standing presentation that I observed pronounced
tremor or shivering of the entire body. This phenomenon, in connection
with pronounced sexual excitement, appears commonly in man, both male
and female. . . . Subsequently as Congo continued to make sex presenta-
tions either on her back or standing, the tremor was observed at least
twice. . . . This behavior, which I characterize as sex aggression, was
exhibited for several minutes. Her insistence on sexual contact was extremely embarrassing . . . and somewhat dangerous because of her enormous strength, but throughout the period of observation she was unusually gentle and friendly, although determined in her efforts to satisfy
her desire. (Yerkes, 1928, pp. 68-69.)

Yerkes also noted attempts on the part of a female chimpanzee to
use a man's hand as a masturbatory object, and Zuckerman describes
similar behavior in a gray-cheeked mangabey at times when she was
in the phase of genital swelling (see Chapters V and XI). Bingham
states that the immature female chimpanzees which he studied often
showed sexual excitement in the presence of male humans. Male
apes appeared to be more responsive to women. According to Hamilton, some female macaques display the sexual presentation and
smack their lips in stereotyped sex invitation when men approach
their living quarters.

Observations of this kind of behavior probably are the source for
many of the superstitions pertaining to the sexual attraction that
human beings are supposed to hold for other primates. Buffon's
Natural History, published in 1775, includes several credulous
accounts of cohabitation between humans and animals. It is stated,
for instance, that African apes show no mercy to native men whom
they may encounter, and kill them without delay. But in their
passion the animals abduct many beautiful women, "which they
keep with them for the pleasure of their company, feeding them
plentifully all the time." The same author describes a captive male
baboon that was ". . . insolently lascivious . . . presenting its pos-

teriors oftener to the spectators than its head; but it was particularly impudent in the presence of women, and plainly showed its immoderate desires before them by an inexpressible lascivity."

In its natural environment each species of primate probably mates exclusively with its own kind; but when several species of monkeys are brought together in captivity, interspecific mating is not uncommon. Zuckerman observed a young male orangutan who repeatedly attempted to copulate with an immature female chimpanzee. G. V. Hamilton recorded frequent intercourse between male macaques and female baboons that lived together in his yard. The female's desire apeared to be insatiable, presumably, according to Hamilton, because the macaque penis is much smaller than that of an adult baboon.

Male and female apes and monkeys will also seek sexual contact with subprimate partners. One of the young female chimpanzees studied by Bingham was given a cat as a cagemate and repeatedly pulled the animal upon her genitalia as she lay on her back. Upon other occasions the ape drew the cat's tail to her vulva. Several times she got down on all fours and, facing away from the cat, determinedly pushed her genitals against the other animal. Some of Hamilton's male monkeys attempted to copulate with snakes, kittens, puppies, and foxes.

Kempf offered partners of several species to male and female primates. He found that a wide variety of animals evoked sexual reactions on the part of monkeys of either sex. Sometimes the attempts at sexual relations led to the formation of relatively protracted periods of close association. "When baboons and monkeys find animals which do not cause fear and are satisfactory sexual objects they tend to associate with them and in a sense to adopt them." (Kempf, 1917, p. 151.) One female macaque copulated repeatedly with a male dog, as described in the following quotation:

A small mongrel dog visited the yard . . . [and] on his approach all of the monkeys would take to the trees and chatter threateningly. But finally Maud descended to the ground and assumed the female position for copulation. The dog mounted her, dog fashion, and partially entered her. She displayed marked sexual excitement, and ever thereafter would descend to the ground and copulate with a dog whenever he entered the yard. . . . Maud finally offered to a strange dog, and the animal bit off her arm. Since then all the monkeys have shown hostility to dogs. (Hamilton, 1914, p. 309.)

According to Zuckerman, captive baboons that South African farmers keep chained to stakes frequently offer themselves sexually to dogs.

Cross-species sexual relations are not frequent among subprimate animals. In the first place the excitatory value of females of a given species is maximally effective only to a male of the same kind; extra-specific partners are rarely as stimulating. Secondly, anatomical differences between most of these species prevent or render difficult any satisfactory copulatory interaction. Nevertheless, partial or complete matings sometimes occur between a female of one species and a male of another. Sometimes this behavior reflects inability to discriminate the species of the sexual partner. For example, different kinds of toads that normally breed in separate habitats may produce fertile hybrids if they are brought together in the same environment.

In other instances cross-species matings occur because intraspecies copulation is prevented. Animals deprived of opportunity for normal intercourse may attempt coitus with almost any other living creature that is available. For instance, some captive male porpoises kept in the same tank with large sea turtles frequently insert the erect penis into the soft tissue at the rear of the turtle's shell. At other times these animals may attempt to copulate with sharks.

Cross-species copulation is rarely complete and even less frequently is it fertile, but there are exceptions. Mexican swordtail fish and platyfish inhabit the same rivers in Mexico but they never crossbreed. However, when males of one species are placed in aquariums containing only females of the other species, sexual activity occurs and may result in the production of fertile offspring. If the male is offered females of both species, he reacts only to intraspecies partners and entirely ignores the foreign species.

Experience and learning influence the tendency of lower animals to respond sexually to partners of a different kind. According to Whitman, ringdoves that are reared by pigeons may refuse to mate with their own kind but readily couple with birds belonging to the same species as their foster parents. Male mammals that are accustomed to receiving receptive females in a particular cage or pen often become so aroused by the general environmental setting that they will attempt cross-species matings. Male rabbits that are regularly given estrous does in their living cages will mount rats, small kittens, and even inanimate objects if these are presented in the same fashion as the receptive female. Male rats that have mated with females in a particular observation cage attempt copulation with almost any animal of appropriate size that is encountered in the experimental cage.

SUMMARY

In this chapter we have shown that different societies maintain quite different standards with respect to the propriety of "bestiality." Sexual activities involving other animals are acceptable to some peoples, ridiculed by others, and strongly condemned by still others. This variation in attitudes toward the practice of sexual activities with lower animals reflects the influence of learning and social channelization. The zoological and cross-cultural evidence combine to suggest that within limits man is biologically equipped to respond sexually to a great range of stimuli and potential partners. But as the individual matures, sexual interests come to be focused primarily upon heterosexual activities, principally coitus, with members of his own species.

Chapter IX

Self-Stimulation

THE various forms of behavior described in preceding chapters involve a relationship between two individuals. At this point we wish to analyze sexual activity in which a person or animal can indulge alone. Masturbation, for example, may be practiced in solitude and for that reason it is discussed in this chapter even though the same response often occurs when several individuals are together.

MASTURBATION

We define masturbation as any sort of bodily stimulation that results in excitation of the genitals. It commonly involves handling, rubbing or mouthing of the sexual organs, or bringing them into contact with some foreign object. Deliberate excitation of one's own genitals is considered a perversion by many members of our society. The majority of adults condemn masturbation among contemporaries and attempt to prevent children from engaging in such activities. Nevertheless, the behavior is extremely common.

American Men. Kinsey, Pomeroy, and Martin report that 92 per cent of American men masturbate to the point of orgasm at least once during their lifetime. Various other workers have estimated that the same statement applies to 85 to 96 per cent of males in European countries. Self-masturbation is responsible for the first ejaculation experienced by most American boys, and this form of stimulation furnishes the chief source of sexual outlet during the early years of adolescence, during which period it occurs an average of 2.4 times per week.

The frequency of masculine masturbation is progressively reduced in postadolescent years, although it may continue throughout adult life. Kinsey and his collaborators found that 69 per cent of American husbands who have graduated from college masturbate at least occasionally. However, males of lower educational levels are apt to stop masturbating at some point in adolescence. They are more likely to consider this practice "unnatural" or "perverted." Men who do not go beyond grade school usually begin to indulge in heterosexual intercourse much earlier than those who are going to college. They have, accordingly, a different source of sexual satisfaction and can dispense with masturbation without becoming sexually inactive. According to Hamilton, autogenital stimulation tends to increase in men during their sixties and may at this time be more frequent than during the preceding two decades. This statement is at variance with the findings of Kinsey and his co-workers.

By far the most common method of masturbation in our society involves manual stimulation of the penis. In a very small proportion of the cases foreign objects are inserted in the urethra or anus as a means of self-stimulation, and a fraction of one per cent of the males studied by Kinsey and his collaborators were capable of taking their own penis in their mouth and thus inducing ejaculation.

American Women.   Self-stimulation is not limited to the masculine sex in our society. Landis and his co-workers questioned 295 American women and found that 54 per cent of them had indulged in masturbation at one time or another. One-quarter of these individuals practiced the habit at least once per week during the period when they were masturbating, and 25 per cent of the positive cases had indulged in genital stimulation regularly "over a period of time." The majority of masturbators had begun self-stimulation early in life and tended to cease after adolescence when heterosexual interests became predominant. Hamilton found that 74 per cent of a selected group of married women had some experience in masturbation, and Dickinson found the habit to be almost universal in widows over forty years of age. Davis examined 1183 unmarried women with college education and discovered that two-thirds of this number had masturbated at one time or another, although many of these had never induced orgasm in this fashion. One-third of the masturbating individuals ceased the behavior within one year of its inception and one-half of them continued for ten to twenty years.

American men who begin to masturbate and then discontinue the practice usually do so because self-stimulation is replaced by heterosexual intercourse. The same does not appear to hold true for women. Davis analyzed the records of nearly 300 unmarried women who had indulged in masturbation and then given up the practice. Of this total, 230 individuals said they had experienced orgasm, and 65 said they had not. Reasons given for discontinuation of masturbation by the two groups were compared, and occurrence or nonoccurrence of climax was rarely mentioned. The most common explanation in both groups was fear of the results in terms of physical or mental deterioration. Among the women who had experienced orgasm the second most common reason advanced was that the self-manipulation engendered feelings of shame and disgust. This particular explanation was less often mentioned by individuals lacking the orgasmic experience. Instead, they said that they had "outgrown the habit," "no longer needed" the stimulation, or "had lost desire for it."

The apparent unimportance of orgasm as a determining factor in the decision to stop masturbating may be deceiving. We wonder whether in the one group the actual occurrence of climax was not sufficiently upsetting to evoke inhibitions (e.g., "shame," "disgust," etc.) that prevented complete enjoyment of self-stimulation, thus leading to discontinuation of the practice. And in the other group, the so-called "loss of desire" may very well represent a reaction against the inability to achieve satisfactory orgasm. Although many women who can induce orgasm by masturbating do give up the habit, there is some reason to believe that ability to reach climax in this fashion increases the probability that the masturbation will be continued. Comparison of those women in the Davis study who had stopped with those who persisted in masturbatory practices shows that 97.1 per cent of the latter group experienced orgasm, whereas only 74.8 per cent of the former reached climax while masturbating.

Additional evidence pointing to the importance of orgasm as a factor affecting duration of masturbatory habits is seen in the fact that 48.8 per cent of the women who had never experienced climax stopped masturbating within one year or less after the habit began. But among the women who were capable of orgasm as a result of masturbation, only 26.2 per cent ceased to indulge in this activity within less than a year from its inception.

At least a few women derive sufficient satisfaction from self-stimulation without climax to continue the practice for long periods of time. Davis describes six long-term masturbators who said they never had an orgasm and two others who were uncertain as to its occurrence. The duration of the habit in these cases ranged from four to 27 years. One 28-year-old woman who had been masturbating for several years wrote, "I believe I have never experienced the orgasm. I have tried in vain to produce it and am still trying."

Masturbatory techniques employed by American women center in most cases around stimulation of the clitoris by means of vulvar friction. Sixty-seven per cent of 419 women reporting to Dickinson stated that this was the preferred means of self-stimulation. In 20 per cent of the group vaginal sensation was preferred and was evoked by insertion of a foreign object into this organ. For 11 per cent of these women masturbation depended upon stimulation of the urethral meatus (external opening of the urinary tract), and in 2 per cent of the cases orgasm was regularly induced by pressing the thighs together rhythmically or it occurred spontaneously during sleep.

Evidence concerning the relationship between technique of self-stimulation and incidence of orgasm is not currently available. Nevertheless, it is probably of considerable significance that clitoris stimulation was stressed by the majority of the women whose masturbatory methods are specified by Dickinson. It might be expected that the most gratifying technique would be the one used by the largest percentage of the women studied. These findings should be compared with our statements in Chapters II and VII concerning the importance of clitoral sensation in heterosexual intercourse and in homosexual relations.

Attitudes of People in Other Societies. The cross-cultural evidence suggests that adults in other societies rarely engage in autogenital stimulation. But in evaluating ethnological reports it is necessary to hold in mind the fact that some social pressure is leveled against masturbation in nearly all the societies on which we have information, and that informants are likely to underestimate the frequency or to deny the occurrence of behavior that is socially condemned. For most peoples masturbation represents an inferior form of sexual activity in which adults should never participate. An apparent exception are the Lesu of New Ireland, who expect the adult woman to engage in a form of masturbation when sexually excited and lacking a sex partner.

Even among some of the peoples whose sex mores are very free, masturbation on the part of mature persons is considered undesirable. Lepcha men say that they never masturbate; they regard semen as a soiling substance. Siriono men are reported never to engage in autogenital stimulation. They may be observed standing and tugging at the foreskin when preoccupied or worried, but the genital manipulation is not accompanied by erection. The Crow Indians interpret masturbation by an adult as a confession of inability to obtain a lover, and it is therefore something of which a man or woman should be ashamed. Malinowski writes of the Trobrianders:

> Masturbation (*ikivayni kwila:* "he manipulates penis," *isulumomoni:* "he makes semen boil over") is a recognized practice often referred to in jokes. The natives maintain, however, that it would be done only by an idiot . . . or one of the unfortunate albinos, or one defective in speech; in other words, only by those who cannot obtain favours from women. The practice is therefore regarded as undignified and unworthy of a man, but in a rather amused and entirely indulgent manner. Exactly the same attitude is adopted towards female masturbation (*ikivayni wila:* "she manipulates cunnus"; *ibasi wila o yamala:* "she pierces vagina with her hand"). (Malinowski, 1929, pp. 475-476.)

While adult masturbation is generally frowned upon in most societies, a different attitude is often taken toward autogenital stimulation on the part of youngsters and adolescents. There are some peoples, in addition to ourselves, who condemn masturbation regardless of the individual's age, but many societies believe that for the young boy or girl masturbation is a natural and normal activity. Wherever this permissive attitude prevails it appears that autogenital stimulation occurs early in life and is then gradually replaced by other sexual activities. This matter is discussed more fully in Chapter X.

Masturbatory Behavior in Other Societies. Despite societal disapproval, there is evidence that adult males masturbate, at least occasionally, in a few societies other than our own. Although this behavior is apparently rare, Trukese men are reported to masturbate secretly, particularly while watching women bathe. The Polynesian peoples of Tikopia express distaste for masturbation, but men do induce orgasm manually, and this sometimes takes place in the company of other men. Although the Dahomeans condemn adult masturbation and it is reported to be rare, men occasionally masturbate in secret. Adult natives of the Marianas are said to stimulate themselves, but for fear of public ridicule they do so only in solitude.

The data available indicate that some women in a few societies other than our own occasionally masturbate, although the practice generally meets with social disapproval. The evidence is too fragmentary to permit generalization, but it is of interest to note that in a few cases vaginal insertion of a penis substitute appears to be more common than manipulation of the clitoris, although there is, of course, no assurance that the latter form of stimulation is not combined with insertion. African Azande women use a phallus fashioned from a wooden root; but if she is caught by her husband while masturbating, a wife may be severely beaten. In Siberia, Chukchee women masturbate with the large calf muscle of a reindeer. Tikopia women occasionally insert a manioc root or a banana for self-stimulation, and Crow women rub the clitoris or insert a finger into the vagina in the attempt to obtain sexual satisfaction. Among the Aranda of Australia, women apparently quite often finger the clitoris as a means of erotic stimulation. Powdermaker makes the following interesting statement concerning Lesu women, the one society in which there appears to be no sanction levied against female masturbation:

A woman will masturbate if she is sexually excited and there is no man to satisfy her. A couple may be having intercourse in the same house, or near enough for her to see them, and she may thus become aroused. She then sits down and bends her right leg so that her heel presses against her genitalia. Even young girls of about six years may do this quite casually as they sit on the ground. The women and men talk about it freely, and there is no shame attached to it. It is a customary position for women to take, and they learn it in childhood. They never use their hands for manipulation. (Powdermaker, 1933, pp. 276-277.)

In this connection it is interesting to note that similar behavior sometimes occurs in American society. After describing certain physical changes in the sexual organs that he considers reliable proof of habits of self-stimulation, R. L. Dickinson adds that puzzling exceptions sometimes occur. Extreme enlargement of the labia minora, which he regards as a sign of masturbatory habits, may occur in female patients who categorically deny that they have ever handled the sex organs or inserted anything in the vagina. The solution is sometimes fairly simple. "For example, there was the patient who constituted a baffling problem because of the extreme frequency of reported orgasm, but without pressure by finger, thighs, pillow or mattress; she was finally observed at one visit to the office to be sitting on her heel." (Dickinson, 1949, p. 55.)

Masturbation in Male Animals. Many animals other than man engage in activities that result in stimulation of their own sexual organs. And in at least a few species it is obvious that masturbation is undertaken with the specific purpose of producing an orgasm. This is particularly true of some subhuman primates. It is well known that some captive male apes and monkeys form habits of self-stimulation. The penis is manipulated with a hand or foot, or is taken into the mouth. Adult males frequently induce ejaculation by one or a combination of these masturbatory techniques. Some of the monkeys studied by E. J. Kempf concluded unsuccessful attempts at copulation by lying and rubbing the penis against the floor until emission took place. The usual external signs of orgasm (e.g., mild convulsions) accompanied this behavior.

Hamilton described masturbation on the part of one of his adult male monkeys but tended to consider this kind of behavior abnormal, and blamed its occurrence upon the "unnatural conditions" under which the animal had lived. Carpenter's field studies of New and Old World monkeys suggest that Hamilton's interpretation was incorrect. Free-living spider monkeys manipulate their sexual organs with the tip of the exceedingly prehensile tail; and comparable reactions occur in several other species.

When he began his observations on free-living rhesus monkeys Carpenter anticipated that some masturbatory behavior would be seen, but only under special conditions. "By *a priori* reasoning it was expected that masturbation would be observed in isolated males or immature males. . . . [However] during this study three observed instances of self-stimulation to the point of ejaculation occurred in adult, mature males during association with females!" (Carpenter, 1942, p. 152.)

Case histories which are presented in conjunction with the foregoing quotation show that at least some males that have ample opportunity to copulate with receptive females will nevertheless occasionally indulge in masturbatory behavior. The same thing apparently is true in the case of male baboons, at least under conditions of captivity. All the males in the colony studied by Zuckerman masturbated fairly frequently. This generalization applies not only to "bachelors" but also to mated animals that could copulate with adult females whenever they wished to do so. Marais stated that free-living male baboons lacking opportunity for coitus often resorted to masturbation, but Zuckerman was unable to confirm this conclusion in his own field studies. Although prepuberal chimpanzees often manipulate their own genitalia, Yerkes believes that masturbation in adulthood is exclusively a substitute for sexual intercourse and will disappear when mature and sexually congenial individuals have free access to opposite-sexed partners.

Male mammals of many subprimate species manipulate the penis with their forepaws or mouths and sometimes employ inanimate objects as a source of genital stimulation. Sexually excited male porcupines, for example, walk about on three legs while holding one forepaw on the genitals. They also rub the penis and scrotum vigorously against the ground or against any projecting objects that are conveniently placed. A third characteristic response is described in the following quotation, which refers to a captive male of this species: "His excitement was evidenced by . . . holding a long stick in his fore paws and straddling it as a child does a broom-stick. The stick was held so that his genitals were stimulated by the contact, and the wood soon accumulated odor from the urine and glandular secretions absorbed. In consequence, it was a natural source of sexual stimulation." (Shadle, 1946, pp. 159-160.)

Male elephants sometimes manipulate their semierect penis with the trunk. Before and after coitus male dogs and cats regularly lick the phallic organ, often showing convulsive pelvic movements which indicate the stimulatory value of the resulting sensations. Male rodents sit upon the hind feet and manipulate their genitals with forepaws and mouth. After each copulation the male shrew assumes a sitting position and forces the penis back into its sheath; until this is done a second intromission is impossible.

Some male mammals possessing no prehensile appendages are known to stimulate their own genitals. McBride and Hebb recorded a good deal of masturbatory behavior on the part of captive dolphins. One male had a habit of holding his erect penis in the jet of the water intake, and other individuals characteristically rubbed the tumescent organ against the floor of the tank.

A very unusual type of self-stimulation has been described for the red deer. Males of this species shed their antlers each spring and a new pair develops during the summer. During rutting season, which occurs in September and October, the hardened antlers apparently constitute an extremely sensitive erotic zone. F. Fraser Darling describes the masturbatory behavior of the stag as follows:

This act is accomplished by lowering the head and gently drawing the tips of the antlers to and fro through the herbage. Erection and extrusion of the penis from the sheath follow in five to seven seconds. There is but little protrusion and retraction of the penis and no oscillating movements of the pelvis. Ejaculation follows about five seconds after the penis is erected, so that the whole act takes ten to fifteen seconds. These antlers, used now so delicately, may within a few minutes be used with all the body's force behind them to clash with the antlers of another stag. These mysterious organs are a paradox; at one moment exquisitely sensitive, they can be apparently without feeling the next. (Darling, 1937, p. 161.)

Darling adds that he has seen a stag masturbate three times in a morning at approximately hourly intervals even though the male had a harem of hinds with whom he could copulate at will.

Masturbatory Behavior in Female Animals. It is of considerable evolutionary significance that female mammals of most subprimate species indulge in self-stimulation much less frequently than do males. Exceptions do occur. For example, during the breeding season females may rub the swollen vulva against available objects or manipulate the labia with forepaws and mouth. And when they are in heat some females drag the vulva over sticks, stones, or bare patches of ground, depositing odoriferous material that serves to attract and excite the male. Furthermore, if specialized prehensile organs are available they may be employed in genital stimulation. Occasionally a female may achieve genital friction in an unusual manner. Female porcupines in estrus sometimes hold one end of a stick in one forepaw and walk about their cage in an erect position while straddling the stick. Vibrations produced in the stick as its lower end bumps along the ground probably are transmitted to the vulva with which it is in close contact. In this and nearly all other instances, the behavior has the appearance of a response to localized irritation in the genitals. It is similar to the autogenital manipulations of subprimate males.

As far as female primates of infrahuman species are concerned, three generalizations seem justified. First, as in lower mammals, masturbatory behavior is less frequent in this sex than in the male. Second, such genital stimulation as can be observed in females never produces the clear-cut climactic results that are seen in masturbating males. And, third, when it does occur, feminine masturbation in subhuman primates, particularly chimpanzees, more nearly resembles the self-stimulatory activity of women than does the similar behavior pattern shown by infraprimate females.

Autogenital manipulation is quite infrequent among female monkeys. Hamilton states that one of his females which at first appeared to show genuine masturbation turned out upon careful examination to be indulging in "mere reflex scratching of the genitalia which were irritated by partially dried menstrual discharge." According to Zuckerman, comparable behavior may occur in other kinds of monkeys: "Female baboons . . . may sometimes be seen examining their ano-genital regions with their fingers, but they have not been observed actually masturbating. The habit is commonly practiced by all the males of the colony including those that are mated." (Zuckerman, 1932, p. 230.) The writer adds, however, that female baboons that are caged alone may masturbate occasionally. During estrus a female gray-cheeked mangabey observed by Zuckerman habitually examined her swollen perineum and often rubbed it on available surfaces.

Self-stimulation appears to be equally rare in wild female monkeys. The female spider monkey may manipulate her elongated clitoris with the prehensile tail, but the reaction is neither frequent, vigorous, nor prolonged. Although he observed several cases of male masturbation in free-living rhesus monkeys, Carpenter never saw the same behavior in females, despite the fact that his records cover the behavior of 40 females and 45 estrous periods.

In the great apes, as in monkeys, the tendency toward autogenital behavior is much weaker in females than in males. Nevertheless, recognizable attempts at masturbation do appear occasionally; and when this occurs the techniques may be similar to the methods adopted by some women. Bingham has collected the evidence on this score, and the following comments are based upon statements in his monograph.

Sexually immature female chimpanzees occasionally engage in behavior that leads to genital stimulation. One animal, for example, sometimes turned her back to the grillwork of the cage door and pressed her genitalia against it as hard as she could. Another prepuberal female who was being tested for ability to construct towers from packing boxes habitually rubbed her sexual parts against the corner of a box. Bingham describes another immature ape who took advantage of unusual external circumstances to stimulate her genitalia. The animal was being carried in a large box which contained a pool ball. She promptly settled down in a squatting position with her vulva touching the ball. Swinging movements of the carrier produced vibrations in the pool ball and caused it to rub back and forth against the female's genitalia.

Adult female apes sometimes devote considerable energy and ingenuity to the achievement of vulvar stimulation. In one instance a full-grown chimpanzee was playing with a mango. First she placed the fruit upon her external genitals. Then, apparently dissatisfied with the results of this procedure, the animal put the mango on the floor, sat down upon it, turning, twisting, and rubbing awkwardly with her hands and continually varying her position, "as though to improve her technique of producing genital friction." Subsequently, the chimpanzee raised and lowered her body repeatedly, bumping her genitals against the fruit. Later she explored the vagina with a finger and also inserted a pebble into the orifice. The most complicated and, perhaps, effective masturbatory procedure shown by the same individual is described in the following quotation:

On another occasion, Malapulga inserted the stem of a leaf . . . [in her vagina], then turned posteriorly to the bars of the cage and swayed back and forth. The leaf was thus pushed from bar to bar. As it slipped from one bar to the next there was set up considerable vibration in the stem, to which the inner walls of the vagina were evidently sensitive. In these scattered observations on masturbatory practices there is evidence of experimental procedure. . . . The variety of methods employed by the female chimpanzee is especially significant. (Bingham, 1928, pp. 150-151.)

Interpretation of Human Masturbation. In view of the extremely widespread occurrence of autogenital stimulation throughout the class Mammalia it seems illogical to classify human masturbation as "abnormal" or "perverted." This form of sexual expression appears to have its evolutionary roots in the perfectly normal and adaptive biological tendency to examine, to manipulate, to clean, and incidentally to stimulate the external sexual organs. In the course of evolution as learning ability increased and individual experience and experimentation became progressively more important, these reactions assumed a more frankly sexual nature. For many male monkeys and apes and for some female chimpanzees masturbation constitutes a supplement to or a substitute for coitus. The human capacity for symbolic behavior has permitted marked increase in the sexual significance of masturbation by linking it with fantasy and imagination. But the basic potentialities are a part of the biological inheritance of the species.

"Spontaneous Orgasm"

One other type of sexual response that occurs without the presence or participation of a second individual is the so-called "spontaneous orgasm." The phrase is set in quotation marks to indicate the difficulty of proving the complete absence of external stimulation. There are a few women and men who say they are capable of inducing a complete sexual climax in themselves by indulging in sexual fantasies. A more common illustration of spontaneous orgasm is the nocturnal emission or "wet dream." Here, however, one cannot entirely rule out the possibility that the genitals have been stimulated to a certain extent by contact with the bedding or night clothes. Nevertheless, the amount of such stimulation probably is not sufficient to account for the resulting phenomenon.

In Chapter XII it will be shown that nocturnal ejaculation occurs in men whose spinal cords have been completely severed. Under such conditions the lower nerve centers responsible for the phenomenon are completely disconnected from the brain. Therefore, erotic dreams are not an essential complement of this response. It seems more probable that sexual dreams associated with genital reflexes are a product of sensations arising in the tumescent phallus.

According to Kinsey, Pomeroy, and Martin, 83 per cent of the postpuberal males in our society have ejaculated during sleep at least once in their lives. Individual differences are great, but during the late teens nocturnal emissions occur on an average of once every four weeks. From this age onward they become progressively less frequent and are rare after the age of forty. Relatively few women experience sexual climax during sleep. But spontaneous orgasm can occur in adult females in the absence of any apparent bodily stimulation. As noted above, they sometimes take place in a few extremely responsive women in connection with sexual fantasy, and they are reported to be common in female morphine addicts during periods of enforced withdrawal.

Nocturnal emissions occur in men of other societies, but information as to their frequency is scarce. In a few societies the first "wet dream" experienced by the adolescent boy is taken to be a signal of his maturity (see Chapter X). Evidence concerning nocturnal emissions is reported primarily in connection with native dream interpretation. Nearly every society about which we have adequate knowledge recognizes the existence of male orgasm experienced during sleep. Dreams involving sexual climax in women, however, are only rarely referred to in the anthropological literature.

Male mammals of several species occasionally display complete erection during sleep. In connection with his description of the genital anatomy of the short-tailed shrew, Pearson writes as follows:

It is not difficult to study the penis because some males experience frequent erections during the mating season. These occur while the animal is lying asleep on its side or back. First, the penis becomes erect; then the animal stirs restlessly and there are twitching movements of the hind legs, although the shrew is not yet fully awake. After several seconds a number of minor thrusts are made, followed by one vigorous, deep thrust which is accompanied by rigid extension of the hind limbs as in actual copulation. This may be repeated two or three times before the animal awakens and scurries off. . . . There may be several of these episodes in a half hour. I have never seen an emission during one of them, but there can be little doubt that they represent an erotic phenomenon closely related to the nocturnal emissions of man. (Pearson, 1944, p. 41.)

Actual ejaculation can occur in some animals while they are asleep. L. R. Aronson has observed erection in sleeping male house cats. Genital tumescence is often accompanied by pelvic movements similar to those occurring in coitus, and fluid collected from the tip of the penis contains large numbers of motile sperm, proving that ejaculation has taken place.

SUMMARY

In this chapter we have considered those forms of sexual behavior that can be indulged in by the individual alone. The activities involved are masturbation and "spontaneous orgasm." It has been shown that societies differ with respect to their attitudes toward self-stimulation; but regardless of the cultural ideals, at least a few members of every society do indulge in masturbatory practices. It appears universally true that men are more likely to practice self-stimulation than are women.

Examination of the cross-species evidence has revealed that self-stimulation occurs in many subhuman mammals. In the case of some other primates the behavior is frankly sexual. Male monkeys and apes sometimes induce ejaculation and orgasm by masturbating themselves. It is considered particularly significant that such behavior occurs in wild male primates despite ample opportunity for heterosexual coitus. Equally important is the fact that female monkeys and apes stimulate their own genitals much less frequently than do males.

Among the lower mammals, nibbling, licking, and pawing of the genitals is extremely common, although perhaps more so for males than for females. At this level of the evolutionary scale, however, the behavior has the appearance of self-cleaning or grooming rather than deliberate self-stimulation. Nevertheless, the genital manipulations of lower mammals probably constitute the prototype of genuine masturbatory behavior which appears at the primate level.

Males of at least a few lower mammalian species sometimes develop a full genital erection during sleep. This reflexive response may be accompanied by copulatory movements and in at least one species it includes the ejaculation of seminal fluid.

The basic mammalian tendencies toward self-stimulation seem sufficiently strong and widespread to justify classifying human masturbation as a normal and natural form of sexual expression. Nevertheless, members of most human societies consider masturbation by adults to be undesirable. We believe that the relative infrequency of self-stimulation among mature people in most societies is a consequence of social conditioning. In the absence of cultural rules against it, such behavior probably would occur much more frequently than it actually does. These generalizations apply particularly to males. The lower frequency of feminine masturbation may well have an evolutionary or biological explanation. The cross-species comparisons strongly suggest that this is the case; the matter will receive additional consideration in Chapter XII.

We have now surveyed the different types of sexual behavior exhibited by adults in various human societies and in a large number of animal species. It has been shown that heterosexual coitus is the dominant mode of sexual expression in all human societies and in all subhuman mammals. At the same time we have pointed out basic tendencies throughout the mammalian scale leading to homosexual behavior, autogenital stimulation, and sexual activities involving members of different species. The frequency and form which all of these activities show in maturity are in part a consequence of the species heredity and in part the result of development during the early years of life. In order better to understand the sexual behavior that appears in adulthood we turn in the next chapter to a consideration of the development of sexual practices in the growing individual.

Chapter X

Development in the Individual

THE various forms of sexual behavior that have been analyzed in preceding chapters do not appear in complete form in the newborn organism. Many of them, in fact, do not appear even in the reproductively mature individual unless the requisite amount of practice and experience has occurred. This chapter is primarily concerned with the ontogeny of sexual habits—with the development of sexual patterns in males and females of our own and other mammalian species. As far as human beings are concerned, the rate and direction of such development may be strongly affected by the social code of the group in which the individual grows up. However, regardless of cultural conditioning, the kinds of sexual responses that are possible are limited by physiological factors. Accordingly, we begin this chapter with a discussion of the physiological processes involved in sexual maturation.

PHYSICAL MATURATION

Directly beneath the brain in a special bony cavity lies the pituitary gland. The forward or anterior portion of this organ is often referred to as the "master gland" because hormones which it secretes control the activity of several other glands located in different parts of the body. Certain of the anterior pituitary hormones that are known as "gonadotrophins" stimulate growth and activity in the male and female gonads or sex glands. The pituitary secretes very little gonadotrophic material during infancy and childhood, but just prior to puberty the production and release of these hormones are increased. This is the initial physiological step toward the achievement of sexual maturity. The exact age at which the change occurs varies from one individual to the next, but it takes place on the average during the thirteenth or fourteenth year in boys and perhaps a year earlier in girls.

The effects of gonadotrophins upon the reproductive glands are twofold. The ovaries and testes respond to the crucial pituitary secretions by beginning to synthesize and secrete their own hormones. In addition, the sex glands start to produce mature germ cells—eggs in the case of the ovaries and sperm in the case of the testes. The increase in the secretion of sex hormones usually antedates by a year or more the appearance of mature sperm and eggs.

Evidence revealing the relationship between pituitary secretion and gonadal function comes from several sources. Analysis of the urine of pre- and postadolescent boys and girls shows that increase in the concentration of pituitary gonadotrophins is closely correlated with the sex gland changes. The same sort of measurements reveals an increase in the secretion of testicular and ovarian hormones shortly after the rise in the level of gonadotrophic substances. Direct examination demonstrates that the reproductive glands become larger at this time, and microscopic study makes it plain that the cellular structure of these organs is altered simultaneously. The presence of motile sperm or of ripe eggs can be demonstrated directly (however, see subsequent sections of this chapter that deal with the first occurrence of ovulation).

Experimental and clinical investigations show that the adolescent changes in testes and ovaries must be preceded by activation of the pituitary function. If the pituitary gland is removed from experimental animals before puberty, the gonads do not develop and other signs of sexual maturation are absent. Similar symptoms accompany the failure of the normal pituitary function in human beings. However, animals deprived of this gland will develop normally if they are injected with pituitary extracts. Finally, it is possible to evoke precocious puberty in some species by pituitary administration. Male chicks only a few days old react to the injection of the appropriate pituitary hormones by growing a comb, crowing, and attempting to mate like an adult rooster. The testes in these animals are strongly stimulated by the pituitary treatment and therefore secrete a sex hormone. It is the male hormone from the testes that causes the physical and behavioral changes characteristic of sexual maturity.

Precocious physical and behavioral maturity has been induced in rats, mice, dogs, monkeys, and other mammals by supplying the immature organism with large quantities of gonadotrophic hormone from the anterior pituitary gland. Similar results can be produced in our own species. Some boys whose testes fail to descend into the scrotum have been treated with pituitary extracts. If too much gonadotrophic hormone is given, the testes may respond by secreting large amounts of the male hormone and this substance in turn induces premature development of the sexual organs and of the secondary sex characters which are defined below.

At the time of puberty several additional glandular changes occur. Although its function is not at all clear, it is known that the thymus gland grows smaller. The thyroid becomes increasingly active as puberty approaches and then grows somewhat less so in the later stages of adolescence. The behavioral consequences of these extragonadal endocrinological changes are of little interest at this point; hence they will not be considered further.

We have seen that the first step toward sexual maturation is increased pituitary function, and that the second is growth and maturation of the gonads, both as sources of a sex hormone and as the site of the production of fertile germ cells. The third phase in this chain of events consists of a variety of bodily responses to the sex hormones that are released from the reproductive glands. Some of these changes are internal and are largely unnoticed except by the experimentalist or the physician. Others are well known and recognized in every human society, and may in fact be defined as signals that call for changing the individual's social status.

The primary sex characters are the gonads—ovaries in the female and testes in the male. Accessory sex structures include the vagina, uterus, and Fallopian tubes of the female, and the penis, seminal vesicles, prostate gland, and epididymis of the male. One effect of the sex hormones is to produce growth of these accessory structures. In girls, the lips or labia of the vulva enlarge at the time of puberty and the uterus gradually assumes its adult form. The first menstruation (menarche) occurs in response to increased concentration of ovarian hormones, usually well in advance of the time that the entire reproductive tract is mature. In boys, the penis grows larger and the seminal vesicles and prostate increase in size and become functional. Not until the latter two organs are developed is the male capable of normal ejaculation, although, as noted below, orgasm can occur at a much earlier age.

The secondary sex characters are numerous and somewhat variable from species to species. In male and female human beings they include pubic and axillary (underarm) hair. Deepening of the voice occurs in both sexes, although it is more marked in the male. Facial hair begins to appear in boys; other body regions including the chest, forearms, and legs may also become more hirsute. The female breast is a secondary sex character and growth of this structure is usually rather rapid at the time of puberty. In males, the shoulders tend to become wider and in females the hips undergo similar alteration.

Proof that the sex hormones are responsible for these developmental changes in accessory and secondary sex structures is abundant. When, in human beings, the gonads fail to undergo the expected growth changes during puberty, the other bodily alterations described above do not occur. Men whose testes never develop do not grow beards; they retain the high-pitched preadolescent voice and fail to acquire the normal masculine bodily conformation. Girls whose ovaries do not mature never menstruate and do not develop prominent breasts. If the reproductive glands are removed from domestic or experimental animals before puberty, the normal physical and behavioral signs of adolescence fail to materialize.

Many of the phenomena usually associated with puberty can be produced in human beings and lower animals by the administration of the appropriate sex hormones. Men without functional testes react to injections of a male hormone by developing a deeper voice, sprouting a light beard, and assuming more masculine bodily proportions. These changes have been produced in some individuals as late as the third decade of life. Women lacking normal ovaries can be caused to menstruate and to develop larger breasts if they are treated with estrin, one of the ovarian hormones.

Finally, many of the accessory and secondary sex characters can be caused to develop prematurely under the influence of sex hormones derived from some source other than the individual's own reproductive glands. Infant male animals treated with testicular hormone display excessive growth of the sexual organs and accentuation of the secondary sex characters, and in general take on the appearance of a miniature adult. Similar changes occur in immature females that are injected with ovarian hormones.

In human beings there sometimes occurs a condition known as precocious puberty. The outward signs of this abnormality are striking. Male children only two or three years of age may show all the physical signs of maturity. In some cases there is a heavy beard growth. The voice is deep and the accessory sexual structures are well developed. In normal human beings one part of the adrenal gland secretes hormones that are very closely related to the testicular hormones. Cases of masculine precocious puberty usually are caused by tumors of the adrenal which cause that gland to produce very large amounts of the male sex hormone.

The fact that the secondary and accessory sex structures in the male respond to the appropriate hormone injections, even though the testes may be immature, indicates that under normal conditions the changes which occur at puberty are due to the male hormone from the gonads. Somewhat similar conditions sometimes occur in female children. Little girls have been known to menstruate as early as three or four years of age, and in such instances other secondary sex characters tend to assume the adult condition. Most of these children suffer from tumors of the ovary which cause that gland to secrete ovarian hormones in amounts equal to those normally produced during adulthood. It is particularly instructive to note that despite the striking advance in physical development, children showing signs of precocious puberty are mentally and emotionally normal for their chronological ages. Furthermore, so far as is known, their sexual behavior is childlike rather than adult. This fact is especially important in connection with the evaluation of the role of learning in normal human sexuality—a topic that is discussed later in this chapter.

Differentiating Puberty from Adolescence

The terms "puberty" and "adolescence" have been used frequently in the foregoing discussion, and it is now necessary to consider their precise meanings. It is sometimes assumed that once an individual has passed through puberty he or she is sexually mature. Actually, however, puberty and maturity are temporally separated. Derived from the word *pubes*, meaning hair, the first term refers to the initial appearance of body hair in the genital region. It signifies the beginning of sexual maturation.

Adolescence is the period extending from puberty to the attainment of full reproductive maturity. Adolescence lasts several years in some species and involves a complex series of changes in several organs and organ systems. Different parts of the reproductive system reach their maximal efficiency at different stages in the life cycle; and, strictly speaking, adolescence is not completed until all the structures and processes necessary to fertilization, conception, gestation, and lactation have become mature. This complex maturational process may stretch over a period of ten years or longer.

The outward signs of puberty occur in most boys during approximately the fourteenth year. Rarely, however, do the testes contain fertile sperm any earlier than the fifteenth year and in many cases fertility may be delayed even longer. Menstruation starts in most girls before their ovaries are capable of producing ripe eggs. And egg production, in turn, begins before the uterus is mature enough to support normal gestation. The attainment of full reproductive maturity is therefore a gradual process, subject, of course, to marked individual differences. For most individuals the menstrual rhythm during the first year or two after its inception is less regular than it will be in adulthood. Very often the period of flow is protracted and several months may intervene between the first few periods.

Relatively few girls are capable of reproduction before fifteen years of age, and even then their reproductive capacity is not as great as it will be later. The average age for full reproductive maturity in women has been estimated at approximately twenty-three years. This means that coitus is less likely to result in conception in the postpuberal girl than in the mature woman. A statistical study of age at first pregnancy in 2535 Scottish wives bears out this general conclusion. The data presented in Table 7 show that women fifteen

TABLE 7

Percentage of Wives Conceiving During the First Two Years of Marriage

NUMBER OF WOMEN	AGE AT MARRIAGE	PER CENT CONCEIVING	
		FIRST YEAR	FIRST TWO YEARS
700	15-19	13.71	43.71
1835	20-24	18.49	90.51

to nineteen years of age are less likely to become pregnant during the first two years of marriage than are wives who are five years older. (These figures are based upon the early findings of J. Mathews Duncan, as summarized by M. F. Ashley Montagu, 1946.)

The phenomenon involved here is customarily referred to as adolescent sterility. It may be the explanation for certain important anthropological observations having to do with sexual behavior. In a number of human societies girls are permitted free sexual activity from puberty until marriage, but there appear to be relatively few conceptions even though contraception is reputedly not practiced. The discrepancy between frequent copulation and infrequent impregnation is particularly striking in the case of the Ifugao natives of the Philippines and the Trobrianders. This matter is discussed in greater detail later in the present chapter.

Some lower animals mature more rapidly and some more slowly than man. Laboratory rats and mice ordinarily become capable of fertile mating within about two months after birth. The age of reproductive maturity is approximately eight months in some breeds of dogs, three years in rhesus monkeys, nine years in female and seven and one-half years in male chimpanzees, and thirteen years in the elephant. A few of the larger mammals mature much less

TABLE 8

Relative Fertility of Adolescent and Adult Female Chimpanzees

	RESULTS OF 78 PAIRINGS OF YOUNGER FEMALES	RESULTS OF 177 PAIRINGS OF OLDER FEMALES
Per cent of matings resulting in pregnancy	14.0	30.0
Per cent of pregnant females aborting within 100 days or less after conception	36.0	18.0

rapidly. For example, fertile mating does not take place in the rhinoceros until the twentieth year. All mammals that have been carefully studied pass through a developmental period of adolescent sterility similar to that which is believed to occur in human beings.

In rhesus monkeys, baboons, and chimpanzees, as in the human female, the first menstrual cycles tend to be longer and less regular than they are in adult animals. The earliest menarche recorded for a chimpanzee is 7.5 years and the latest 10 years. The first few cycles in this species are usually 46 to 54 days long, whereas those of the healthy, mature female rarely exceed 36 days and usually average about 32 to 34 days. The period of adolescent sterility lasts from four months to more than two years in different individuals. Young and Yerkes collected data that show the relative fertility of adolescent and adult chimpanzees. The figures presented in Table 8 demonstrate that the differences seen in women have their parallel in the ape.

PUBERTY CEREMONIES IN DIFFERENT SOCIETIES

In contrast to the gradual developmental changes that characterize the period of adolescence, the onset of puberty is comparatively abrupt and has therefore claimed the attention of human beings in many societies. Special ceremonies are designed to mark this phase of the individual's life.

Girls. The onset of menstruation furnishes an obvious and dramatic signal of approaching physiological maturity in girls. In a large number of societies[1] the first menses are an occasion for more or less elaborate ceremonial. One common feature of many such ceremonies is the seclusion of the girl, particularly from any contact with men. The period of seclusion may last for only a few days or it may continue for several months.

In many instances the secluded girl receives special instruction from an older woman in matters pertaining to sex and marriage. The tuition generally includes an explanation of the social regulations governing proper conduct in sexual affairs, a description and sometimes a demonstration in pantomime of the techniques of lovemaking, advice on how to get along in married life, methods of avoiding conception, and what to expect in childbirth. In some societies the pubescent girl must undergo certain hardships while she is in seclusion. She may be "deflowered" and subjected to genital mutilation. Her ears may be pierced, her skin tattooed or scarified, her hair cut off, and her teeth filed or blackened. Very often the conclusion of the period is marked by a feast or dance at which the girl, after bathing or going through ritual purification, publicly dons the clothes of a mature woman.

Some comprehension of the nature of puberty ceremonies for girls can be gained from the following examples. Among the northern Thonga of Africa, the girl at the time of her first menstruation goes to an older woman of her own choice and announces that she is of age. Subsequent events are described by Junod as follows:

[1] Aleut, Andamanese, Apache, Arapaho, Arikara, Ashanti, Barama, Bena, Chagga, Chewa, Cheyenne, Chiricahua, Cree, Cuna, Dahomeans, Flathead, Fox, Havasupai, Hopi, Ila, Kiwai, Kurtatchi (nobility), Kutchin, Kutenai, Lamba, Macusi, Manus, Maricopa, Marshallese, Mataco, Nama, Nauruans, Navaho, Oto, Papago, Pima, Sinkaietk, Swazi, Thompson, Thonga, Tikopia, Toba, Tolowa, Trobrianders, Trukese, Wogeo, Yapese, Zulu. Inferred: Abipone, Aranda, Choroti, Dieri, Dusun, Goajiro, Kamilaroi, Kwakiutl, Lenge, Loyalty Islanders, Mbundu, Miriam, Nandi. Orokaiva, Palauans, Pedi, Seniang, Tehuelche. Toda, Tswana, Wolof, Yuma.

They will begin a *seclusion period* of one month. Three or four girls receive the initiation together. They are shut up in a hut, and when they come out, must always wear over their face a veil consisting of a very dirty and greasy cloth. Every morning they are led to the pool, and their whole body is immersed in the water as far as the neck. Other initiated girls or women accompany them singing obscene songs, and drive away with sticks any man who happens to be on the road, as no man is allowed to see a girl during this period. If a man happens to come near the group, the women ask him the secret formulae of the circumcision school, not the long ones but the short ones, probably those which contain licentious words. Should he be unable to answer, they beat him. It is said that a man who sees a girl during this month becomes blind! When the cortege of women accompanying the initiated has returned home, the nubile girls are imprisoned in the hut. They are teased, pinched, scratched by the adoptive mothers or by other women; they must also listen to the licentious songs which are sung to them. Though they are trembling from cold, being still wet, they are not allowed to come near the fire. They are also instructed in sexual matters, and told that they must never reveal anything about the blood of the menses to a man. They are also exhorted to be very polite to every grown up person, and must salute everybody entering the hut, even those passing before the door, by clapping their hands. Sometimes the wind moves some dead leaves; they mistake this noise for the sound of steps and salute reverently!

At the end of the month the adoptive mother brings the girl home to her true mother. She also presents her with a pot of beer. A feast takes place on this occasion.... (Junod, 1927, Vol. I, pp. 177-178.)

At menarche the Marshallese girl retires to a specially built hut, accompanied by a number of immature girls who are to act as her maids-in-waiting. The pubescent girl wears two loin mats in the fashion of an adult woman and underneath them a wadding to absorb the menstrual blood. For fifteen days she remains secluded and during this time she may not eat fish or meat. All cooking for the girl and her attendants must take place outside the hut. They are looked after by an elderly woman who teaches them songs and tells them moralistic stories. Every morning before dawn the girls go down to the sea to bathe and put on clean mats. When they return to the hut the elderly woman purifies and perfumes the pubescent girl by burning sweet-smelling leaves and passing them between her legs. On the fifteenth day a final ceremony takes place which releases the girl from seclusion and marks the end of her girlhood.

Lenge girls go through an elaborate puberty ceremonial. They are "deflowered" with a special tool made of horn and remain in an initiation school for an entire month during which they may not eat meat or salt. Sexual instruction is given indirectly through the recitation of magical formulas. At the close of the period a day is spent bathing in the sea. Fertility medicine is given to the girls and they then return home to remain in seclusion for two or more months.

Practices similar to those occurring at the time of puberty take place in some societies at times other than at menarche. Attempts to enlarge the labia, ear piercing, tattooing, and scarification may take place either before or sometimes after first menstruation. Among the Alorese, for example, girls are tattooed at any time between the ages of ten to fourteen. Before puberty, girls on Ponape undergo treatment designed to lengthen the labia minora and to enlarge the clitoris. Old impotent men pull, beat, and suck the labia to lengthen them. Black ants are put in the vulva; their stinging causes the labia and clitoris to swell. These procedures are repeated until the desired results are attained. At the age of about fifteen Jukun girls have their ears pierced during a minor ceremony. Prior to this time and for three weeks thereafter they may not indulge in sexual intercourse. When Venda girls attain the age of ten to twelve years they begin to practice the custom of pulling out and lengthening the labia minora. Girls who fail to do so are criticized as being lazy. "You will remain nothing better than a post one smears one's dirt on. You are a tree that lends no hold. Just a hole without anything."

Like "coming-out parties" in our society, puberty ceremonies for girls serve among other things to announce to the public that these young women have now attained adult status. In some societies the initiation rite marks the point at which girls are permitted to begin indulging in sexual intercourse. If sexual life for girls begins before puberty, such ceremonies may signalize the young woman's eligibility for marriage.

Boys. A number of societies provide initiation rites for boys. In some cultures the only ritual is the adoption of some symbol of manhood. On Truk, for example, when the boy's pubic and facial hair becomes sufficiently noticeable, he merely adopts a red loin cloth and goes to live in the men's dormitory. Among some other peoples, however, the ceremonial is very complicated and extends over a considerable period of time.[2] For boys there is no event comparable to menarche in girls that can be seized upon as an indication of maturity. Nevertheless, such physical signs as the appearance of facial and other bodily hair or the first nocturnal emission are sometimes taken as an indication of masculine maturity, and boys may at that time undergo an initiation ceremony. On the other hand, many of the societies which subject boys to complex initiation ceremonies pay little attention to the time at which the rite takes place. Quite frequently boys are initiated in groups, and the ceremonies are conducted at any time when enough boys are considered sufficiently mature.

In a large number of societies, initiation for boys consists primarily of a period of seclusion during which the neophyte undergoes ordeals and receives instruction on sexual matters. In some, genital mutilations including circumcision, subincision (slitting a section of the urethra), and in one society at least (Ponapeans) hemicastration (the removal of one testis), form a part of the initiation ceremony. Sodomy constitutes part of the puberty initiation for boys in a few societies (see also Chapter VII). Women are usually excluded from these ceremonies, and the practices which take place are carefully kept secret from all feminine members of the society. The following examples illustrate the nature of initiation ceremonies for boys.

Among the Keraki, boys undergo a most complicated initiation, which we can only summarize briefly. The initiates are several in number, about thirteen years old. In preparation for the period of initiation a space is cleared in the bush, and by the edge of the clearing a structure is built as a dormitory. The first important rite is the revelation of the bull-roarer (a primitive musical instrument) to the uninitiated; while this is being done each boy must remain perfectly silent and motionless. Following this the boys submit to a blow on the back with a heavy banana stalk. Next come a feast and a parade through the village, after which the initiates return to

[2] Ainu, Aleut, Alorese, Andamanese, Apache, Apinaye, Aranda, Arikara, Azande, Balinese, Chagga, Cherente, Chewa, Colorado, Creek, Dahomeans, Delaware, Dieri, Dusun, Gilbertese, Hopi, Ila, Jivaro, Jukun, Kababish, Kamilaroi, Kansa, Keraki, Kiwai, Kurtatchi, Kusaians, Kwoma, Lango, Lesu, Marshallese, Masai, Mbundu, Menomini, Miriam, Nama, Nandi, Orokaiva, Oto, Pedi, Ponapeans, Pukapukans, Purari, Seminole, Seniang, Sinkaietk, Swazi, Tanala, Taos, Tasmanians, Thompson, Thonga, Tikopia, Tokelauans, Tongans, Tswana, Venda, Wogeo, Wolof, Xosa, Yuma, Yungar, Zulu, Zuñi.

the dormitory. That night begins a period of nearly a year during which the boys play a passive role in sodomy with older men. During this time they may not even be seen by women but are constantly at the service of older men, who may be fellow villagers or visitors wishing to have anal intercourse with the initiates. At the end of the period a second feast occurs and the boys are released from seclusion to return home, entitled now to assume the role of an adult male.

When the Chewa youth reaches the age of puberty the chief of his village is advised of this fact by the boy's maternal uncle. Preparations are made for the initiation, which is usually delayed until several boys are ready to undergo the ceremony. When the day arrives the boys are led blindfolded to a secluded spot where the cult figures are made and kept. Of the boy's treatment there Steytler writes:

Here the boy is kept for about a week and he is cruelly treated. He is swung over a slow burning fire, drawn prostrate over the hard ground, beaten with rods, rolled in ants and itching beans, pulled about with a string tied to his private parts, made to eat excrement and drink urine, etc. The test is very severe and if the boy in pre-puberty days happened to be disobedient . . . he is more severely treated still. . . . When everything is over and past the boy is taken to the chief, presents are exchanged between relations and the chief and the boy receives his new name. (Steytler, 1934, p. 95.)

DEVELOPMENT OF SEXUAL BEHAVIOR IN HUMAN BEINGS

It has been explained that the attainment of sexual maturity is a gradual process and that the various organs and organ systems involved in reproduction become functional at different stages in the life of the individual. We have further noted that in many societies the individual's entrance into adolescence receives public recognition in the form of puberty ceremonials. But up to this point very little has been said about sexual behavior per se. The nervous and muscular mechanisms involved in sexual arousal and its overt expression can properly be classified as very important elements in the interrelated system of physiological factors that must become mature before reproduction can occur.

Reflexive Components. Some of these mechanisms for behavior are reflexive, whereas others develop only as a result of practice and learning. For example, the human male does not have to learn how to fill his penis with blood so that it becomes erect and rigid, but he may have to learn how to copulate; the conditions under which an adult man experiences erection undoubtedly are influenced by his life experiences. There are decided differences between various animal species as regards the extent to which mating responses depend upon or are modified by learning and conditioning.

It is possible to analyze separately the several reflexes and more complex reactions that normally appear simultaneously or sequentially in the sexual act of adult males and females. When this is done it becomes obvious that different segments of the total response mature at different rates. In the human male, for example, complete genital erection is possible from the day of birth, and baby boys frequently show this reaction under the influence of bladder distention or in response to manipulation of the phallus. The power of ejaculation, in contrast, is not acquired until puberty, and the production of normal sperm is delayed until even later in life.

In grown men orgasm and ejaculation usually occur together, but they are not necessarily mutually dependent. As a matter of fact, it is reported that sexual climax or orgasm can be produced in very young human infants of either sex. Kinsey, Pomeroy, and Martin state that male infants less than one year of age respond to manipulation of the genitals by making thrusting movements with the pelvic muscles; and if the stimulation is continued the baby's movements become more rapid and vigorous and culminate in a general spasm quite similar to that which characterizes climax in most adults.

The evidence therefore suggests that the neuromuscular system of the human animal is capable at birth of mediating at least two of the basic reflexive patterns that will later be woven into the complete sexual act. But adult patterns of sexual behavior consist of a great deal more than genital and pelvic reflexes. What other mechanisms are involved, how do they develop, and when do they become mature? How are the simple, inherited reflexes elaborated into the much more complex and variable forms of sexual expression that characterize adults in different societies? A fully satisfactory answer to these questions could be obtained only by studying the sexual play of many children of varying ages in a large number of different cultural settings. Unfortunately, however, the amount of such activity that occurs and the ease with which the observer can obtain information concerning it are controlled to a large extent by the attitudes of adults. And these attitudes vary to a great extent from one society to the next.

Restrictive Societies. In a minority of the societies concerning which we have adequate information adults attempt to deny young children any form of sexual expression.[3] As will be explained later, this is the prevailing attitude in American society, although there is considerable variance between actual behavior and the idealized standards of the moral code.

The severity of restrictions and punishments associated with sexual transgressions in childhood varies from one restrictive society to another. Among the Apinaye, for example, boys and girls are warned from infancy not to masturbate and a severe thrashing awaits the child suspected of such behavior. In Africa, Ashanti boys are told by their fathers at an early age not to masturbate or engage in any sexual play. In New Guinea, Kwoma boys are constantly warned not to finger their genitals; if a woman sees a boy with an erection she will beat his penis with a stick, and boys soon learn to refrain from touching their genitals even while urinating. Kwoma girls also are told not to finger their genitals but are not punished for so doing. The Cuna specifically forbid their children to engage in either homosexual or heterosexual play; and youngsters among the Chiricahua are whipped if they are detected playing sex games.

Most of these restrictive societies maintain a public conspiracy against the acquisition of any sexual knowledge by children. Adults avoid mentioning matters of sexual significance in their presence, and make every attempt to keep them in total ignorance of the reproductive process. Among the natives of the western Carolines sex is never discussed before children, especially girls. Cuna children remain ignorant of sexual matters (as far as adult instruction is concerned) until the last stages of the marriage ceremony. They are not even allowed to watch animals give birth. Chagga children are told that babies come out of the forest.

In a number of these societies particular pains are taken to prevent young children from accidentally observing sexual behavior. In some instances, as among the Murngin of Australia, boys are removed from the dwelling to the boys' house or bachelors' hut when they are four or five years old; this is done for the specific purpose of preventing them from witnessing sexual behavior at home. The Kwoma husband and wife are always careful to wait until the children are asleep before indulging in sexual intercourse.

[3] Abelam, Apinaye, Ashanti, Chagga, Chiricahua, Cuna, Dahomeans, Haitians, Kwoma, Manus, Murngin, Penobscot, Rengma, Trukese.

Such adult attitudes toward childhood sexuality may prevent youngsters from engaging in sexual practices in the presence of their elders, but whether they successfully suppress sexual activity in secret is another matter. There is evidence that in some of these societies children do engage in a certain amount of sexual behavior despite strong adult disapproval. In Haiti little boys and girls privately experiment in sexual activity from early childhood until puberty. Manus children masturbate, but always in solitude and surrounded by shame. When they are alone in the bush Kwoma boys scrape the penis with nettles. And on Truk, children play at intercourse at an early age, although their parents will beat them if they are caught. In Trukese society children do sometimes observe their elders engaging in sexual activities at night. Apinaye boys and girls masturbate frequently even though such play is punished whenever it happens to be observed, and despite the fact that at a ceremony which is conducted when they are half grown their genitalia are examined and the children are flogged if there appears to be evidence of masturbation. In the case of boys, this "evidence" is described as "retractibility of the prepuce." But the validity of such criteria is questionable. Actually, there are no known physical stigmata that constitute reliable evidence of habitual masturbation as far as the male is concerned. R. L. Dickinson has long held that prolonged habits of feminine masturbation involving vulvar traction and friction leave permanent signs in the form of lengthened and corrugated labia. However, Dickinson's thesis is not accepted by all authorities, and in any event it applies to mature women and not to "half-grown" girls.

Some peoples make a sharp distinction between socially immature and mature persons with respect to permissible sexual activity. These societies take the attitude that sexual intercourse before adulthood must be avoided; but once the person is mature by their standards, considerable freedom in sexual matters may be allowed.[4] For the most part these peoples seem particularly concerned with the prepubescent girl, believing that intercourse before the menarche may be injurious to her. Girls of the east central Carolines are strictly forbidden intercourse before puberty, but after that they enjoy almost complete sexual freedom. After menarche, Ao girls begin to

[4] Ao (girls), Ashanti (girls), Choroti (girls), Chukchee (girls), Haitians (boys), Jukun (girls), Lamba (girls), Mataco (girls), Seniang, Siriono (girls), Swazi, Toba (girls), Tupinamba (girls).

sleep in dormitories where they indulge in intercourse with partners of their choice. Among the Siriono intercourse before puberty is forbidden, but premarital affairs are customary once the girl has menstruated. The Chukchee believe that intercourse will harm a girl until her breasts are fully developed or until she begins to menstruate. However, immature girls often engage in coitus despite this belief. In this society it is considered proper for a girl to carry on serious love affairs between the time of the first menstruation and marriage. The Ashanti are convinced that sexual intercourse with a girl who has not undergone the puberty ceremony is so harmful to the community that the offense is punishable by death for both partners. Premarital intercourse is also forbidden to the postpubescent Ashanti girl, but this rule is not nearly so strictly enforced.

In most of the African societies in our sample[5] boys are strictly forbidden to have intercourse before undergoing the puberty ceremony or initiation rite. The Chagga boy, for example, cannot have intercourse until he has been circumcised and properly initiated into adult status. If caught in the act the boy and his partner are laid one on the other and staked to the ground. After circumcision all Chagga boys have intercourse with a barren woman and subsequently they sally forth to seek other sex partners. Until marriage they are instructed to practice either interfemoral intercourse or coitus interruptus unless the girl places a pad in the vagina to avoid conception. A comparable attitude is taken by the Jivaro of Ecuador, who strictly forbid boys to engage in intimate relationships with girls until they have gone through an initiation ceremony at puberty.

In other societies the prohibitions against sexual intercourse continue unabated or, in some instances, are intensified after puberty and remain in force until marriage or at least until betrothal. The methods used to prevent premarital sexual activity during adolescence include segregation of the sexes, strict chaperonage of girls, and threats of severe disgrace or physical punishment. The extreme pains to which adults in these societies are forced to go in order to control the sexual behavior of young people is an eloquent expression of the strength of the tendency on the part of older children and adolescents to engage in such activity. There are indeed very few societies in which any method of control appears to be completely effective in preventing heterosexual intercourse among young unmarried couples.

[5] Chagga, Masai, Pedi, Swazi, Thonga (inferred), Wolof.

Perhaps the most nearly successful method of controlling the sexual activity of young people is to separate the sexes and keep the girls under constant surveillance. Among the Abipone, for example, boys and girls were strictly segregated at all times and premarital chastity is said to have been universal. A similar situation exists among the Arapaho, Cheyenne, Papago, and Wapisiana, all of whom keep the sexes strictly apart from childhood. Boys and girls never play together, and until marriage young men and women never associate in the absence of chaperones. The only completely effective prevention of premarital relations has been devised by the Wapisiana. They define cohabitation as marriage, and thus rule out the possibility of intercourse between two unmarried people. At the same time, of course, they eliminate the problem of the unmarried mother.

In most of the societies that practice segregation and chaperonage to control the sexual behavior of adolescents, boys are less carefully watched than girls; and, in some cases at least, it appears that youths are able to circumvent the barriers, with the result that sexual intercourse before marriage not infrequently occurs. For example, among the Hopi a strong attempt is made to keep boys and girls apart from the age of ten until marriage; the girls are kept at home and are accompanied by an older woman whenever they go out. Girls are expected to be chaste until marriage. Boys, however, are not similarly restricted, and, whenever possible, they defeat the chaperonage system by crawling into the girl's house stealthily at night or by holding clandestine prearranged meetings. The Hopi place all the blame for illegitimate pregnancy squarely upon the girl who is involved. Her friends ignore her and her family scolds her, but the lover is not regarded as at fault and is neither forced nor expected to marry her.

A similar situation exists among the Kiwai Papuans of New Guinea. There, girls are carefully chaperoned by their parents and usually kept in ignorance of love-making for some time. The boy, however, is not similarly restricted and will take the initiative in attempting to get around the rules. The young pair have to be very clever to meet; they usually are able to do so only at night. The girl may slip out of the house after her parents are asleep or the boy may sneak into her house through the floor. And apparently, despite every effort on the part of adults, many couples find it possible to carry on love affairs in secret.

Threats of the most severe disgrace and punishment do not appear to be completely effective in preventing young people from engaging in sexual activity before marriage. In the Gilberts, for example, great emphasis is placed on a girl's chastity before marriage. If a girl is seduced and it becomes public knowledge, both parties are put to death. Nevertheless, the evidence indicates that many transgressions take place in secret. In only a few societies—namely, the Vedda, Keraki, Chiricahua, and Sanpoil—is the burden of guilt placed upon the boy. Among the Vedda, for example, if a man were seen even talking to an unmarried girl her relatives would kill him. In most of these restrictive societies, however, the threats of disgrace and punishment are specifically directed toward misbehavior on the part of the girl.

The attempts of adults to restrict the sexual behavior of adolescents seem, in many of these societies, to be intended primarily as a means of insuring the virginity of the unmarried girl. Some peoples attempt to determine whether or not a girl has remained chaste by conducting a crude examination of her sexual organs. The hymen or "maidenhead" is a tab of tissue which, in most virgins, partially obstructs the entrance of the vagina. Very often this structure is nicked or stretched when the vagina is sufficiently penetrated for the first time, and a certain amount of blood may be lost. However, the size and thickness of the hymen vary from individual to individual. As a result, some fully virginal girls may bleed very little if at all during the first intercourse, whereas in other women a great deal of stretching is necessary before the obstruction offered by this tissue is completely removed.

Despite the actual unreliability of their tests, some societies use the occurrence of bleeding in response to vaginal penetration as an important index to chastity. Among the Kurd, for example, when the bridegroom has intercourse with the bride the nuptial cloth is examined for blood. If a girl is shown to have been a virgin, the cloth is paraded on a stick through the village and the bride price is then paid. If, however, the bridegroom finds himself disappointed, the girl is heaped with abuse, given back to her parents, and in some instances subjected to further public disgrace. Yungar girls are "deflowered" a week before marriage by two old women. If, at this time, examination fails to indicate chastity severe penalties are meted out to the girl, including starvation, mutilation, torture, and even death.

American Society.   The social code pertaining to sexual behavior of children and unmarried adolescents in the United States is clearly a restrictive one. In this country, constant pressure is exerted, ideally at least, to prevent any form of sexual behavior until it is legalized and can occur in the bonds of matrimony. In this society, as in many others, there is a tendency toward a double standard in respect to premarital sexual behavior. More pressure is brought to bear upon unmarried girls than upon boys. In actual practice, furthermore, the burden of protecting young persons from indulging in sexual activity falls somewhat more heavily upon the parents of American girls than upon the parents of boys. This tendency toward a double sex standard is also reflected in attitudes toward extramarital sexual activity. As has been shown, a double sex standard during late childhood and adolescence is characteristic of many societies, but not of human beings in general. There are societies in which there is little if any difference in the premarital sexual restrictions placed upon girls and boys, and in a few societies the more severe restrictions confine the male rather than the female.

Kinsey and his associates have shown in statistical fashion what has generally been recognized for many years, namely, that in spite of the attitudes of adults, children in our society frequently indulge in many forms of sexual activity. Although the strictness with which the moral code is enforced varies considerably from one social class to another, a more or less concerted attempt to prevent children from indulging in any form of sex play continues well into adolescence and up to the time of marriage. And, as we have noted, most other societies that discourage infantile and childhood sex play also attempt to control premarital experimentation in sexual matters on the part of adolescents or young adults.

Although this attitude is characteristic in America, the strength of condemnation varies somewhat from one social group to another However, regardless of the prohibitions against it, premarital sexual behavior does occur in a fairly large proportion of the population. It does not necessarily involve actual copulation. Landis and his co-workers report that 59 per cent of the married women whom they questioned had indulged in extensive heterosexual play without coitus prior to marriage. Forty-two per cent of the unmarried women in this study admitted the occurrence of sex play.

According to Kinsey, Pomeroy, and Martin, more than 80 per cent of American males engage in petting before they are twenty years old. By the age of twenty-five, approximately one-third of the male population has achieved orgasm in this fashion. Men from the higher educational levels are likely to confine their adolescent activity to noncoital techniques, whereas individuals from the lower socio-educational strata tend to proceed more or less directly to coitus and indulge in a minimum of petting.

As far as actual copulation is concerned, Kinsey and his collaborators report that it was attempted during or before adolescence by 22 per cent of the American boys they interviewed. The first experiment usually takes place between the ages of 10 and 14. By the time he is 12 years old approximately one boy in every four or five has at least tried to copulate with a girl or woman. More than 10 per cent of these youths experience their first ejaculation in connection with heterosexual intercourse. Considering all the men interviewed in Kinsey's study, it becomes apparent that more than two-thirds of them had at least one premarital experience involving copulation. The incidence of such behavior varies with the individual's socioeducational level, being least frequent in college-educated groups, and nearly universal among men who have no more than an eighth-grade education.

Terman found that approximately one half of 760 American husbands whom he studied admitted premarital intercourse with the women they later married. Seven per cent of this group said they had copulated with at least one other woman prior to marriage, and 26 per cent mentioned intercourse with five or more women before marriage. Only 13.3 per cent of the 777 wives represented in Terman's sample admitted premarital relations with the husband, and much smaller percentages listed intercourse with other males before marriage. The lack of agreement between accounts given by husbands and wives probably reflects chiefly a different degree of resistance to confessing premarital freedom. Terman was particularly impressed with differences between older and younger married couples as regards premarital behavior. He noted that the proportion of men and women who were virgins at marriage had steadily decreased between the approximate dates of 1910 and the early 1930's.

If the drop should continue at the average rate shown for those born since 1890 virginity at marriage will be close to the vanishing point for males born after 1930 and for females born after 1940. It is more likely that the rate of change will become somewhat retarded as the zero point is approached and that an occasional virgin will come to the marriage bed for a few decades beyond the dates indicated by the curves. It will be of no small interest to see how long the cultural ideal of virgin marriage will survive as a moral code after its observance has passed into history. (Terman, 1938, p. 323.)

Semirestrictive Societies. There is no clear-cut dividing line between restrictive and semirestrictive societies; and often, as we have pointed out, the sexual codes that adults attempt to enforce on immature members of the group differ according to the young person's sex or age. There are, however, many societies[6] in which the adult attitudes toward sex play in children or toward premarital affairs in adolescents are characterized by formal prohibitions that are apparently not very serious and in fact are not enforced. In such cases sexual experimentation may take place in secrecy without incurring punishment, even though the parents know perfectly well what is going on. The Alorese formally object to any form of sex play on the part of older children. But overt homosexual and heterosexual practices on the part of boys and girls occur, and children playing together in field houses imitate the sexual intercourse of their parents. Unless this is brought flagrantly to the attention of the adults they do nothing about it.

Among the Andamanese premarital promiscuity is common and the parents do not object as long as the love affairs are kept secret. Parents object to such activities in theory, but unless they are practiced openly no punishment is involved. Should a girl become pregnant, however, the parents of the couple usually arrange for them to be married. The Huichol uphold an ideal of premarital chastity for both sexes, but in practice this is rarely realized. If an adolescent couple is caught in sexual intimacy both individuals are beaten and they are forced to marry; but parents do not keep close surveillance over the activities of young people, and the latter have many opportunities to slip off into the bush in the evening during feasts and dances.

In some societies the only recognized sign of sexual transgression on the part of young people is premarital pregnancy. Among such peoples it appears that intercourse frequently takes place between

[6] Alorese (older children), Andamanese, Aranda (girls), Azande, Bena, Chagga (girls), Colorado (girls), Cree, Creek, Crow (girls), Dusun (girls), Flathead, Ganda (girls), Havasupai, Huichol, Kickapoo, Kiowa Apache, Kiwai, Klamath, Kurtatchi (girls), Kutchin, Kutenai, Kwoma, Lango, Mailu, Mandan, Mangarevans (now), Manus, Mbundu, Menomini, Omaha, Orokaiva (girls), Papago, Pedi (girls), Purari (girls), Ramkokamekra, Reddi, Rengma (girls), Seminole, Sinkaietk (girls), Tinguian, Tokelauans, Venda, Wappo, Yagua, Yako, Zulu (older children).

unmarried couples, but numerous devices and techniques are employed either to prevent conception or to abort an unwanted fetus.
In a number of African societies it is customary for adolescent boys
to practice interfemoral intercourse or coitus interruptus to avoid
impregnating the girl. Contraceptive measures used by young people
in these societies include placing a pad of absorbent material in the
vagina, washing the passage after intercourse, and orally ingesting
certain medicines believed to insure temporary sterility. Should these
fail to prevent conception the girl may resort to an abortion.

Permissive Societies.   Adults in a large number of societies take
a completely tolerant and permissive attitude toward sex expression
in childhood.[7] Under such conditions youngsters engage in a certain
amount of sexual play in public. The fingering of the child's own
genitals follows exploratory movements of the hands which contact
the various parts of the body. If adults do not attempt to discourage
such behavior, fingering the genitals becomes an established habit
of occasional occurrence. As the child grows old enough to walk
about and play with others, he tends to extend the range and to
increase the variety of sexual activities. Handling the genitals of
others of the same or opposite sex occurs frequently under conditions of free sex play. Additional forms of sexual activity on the part
of young children sometimes include oral-genital contacts and
attempted copulation with a sex partner.

In a few permissive societies adults participate actively in the
sexual stimulation of infants and young children. Hopi and Siriono
parents masturbate their youngsters frequently. And in these societies self-masturbation passes practically unnoticed during early
childhood, adults taking a tolerant and permissive attitude toward
all sexual behavior at least until the age of puberty. Among the
Kazak, adults who are playing with small children, especially boys,
excite the young one's genitals by rubbing and playing with them.
In this society autogenital stimulation on the part of young children
is accepted as a normal practice. Mothers in Alorese society occasionally fondle the genitals of their infant while nursing it. During
early childhood Alorese boys masturbate freely and occasionally they
imitate intercourse with a little girl. As the children grow older,

[7] Alorese, Chewa, Copper Eskimo, Crow (boys), Easter Islanders, Hopi, Ifugao,
Ila, Kazak, Kwakiutl, Lepcha, Lesu, Mangarevans (formerly), Maori, Marquesans,
Marshallese, Masai, Nama, Ojibwa, Palauans, Ponapeans, Pukapukans, Samoans,
Seniang, Siriono, Tikopia, Trobrianders, Walapai, Wogeo, Yapese, Yaruro, Zulu.

however, sexual activity is frowned upon and during late childhood such behavior is forbidden to both boy and girl. Actually, however, they continue their sexual behavior, but in secret.

Among the Pukapukans of Polynesia where parents simply ignore the sexual activities of young children, boys and girls masturbate freely and openly in public. Among the Nama Hottentot no secret is made of autogenital stimulation in early childhood. Young Trobriand children engage in a variety of sexual activities. In the absence of adult control, typical forms of amusement for Trobriand girls and boys include manual and oral stimulation of the genitals and simu-lated coitus. Young Seniang children publicly simulate adult copu-lation without being reproved; older boys masturbate freely and play sexual games with little girls, but the boys are warned not to copulate on the grounds that this behavior would weaken them. Lesu children playing on the beach give imitations of adult sexual intercourse, and adults in this society regard this to be a natural and normal game. On Tikopia small boys induce erections in them-selves through manual manipulation, and this is ignored or at most mildly reproved by adults. Little girls also may masturbate in this society without being punished for such behavior.

Most of the societies that permit children free sex play (and some that are semirestrictive) also allow them opportunity to observe adult sexual behavior and to participate in discussions of sexual matters.[8] Among the Alorese sex knowledge is completely accessible to young children and by the age of five they are well informed on all details of the entire reproductive act. All members of the Puka-pukan household sleep in the same room under one mosquito net; and although some parents wait until they think the children are asleep, there are frequent opportunities for youngsters to observe adult sexual activities and sexual matters are often talked about. Lesu children are free to observe adults copulate, with the specific exception that they may not watch their own mothers having inter-course. On Ponape children are given careful instruction in sexual intercourse from the fourth or fifth year. Trukese children receive no formal tutelage, but they learn a great deal by watching adults at night and by asking their elders about sexual matters. Among the

[8] Alorese, Copper Eskimo, Cree, Dusun, Easter Islanders, Flathead, Ganda, Hopi, Ifugao, Lesu, Marquesans, Ojibwa, Ponapeans, Pukapukans, Samoans, Tikopia, Tinguian, Trobrianders, Trukese, Wogeo, Yapese.

Wogeo sexual matters are freely discussed by adults in the presence of children. In this society, however, parents take some precautions against their own children observing them in intercourse.

In the societies where they are permitted to do so, children gradually increase their sexual activities both as they approach puberty and during adolescence. There are, indeed, some societies in which enforcement of the prevailing incest regulations is the only major restriction on sexual activity among adolescents.[9] As in the case of very young children, their sex play first includes autogenital stimulation and mutual masturbation with the same and opposite sex, but with increasing age it is characterized more and more by attempts at heterosexual copulation. By the time of puberty in most of these societies expressions of sexuality on the part of older children consist predominantly of the accepted adult form of heterosexual intercourse, the pattern which they will continue to follow throughout their sexually active years of life.

Among the Chewa of Africa parents believe that unless children begin to exercise themselves sexually early in life they will never beget offspring. Older children build little huts some distance from the village, and there, with the complete approval of their parents, boys and girls play at being husband and wife. Such trial matings may extend well into adolescence, with periodic exchanges of partners until marriage occurs. The Ifugao head-hunters of the Philippines maintain a similar attitude toward the sex play of older children and adolescents. In this society unmarried individuals live in separate dormitories from early childhood. It is customary for each boy to sleep with a girl every night. The only check on promiscuity is that imposed by the girls themselves. Usually a girl is unwilling to form too prolonged an attachment to one boy until she is ready to be married. Boys are urged by their fathers to begin sexual activities early, and a man may shame his son if the latter is backward in this respect. Even after puberty there seem to be relatively few instances of conception resulting from this free sexual activity. Pregnancies do occasionally occur, however, and in that event one of the girl's lovers must marry her.

[9] Ainu, Aymara, Balinese, Barama, Chewa, Copper Eskimo, Crow (boys), Dobuans, Easter Islanders, Futunans, Gilyak, Goajiro, Gond, Ifugao, Ila, Lapps, Lepcha, Lesu, Macusi, Mangarevans (formerly), Maori, Marquesans, Marshallese, Mongols, Nandi, Naskapi, Natchez, Nauruans (commoners), Palauans, Palaung, Ponapeans, Pukapukans, Seniang, Siriono (boys), Taos, Tarahumara, Thonga (girls), Toda, Tongans (boys), Trobrianders, Trukese, Tuareg, Walapai, Wogeo, Yakut, Yapese, Yaruro, Yukaghir.

The Lepcha of India believe that girls will not mature without benefit of sexual intercourse. Early sex play among boys and girls characteristically involves many forms of mutual masturbation and usually ends in attempted copulation. By the time they are eleven or twelve years old, most girls regularly engage in full intercourse. Older men occasionally copulate with girls as young as eight years of age. Instead of being regarded as a criminal offense, such behavior is considered amusing by the Lepcha. Sexual life begins in earnest among the Trobrianders at six to eight years for girls, ten to twelve for boys. Both sexes receive explicit instruction from older companions whom they imitate in sex activities. Sex play includes masturbation, oral stimulation of the genitals of the same and opposite sex, and heterosexual copulation. At any time a couple may retire to the bush, the bachelor's hut, an isolated yam house, or any other convenient place and there engage in prolonged sexual play with full approval of their parents. No marriage is consummated in Trobriand society without a protracted preliminary period of sexual intimacy during which both sincerity of affection and sexual compatibility are tested. Premarital pregnancy is said to be rare in this society, despite postpuberal sexual intercourse over a period of three years or more before marriage. This experience has led the Trobrianders to doubt a causal relationship between coitus and conception. Instead they consider supernatural influences to be far more significant in causing a child to be conceived.

In this instance, as in other cases of frequent but infertile coitus among postpubescent males and females, the phenomenon of adolescent sterility would appear to be particularly pertinent. It may well be that although they have passed the menarche, the girls involved in this activity are not yet ovulating, or at least are incapable of carrying a fetus to term. Any such interpretation must remain speculative, however, until there is more satisfactory proof for the absence of any form of contraception.

An interesting attitude toward the sexual activity of adolescents is taken by the Ila-speaking peoples of Africa. Childhood is regarded as a time of preparation for adult life and mature sexual functions. At harvest time each girl is given a house to which she takes a boy of her choice, and there they play as man and wife. It is reported that there are no virgins among these people after the age of ten. On Easter Island children from the age of six on imitate the sexual behavior of adults without censure; and young people among the

Maori play together at being husband and wife at night in the bush. Full copulation frequently occurs before puberty. Lesu adults regard as natural the attempts at intercourse in which children engage, and they give full approval to free sexual activity on the part of adolescents.

DEVELOPMENT OF SEXUAL BEHAVIOR IN SUBHUMAN SPECIES

Unhampered by social restrictions, young animals of many species display sexual behavior similar to that seen in human children in permissive societies. This is particularly true in the case of the other primates, the anthropoid apes and monkeys.

Subhuman Primates. Systematic observations of infant and adolescent chimpanzees have shown that they engage in a great deal of sexual play. Although reproductive maturity is not attained until the eighth year or later, three-year-old chimpanzees show many autoerotic, homosexual, and heterosexual responses. Masturbatory play appears in both sexes prior to puberty. According to Yerkes, solitary masturbation is more common in the male; when females show comparable behavior they tend to do so in association with companions (see Chapter IX).

Like human children, little male and female chimpanzees play sexual games involving erotic advances by either or both partners and including attempts to effect actual copulation. Several different copulatory positions are experimented with and partial intromission is sometimes achieved. Some young males practice manual and oral stimulation of the feminine genitalia and females may handle the erect penis of their immature partners.

Other primates also engage in a great deal of sex play during infancy and childhood; in fact Zuckerman concludes that before puberty the young monkey reproduces all the sexual activities of its elders, as far as is physically possible. This worker studied the development of sexual patterns in several primate species. He describes a six-months-old male pigtailed monkey that formed a habit of mounting his mother in copulatory fashion whenever she adopted the coital posture. When seven months old this animal displayed erections and pelvic thrusts while covering the adult female. At this time the young one was still nursing; his age was roughly equivalent to that of a two-year-old child.

All manifestations of sexual behavior are present in male and female baboons by the ninth month, at which time the milk teeth have just appeared. Carpenter reports observations of autogenital manipulation in infant spider monkeys living in their native environment. During the first year of life the captive male macaque displays sexual reactions to other animals and even to inanimate playthings. In the course of infantile play female monkeys often execute the adult sexual presentation. Immature animals of either sex may react sexually to the advances of a full-grown partner. Preadolescent female baboons may form lasting sexual partnerships with an adult male long before reproduction is a physical possibility.

Lower Mammals. Males of many subprimate mammalian species frequently execute portions of the adult copulatory pattern long before they are mature. In the course of the mock fighting, wrestling, and chasing which characterize the preadolescent animal, young males often grasp another individual and make one or two coital movements before dismounting. This type of behavior has been observed under laboratory conditions in rats, guinea pigs, and golden hamsters, and comparable reactions are seen in many domesticated species. The male lamb may mount other young sheep as early as the first week of life, although puberty is not attained until several months later. Male calves react similarly, and so do male lion cubs. In no instance is the behavior complete, for the ejaculatory response is lacking, and these fragmentary mating reactions do not give the impression of intense arousal or satisfaction. Instead, they appear to be parts of a broader pattern of play involving generalized excitement.

It is most significant that female mammals of subprimate species do not display any of the adult feminine sex pattern prior to puberty. Only with the occurrence of the first heat period do the female's sexually receptive responses appear. This is in marked contrast to the frequent occurrence of masculine reactions in males of the same species and the fact that immature female primates are as active sexually as males. The cause of these differences is not fully understood, but some clues are available; they will be discussed in Chapters XI and XII.

FUNCTIONAL SIGNIFICANCE OF EARLY SEX PLAY

Having noted that sex play is common among young animals of many species and among human children as well, it is reasonable for us to inquire concerning the possible significance of this phenomenon. For example, does early practice prepare the individual for successful sexual performance in adulthood? Does each animal have to learn how to court and mate?

The answer depends upon the species and sex of the individual. As far as females of species below the primates are concerned, the answer is obvious. They do not practice the adult feminine mating pattern before puberty; nevertheless, when the first estrus occurs they are capable of effective coitus. In several experiments males of the same species have been reared in isolation from other animals from the time of weaning until the attainment of maturity. Despite the lack of opportunity to engage in prepuberal sex play, these animals can copulate effectively the first time they are placed with a receptive female. Apparently no practice is necessary for successful coitus.

The copulatory behavior of male primates is more dependent upon learning than is that of lower animals. Adult monkeys and chimpanzees that have had no heterosexual experience often are unable to copulate with the estrous female. The inexperienced male may be sexually aroused and may attempt to mate when the opportunity arises; but even when the female is thoroughly receptive, the male seems incapable of fulfilling his sexual role. Often he starts to cover the female and then is so awkward in attempting intromission that the mating is never completed. As far as the male chimpanzee is concerned, several months or even years of practice and experience in sexual performance appear essential to the development of maximal coital efficiency.

It is somewhat surprising that similar behavioral deficiencies have never been observed in the mating of sexually inexperienced female monkeys and apes. When they are fully receptive, naïve females invite, accept, and respond appropriately to the sexual advances of an experienced male. And if equally inexperienced males and females are put together after puberty, the female is obviously better prepared to carry out her part of the coital relationship. As a matter of fact she not only performs all the necessary feminine responses, but may attempt to assist the male in the execution of his part of the pattern. Yerkes and Elder summarized the evidence on this point in the following words:

Our data justify the following statements of fact. Prior to sexual maturation, the female chimpanzee, if with other members of her species of comparable age and both sexes, learns from social contacts all that is necessary to enable her to behave wholly appropriately and effectively in the mating situation, and even to encourage, direct, or definitely to aid the male in copulation. By contrast, and this seems strange indeed, the recently matured male who is inexperienced in mating with a mature and receptive female commonly acts initially as does the sexually immature male, somewhat playfully, puzzled, and as if at a loss how to meet the situation. Even if, with the cooperation of the female, he attempts to copulate, he usually fails. . . . Our data indicate that the role of the sexually competent male is not taken by reason of maturation solely, but instead that experience and practice are essential to biological adequacy of performance and still more to perfection and skill. Seemingly it requires months for the mating pattern of the male chimpanzee to become so far perfected that it is satisfactory to the experienced female and in highest degree efficient as reproductive function. (Yerkes and Elder, 1936, pp. 12-13.)

The zoological evidence permits two generalizations concerning the role of practice in the formation of sexual patterns. First, that the importance of individual experience tends to be greater for the higher mammals than for the lower. Second, that among the sub-human primates the male is more dependent upon specific hetero-sexual learning than is the female.

The question of the probable contributions of early experience to the capacity for effective coitus in the human species arises next. The evolutionary data strongly suggest that human sexual patterns are not completely organized on a strictly inherited level. Instead, it is highly probable that practice is essential to complete arousal and particularly to satisfactory expression of sexual excitement. It follows, therefore, that if they are ever to derive maximal satisfaction from sexual relations, individuals who are reared under conditions that prevent or seriously reduce experimentation and practice during childhood and adolescence will be forced to go through the essential learning processes after adulthood has been attained.

This type of adjustment may be exceedingly difficult for young adults of either sex, particularly if they belong to a society that inculcates manifold sexual inhibitions in the developing individual. The man or woman who learned during childhood and adolescence that it was "wrong" to examine or stimulate his or her own genitals, that it was even "worse" to have any contact with those of another person, and, particularly, that attempts at heterosexual relations were immoral, is expected to reverse completely at least some of these attitudes on the wedding night or shortly thereafter. This expectation is difficult to fulfill. If the initial lessons have been well learned, the unlearning is bound to take a long time and may never be completed.

Even the simplest sorts of preliminary sexual instruction seem to help intelligent people to make at least partially satisfactory adjustments to the marital relationship. Dickinson compared wives who before marriage had been examined by a physician and instructed concerning the physical relations involved in intercourse, with other women who had received no such preparation. Of fifteen "instructed" wives, 12 reported the occurrence of orgasm during marital coitus, whereas only 10 of 35 "uninstructed" women had a similar experience.

Davis asked 992 American wives if they felt they had been "at all adequately prepared by instruction for the sex side of marriage." Slightly more than one-half of them replied in the affirmative, but the wording of the question was so ambiguous as to result in contradictory answers. For example, one individual who said she had been well prepared added the following explanation: "My mother taught me what to expect. The necessity of yielding to her husband's demands had been a great cross in her own life." Others who stated that their preparation had been adequate offered comments to the effect that they had known in advance that "men were chiefly animals" or that "most men must be beasts." The adequacy of instructions that produce these attitudes is, to say the least, open to debate.

Some wives answering Dr. Davis' questionnaire stated that their ignorance of the facts about sexual relations had cost them dearly, and that instruction "would have saved years of difficult adjustment." But other women pointed out that their knowledge of the "facts" was sufficient. The difficulty was that they "knew nothing about *sex emotions*" which subsequently proved to be of primary importance. However, regardless of the validity of their judgments concerning the adequacy of premarital preparation, the women who said it had been adequate were, as a group, inclined to view their own marriages as relatively happy. The wives whose instruction was considered inadequate tended to describe their marital relationship as unhappy.

We have no intention of implying that the happiness or success of a marriage rests solely upon sexual factors. On the contrary, some American wives consider their marriages happy although sexual relations are described as invariably distasteful and unsatisfactory. And, contrariwise, other women find the sexual side of marriage totally satisfying but say that other elements in the relationship render their marriages unhappy. The points that seem worth making are (1) that satisfactory sex adjustment appears to increase the likelihood of successful marriage, (2) that ignorance and lack of preparation reduce the probability that such adjustment will occur, and (3) that a society which permits extensive sex play in childhood and adolescence may thereby increase the chances that sexual relations in marriage will be pleasant and mutually satisfying.

SUMMARY

In this chapter we have outlined the physiological changes that lead to achievement of full reproductive maturity. It has been shown that they are gradual rather than abrupt, and that the outward signs of puberty are indices to the onset of adolescence, which actually extends over a period of eight to ten years and precedes the life stage of maximal reproductive efficiency. Nevertheless, many human societies recognize the puberal changes as socially significant and use them as indicators of the individual's readiness to enter adult life. Among many peoples the appearance of these signs is marked by ceremonials and initiation rites.

As far as actual sexual behavior is concerned, it develops somewhat more rapidly in certain societies than in others. Some cultures fully approve of a variety of sexual practices among young boys and girls and between adolescents of both sexes. When there is any difference in treatment, the behavior of girls is more carefully controlled than is that of boys. As long as the adult members of a society permit them to do so, immature males and females engage in practically every type of sexual behavior found in grown men and women.

There are other societies, including that of the United States, which attempt to restrict severely the sexual activities of prepubescent and adolescent individuals. Cultural ideals may include disapproval of any sexual life whatsoever for all unmarried persons. However, even under the most severe restrictions some individuals do engage in a certain amount of erotic play.

Males and females of several subhuman primate species are known to indulge in a great deal of sexual play which leads eventually to the perfection of adult patterns of heterosexual coitus. There is some reason to believe that the practice thus acquired is essential to the performance of biologically effective intercourse in adult life. The contribution of sexual experimentation and learning in human sexual relations is unknown. But the zoological data suggest that personal experience in coitus may be very important. Such experience may be gained early in life under certain social conditions, or deferred until after marriage in other circumstances.

After reviewing the cross-species and cross-cultural evidence, we are convinced that tendencies toward sexual behavior before maturity and even before puberty are genetically determined in many primates, including human beings. The degree to which such tendencies find overt expression is in part a function of the rules of the society in which the individual grows up, but some expression is very likely to occur under any circumstances.

Chapter XI

Feminine Fertility Cycles

W E EXPLAINED in Chapter X that the various physiological changes associated with the attainment of physical and reproductive maturity produce alterations in sexual behavior. The appearance of completely adult sexual performance in lower animals and, to a certain degree, in our own species depends in part upon the gradual development of certain glands and other organs involved in reproduction. This chapter and the one that follows are devoted to an analysis of the physiological forces that continue to influence the desire and capacity for sexual activity after adulthood is reached. One of the most obvious and powerful types of physiological control over behavior is exerted by the female sex glands; the present chapter deals with this topic.

PHYSIOLOGY OF THE FEMALE SEX CYCLE

Periodic menstruation occurs in human beings, in all species of apes, and in some kinds of monkeys. It is governed by the rhythmic secretion of certain hormones. Prime movers in the menstrual rhythm are two hormones produced by the anterior pituitary gland. These are the gonadotrophins which were described in Chapter X. Stimulated by the pituitary hormones, the ovaries produce and release into the circulatory system a hormone known as estrogen or, more accurately, estrone,[1] which produces a series of changes in the

[1] There are a number of closely related hormones that have the same effects as estrone. They are called "estrogenic hormones" or, generically, "estrogen," the term that is used in this book.

walls of the uterus. Under the influence of estrogen the inner lining of the uterus grows thicker and develops a very rich blood supply (see Figure 7). The ovary's secretion of hormones is a cyclic affair. A week or so after the cessation of the menstrual flow the production of estrogen begins to increase, and it reaches a high point approximately fourteen days after the beginning of the preceding period of bleeding. This is about two weeks before the next flow begins. In most women ovulation occurs at or near this stage of the cycle, and one or occasionally several eggs are released from the ovary to enter the Fallopian tubes.

Just before or shortly after ovulation the ovary begins to secrete increasing amounts of a second hormone, progesterone. Progesterone prepares the uterus for the "implantation" of any egg which may be fertilized. When conception occurs, the fertilized egg descends the Fallopian tubes, eventually comes to rest against the wall of the uterus, and is embedded there. Later the placenta develops and connects the maternal and fetal organisms. If fertile copulation does not take place, the lining of the uterus, which has been built up by estrogen and further stimulated by progesterone, disintegrates and

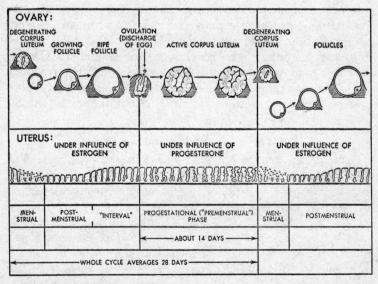

FIG. 7. Diagram illustrating the sequence of events in the menstrual cycle. (Courtesy of Dr. George Corner, The Princeton University Press.)

is shed into the uterine cavity. Preceding this degenerative change there occurs a temporary shutting off of the coiled arteries that supply the new tissue with blood. Circulation is re-established within a few hours, but in the interim the capillary blood vessels that were temporarily deprived of their blood supply have suffered. They burst when the blood flow is resumed. Little pools of blood collect and drain off with the dying tissues which cannot survive without the blood formerly carried by the capillaries. This sequence of changes produces the external signs of menstruation. Except when pregnancy intervenes, the cycle is repeated every twenty-eight days, more or less, from the time of puberty until the onset of the menopause.

The menstruation of apes and Old World monkeys is characterized by the same physiological events that occur in women. New World monkeys do not bleed externally but they do show a regular rhythm of slight internal blood flow. The length of the cycle in infrahuman primates varies from approximately three weeks to thirty days depending upon the species, but in all species, as in human females, differences between individuals are pronounced. Ovulation occurs during the mid-menstrual interval and in some primates it is accompanied by conspicuous swelling of the sex skin which lies next to the external sex organs.[2] Sex-skin stimulation is due at least in part to increase in the amount of estrogen. Within two or three days after ovulation, by which time the estrogen level has been markedly lowered, the swelling of the sex skin is greatly reduced. Sensory nerves in the sex skin arise from the same spinal roots whose motor fibers innervate the vagina. Zuckerman suggests that when this area is swollen and congested, the nerve endings may be stimulated by pressure and the resulting sensations may direct the animal's attention to its own genitalia. In addition, there may occur reflex excitation of the motor nerves to the vagina which evoke increased tonicity and perhaps movement of the muscular walls.

Menstruation does not occur in mammals that are below primates on the evolutionary scale, but the remaining features of the ovarian cycle are present in modified form.[3] The ovaries of guinea pigs, rats,

[2] In some kinds of monkeys the sex skin does not swell appreciably but it may become brilliantly colored during estrus.

[3] Female mammals of subprimate species do not menstruate but may nevertheless show some vaginal bleeding at a particular stage in the reproductive cycle. This occurs, however, at the time of estrus and ovulation rather than during the period of infertility. The bleeding of ovulation and the menstrual bleeding are quite different phenomena.

cows, dogs, and other lower mammals secrete estrogen in gradually increasing amounts as the time for ovulation approaches, and then progesterone is secreted for a while. In these species as in the higher mammals, progesterone prepares the uterus for implantation of the fertilized egg.

Females of our own and other primate species display regular ovarian cycles throughout the year and may conceive during any season, although in some cases, at least in rhesus monkeys, cycles without ovulation are more common during warm summer weather. Absence of a well-marked breeding season is also characteristic of some domesticated animals. Female cattle come into heat periodically throughout the year. Except when pregnancy occurs, the ovaries produce ripe eggs and secrete large amounts of estrogen, and the cow is sexually receptive at intervals of approximately nineteen or twenty days. According to Asdell, the breeding season of the sow probably extends over the whole year. Unless she is pregnant or suckling, estrus occurs every eighteen to twenty-four days. Marshall and Hammond state that the mare, goat, and ewe belong in this same general category of polyestrous mammals. Some wild animals are also polyestrous. Female lions, for example, come into heat at irregular intervals throughout the year, although heat periods tend to be more frequent during the spring.

Unlike the animals discussed thus far, the vast majority of mammals and nearly all the lower vertebrates are fertile for only one or two relatively short periods in each year. The remainder of the time the reproductive glands in these species produce relatively little hormone and sexual behavior does not occur. It is in these "seasonally breeding species" that the relationships between the secretory activity of the ovaries and the appearance of sexual behavior are most obvious.

RHYTHMS OF SEXUAL BEHAVIOR

Lower Mammals.   Female cats and dogs usually come into heat, or estrus, twice a year. At these times the sex glands manufacture and pour into the blood stream relatively large amounts of their hormonal products. As the level of estrogen increases, the female becomes sexually attractive to males, and it is only at this time that she actively seeks a sex partner and readily engages in intercourse. As a matter of fact in some species, such as the guinea pig and chinchilla, the vaginal orifice is completely closed by an epithelial membrane except when the female is in estrus. At other times the penis cannot penetrate the vagina. Only while the appropriate ovarian hormones are present in adequate amounts does the female desire sexual stimulation. And, of course, it is precisely at this time that her ovaries contain ripe eggs and she is capable of conceiving as a result of copulation with a fertile male.

In lower mammals, therefore, the female's sexual urge is rigidly tied to reproductive functions by means of chemical control through the ovarian hormones. In most of these animals the duration of the female's receptive period is predetermined by hormonal rhythms and is not affected by the occurrence of fertile mating. Many coital acts usually take place during this period. In a few species, however, this is not the case. Instead, the female loses her desire for sexual stimulation within a few hours or days after copulating. And at the same time she ceases to attract and arouse the male. The cat stays in heat several days if she is not mated, but she becomes unreceptive within approximately twelve hours after intercourse. Coitus apparently shortens the period of heat in several other species including the shrew, porcupine, and Alaskan seal.

An important exception to the foregoing generalizations concerning hormonal control of sexual responsiveness must be noted at this point. In many if not all subprimate species there seem to be a few aberrant or abnormal females that never become sexually receptive in spite of the fact that, as far as can be determined, they show normal hormonal rhythms. That is to say, they present all the physiological signs of estrus, including the normal vaginal cycle and ovulation, but they consistently refuse to accept the male. A complete explanation for the behavior of these deviant individuals is not presently available. In one species, the guinea pig, it appears that the difficulty lies in a low sensitivity to ovarian hormones. The neuromuscular mechanisms necessary for sexual responses are present, but they do not react to normal amounts of ovarian hormone. If these chronically nonreceptive females are injected with extremely large doses of the appropriate hormones they may display normal mating responses. The psychological significance of these findings lies in the existence of similar barriers to sexual behavior in the more highly evolved species that are discussed later in this chapter.

Subhuman Primates.   Like females of lower mammalian species, apes and monkeys show a clear-cut rhythm of sexual desire. The female is maximally attractive to the male and most eager for sexual contact at those times when ovulation is imminent and copulation can result in conception (see Chapter V). But the relation between reproductive physiology and sexual behavior is less rigid in primates than in lower mammals, and the result is that under certain conditions female monkeys and apes may accept the male when they are infertile and physiologically not in estrus.

The female mangabey's pudendal area increases in size during the middle of the ovarian cycle between two periods of flow. According to Zuckerman, however, males and females of this species may copulate at any point in the cycle, although sexual activity is most frequent at the time of genital swelling when the estrogen level is elevated and the female is likely to be fertile. The bonnet monkey, Moore monkey, and pigtailed monkey all copulate at every stage of the female's cycle, but do so more often and more vigorously during her physiological estrus.

Ball and Hartman measured sexual receptivity in female macaques and correlated fluctuations in this behavioral function with the ovarian condition of the monkey. They found that the peak of sexual responsiveness appears from two to five days before ovulation. But it was observed that under special conditions the female may receive the male at any time regardless of her reproductive status. The menstrual cycle of the baboon ranges from twenty-three to forty days in length, the average being thirty and one-half days. The period of flow extends from two to four days. The perineal region is enlarged before and during the approximate time of ovulation and the sex skin is quiescent throughout the second half of the cycle. The male baboon usually controls the time of mating because the females are completely subjugated and passive. Zuckerman has noted, however, that copulation is most likely to occur while the female's sex skin is engorged. Within a baboon harem, the temporary "chief wife" of the male overlord is the female whose genital skin shows the greatest swelling (see Chapter VI). But if none of his females are in this condition a male may copulate with them anyway.

Since the anthropoid apes are man's nearest living relatives, evidence concerning the behavioral effects of the feminine sex cycle in these animals is of particular importance in formulating an evolutionary interpretation of human activities. Fox describes copulation in a pair of caged orangutans as a daily occurrence irrespective of the female's physiological condition. Carpenter states that captive gibbons copulate throughout the year and do not restrict their intercourse to the female's fertile period. Young and Orbison studied various types of social interaction between male and female chimpanzees at different stages in the female's menstrual cycle. They observed not only copulation but a variety of other interpersonal responses including the following: signs of excitement on the part of the male prior to his access to the female, tendency of the male to move toward the female when allowed to do so and to attempt coitus, tendency of the female to move toward the male and to adopt the sexual presentation posture which serves as an invitation to mate, and tendency of the pair to remain close together. Scores on all of these items were high during the period when the female was in physiological estrus and capable of conception. During the subsequent phases of her cycle each of the various items of behavior occurred less frequently, although none of them disappeared entirely in every pair. The conclusions reached by Young and Orbison deserve quotation.

A well defined period of sexual desire and responsiveness is still present in the chimpanzee and it coincides with the follicular [i.e., high estrogen] phase of the cycle rather than with the days shortly before or after menstruation as in many human females. On the other hand, the chimpanzee may resemble man in that differences between individuals appear to be more important than sexual [i.e., reproductive] status in determining the character of the pattern of behavior when individuals of opposite sex are brought together. . . . Differences between individuals and the consort, [also] affect the pattern of sexual behavior in lower mammals. . . . [But] we assume the influence of the consort becomes progressively greater as man is approached, with a greatly accelerated change during the later stages of his evolution. It seems probable that the corresponding assumption may be made for differences between individuals. (Young and Orbison, 1944, p. 139.)

It is of major significance that these writers, and other workers before them, discovered a few adult female chimpanzees that would never mate although they showed normal cycles of ovarian secretion and menstruation. No explanation is available as yet. It may be that such individuals, like the guinea pigs mentioned earlier, secrete average amounts of ovarian hormone but are relatively insensitive to them. If this were the case the failure to copulate might be corrected by administration of supranormal concentrations of the essential substances. However, there remains the very real possibility that the difficulty is not as simple as this interpretation would indicate, but that a more complex psychological inhibition prevents indulgence in normal sexual relations.

There is the further observation that when they are fully in estrus some female apes show marked reluctance to engage in sexual relations with certain males, although other masculine consorts may be eagerly accepted. Yerkes writes of one female, Wendy, who, when in the phase of maximal swelling, was fully receptive and willing to copulate with a male named Bokar. She rejected Pan, a second male, although he desired and apparently expected coitus. When Pan solicited copulation, Wendy descended from the netting of the cage wall and assumed the coital position. Pan approached, but before he reached her Wendy sprang up and attacked him. Yerkes interpreted this paradoxical behavior as a case in which the female was temporarily dominated by her physiological condition, which was conducive to sexual receptivity, and started to respond appropriately, but then her negative feelings about that particular male suddenly overcame the purely biological determinants of behavior.

All observers appear to agree that individual differences in responsiveness to different consorts are of great importance in sexual relations between male and female chimpanzees. Yerkes has pointed out that completion of the mating pattern does not necessarily imply female receptivity even in low degree:

. . . Since the male consort may dominate and command the female . . . she may respond defensively, protectively, or accommodatingly *in the experimental mating situation*, whatever her sexual status, desire, or preference. A fully receptive female may on occasion repulse the advances of a responsive male, or the reverse may occur. In either case the consort which was non-coöperative may mate promptly with another individual. Such selectiveness usually seems to be due to physical incompatibility, individual preference, or unfavorable affective relations. The ability of females to control a male in the mating situation differs extremely. (Yerkes, 1939, p. 110.)

The following additional illustration of variable behavior by a female toward different consorts is taken from Yerkes and Elder's monograph on the subject:

Mona, a large and courageous, mature, experienced female, was many times given opportunity to mate with Bokar, Pan, and Jack. For each pair of consorts the pattern was distinctive. When receptive she accepted any one of them eagerly and copulation occurred typically with only slight differences in behavior. But when she was slightly or non-receptive, Mona exhibited the following differential behavior: Bokar's advances she met aggressively, and by intimidating him she completely controlled the mating situation. Pan she treated somewhat indifferently, if he chanced to exhibit sexual interest or desire. Her attitude and behavior toward him indicated familiarity and confidence in his self-control. But in the presence of Jack she was alert, cautious, conciliatory, and defensive, and if necessary she would permit copulation. (Yerkes and Elder, 1936, pp. 31-32.)

Male chimpanzees show clear-cut preferences for certain feminine sex partners and individuals vary in the degree of their selectiveness. Apparently all males prefer copulation with a female when she is in the stage of greatest genital swelling, but some apes are sufficiently motivated sexually to copulate at other times if the female will co-operate.

In the sexual behavior of monkeys there first appears some evidence of a low degree of social control over responses that are almost completely dependent upon hormonal secretions as far as lower mammals are concerned. The more highly evolved apes display an even greater degree of emancipation from endocrinological domination of their mating activities. These observations correlate with others presented in Chapter X. There it was pointed out that immature female mammals of subprimate species display none of the sexual reactions characteristic of the adult individual during her estrous period, whereas, in contrast, immature female monkeys and apes do engage in sexual games that involve assumption of the mating posture, manipulation of the partner's genitalia, and on occasion even attempts at heterosexual coitus. The infrequent but recognizable sexual activities of the nonestrous adult female and the incomplete mating attempts of the immature animal both indicate that in primates the role of the ovarian hormones, although still very important, is less marked than it is in lower mammals.

Human Females. The growing evolutionary importance of non-physiological factors which becomes obvious in monkeys and apes is tremendously increased in our own species. As a matter of fact, it is difficult to differentiate between the physiological and social influences that combine to govern erotic responsiveness in the human female.

Many women in American society experience regular cycles of sexual desire that appear to be correlated with the rhythms of ovarian hormone secretion. Various investigators who have questioned hundreds of married women report that for most of the wives who recognize such cycles, the peak of excitability occurs just before or just after the period of menstrual flow. In some individuals there are two times at which erotic responsiveness is greatest—one just before and one immediately after menstruation. A much smaller number of women experience the most intense satisfaction from intercourse during the mid-interval between two periods of flow, at the time when ovulation is most likely to occur and when the ovaries are secreting maximal amounts of estrogenic hormone.

Figure 8 presents a comparison between variations in certain indices of the sexual responsiveness of human and chimpanzee females. The data pertaining to apes are taken from Yerkes and Elder's monograph. These workers gave three male and nine female apes opportunity to copulate at every stage of the female's sexual cycle. The 174 matings that occurred were not evenly distributed over the five stages of the menstrual cycle. On the contrary, only 8.3 per cent of the copulations took place while the female was in the premenstrual phase and 12.2 per cent occurred during menstruation or immediately thereafter. By far the highest number of coital acts were observed at times when the female was in the stage of maximal genital swelling, and when ovulation was imminent.

Evidence concerning rhythmic variations in the sexual desire of human females has been borrowed from two studies of American women. Katharine Davis queried 287 women who stated that they were conscious of fairly regular fluctuations in their desire for sexual stimulation. A small proportion of these women reported more than one peak of desire in each menstrual cycle. But in preparing Figure 8 each case is represented only once, and the time selected is that at which desire was said to be greatest. The second investigation of this phenomenon is that of Terman, who studied the replies of 619 wives to a similar question. It is apparent from the graph that for both groups maximal sexual desire most commonly occurs either a day or so before or after the period of menstrual flow, and is least likely to be present in the phase of the cycle when ovulation is impending.

These curves for two primate species are almost directly opposed, but several details must be considered before the difference can be evaluated. First, the line representing coital behavior in apes does not reflect exclusively the desire of the female for copulation. It simply shows when coitus took place, and we have seen that in some

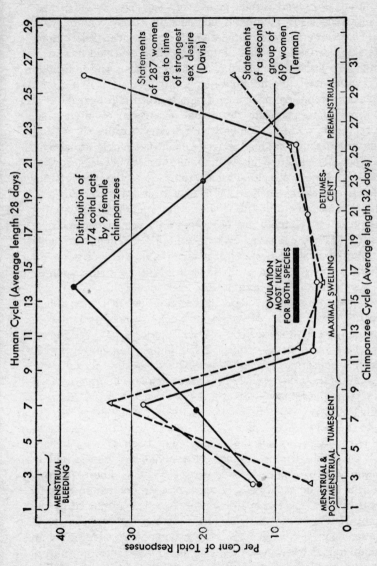

FIG. 8. Cycles of erotic desire described by 906 American women compared with cycles of coital behavior shown by 9 female chimpanzees. See text for detailed explanation.

circumstances the male may control this event. In other words, matings during the premenstrual, menstrual, and detumescent phases probably reflect the modifying influence of social conditions. A theoretical curve showing copulations that depended solely upon the female's desire for sexual contact might be expected to have a much higher peak for the phase of maximal swelling, and to include even fewer contacts at other times.

The curves representing women's reports about their sexual desire do not, of course, indicate the actual occurrence of intercourse. Data reported by Kinsey, Pomeroy, and Martin as well as by several earlier writers show that for the average married couple sexual relations occur much more regularly than this graph might suggest. This is due to at least two factors. First, the desire of the male partner exerts an appreciable degree of control over the frequency and timing of intercourse. Second, women who experience recognizable peaks of erotic reactivity are not necessarily totally unresponsive at other times in the monthly cycle. Despite these obstacles to facile interpretation of it, Figure 8 clearly suggests that the physiological factors governing human eroticism and those controlling similar phenomena in other primates are far from identical.

This generalization involves the assumption that conclusions based upon two studies of American women can be extended to human females in other societies. Within the limits of our evidence this generalization seems justified. It should be noted, however, that statements concerning cycles of feminine desire are available for only a few of the societies included in our sample. The Aranda claim that a woman's responsiveness is low before menstruation and rises sharply just after the period. Members of Lepcha and Masai societies hold to the same belief. Among the Hopi, in contrast, a woman is said to be most ardent both before and immediately after menstruating. Both points of view, as has been noted, are represented in different types of women in our own society, but either pattern is difficult to explain exclusively in terms of reproductive physiology.

If the human female's sex drive were strongly conditioned by the same ovarian hormones that produce heat and mating behavior in other mammals, one would expect it to attain a maximal level during the mid-interval when ovulation is about to occur and the concentration of estrogen has recently increased. It has been stated that a few women do experience the greatest degree of responsiveness during this time. In a purely biological sense this kind of relationship is adaptive, since, other things being equal, it would lead to more frequent intercourse in the woman's fertile period and thus increase the probability of conception. In other words, it favors perpetuation of the species. Why, then, is it true of only a small minority of those women whose attitude has been studied?

Various explanations for the differential importance of estrogenic stimulation in human females and other primates might be suggested. The factors involved undoubtedly are numerous and complex, but one significant fact may be that women in nearly every society are prohibited from engaging in any form of sexual activity during the period of menstrual flow. This interval becomes, therefore, one of total deprivation as far as sexual stimulation is concerned.

Restrictions Placed upon the Menstruating Woman. The attitudes taken by members of different societies toward menstruation furnish an excellent example of one way in which social forces influence human sexual life. In very few societies is the menstruating woman regarded as a suitable sex partner. Among the Marquesans the head husband has intercourse with a wife whose menstrual flow is unduly prolonged. This is thought to stop the blood and is considered a prophylactic measure undertaken for the sake of the woman, although menstrual blood is considered unclean. It is reported that the Trukese of the Carolines commonly engage in sexual relations during the wife's menstruation, and such behavior is permissible among the Walapai, with the specific exception of the woman's first menstrual period after marriage. The Maori wife who is menstruating is permitted to receive her husband if she so desires. Much more commonly, however, the menstruating woman is considered "unclean" and is expected to modify her behavior in a variety of ways. In some cases she is only moderately controlled, but in others she is surrounded by a multiplicity of restrictions that bring major changes in her daily life.

The most lenient mores merely direct that women forego sexual intercourse; they need make no other changes in their routine activities during menstruation. In some other societies there are additional minor interruptions of the usual schedule. These may include the avoidance of certain dietary items such as meat and salt, or temporary discontinuation of bathing, or discontinuation of special activities such as dancing. In contrast, a number of societies enforce a great number of restrictive rules that severely circumscribe the female's activities during menstruation, and some compel her to remain in virtual isolation from other members of the community.

Attitudes taken by different societies toward menstruation are rationalized in various ways, but the reasons advanced almost always are based upon the attitude of the woman's masculine partner or other associates; rarely do they seem to arise from any recognized alteration in her own desires or tendencies. Intercourse with a menstruating woman is believed by the Lepcha to affect a man so adversely as to render him ill and doltish for a long period thereafter. According to the Mataco, such behavior is certain to make a man's loins and head ache. The Thonga of Africa affirm that men who sleep with a woman during her period of flow are later afflicted with failing health and become so fearful that they tremble before battle and cannot fight. Virulent sickness is the result of copulating with a menstruating woman according to the Tswana.

Occasionally, there appears the belief that the woman will be the one to suffer if she has relations with a male while she is menstruating. The Reindeer Chukchee, for instance, are certain that any woman who makes this mistake will shortly become sickly and sterile. It is much more common, however, to consider the woman a potential source of contamination—so powerful a source, in fact, that she may affect other people without the occurrence of any sexual relations. The Ila consider the menstruating woman so dangerous that she is not allowed to eat in mixed company, for were she to do so any man present might lose his virility. During the period of bleeding a woman is not allowed to tend fire or carry water or food; she is forbidden even to approach the camp. The Maritime Chukchee believe that during her menses the wife should avoid her husband because her impure breath can contaminate him and reduce his effectiveness as a hunter.

Because coitus during menstruation is an accepted practice in so few societies, and because there is no detailed evidence regarding the wife's responsiveness in such instances, it is impossible to draw any conclusions concerning the effects of menstruation upon feminine erotic capacity. We have noted, however, that for other primate species in which menstruation occurs, copulation during the period of bleeding is rare. And when it does take place it appears to reflect the male's insistence rather than any genuine receptivity on the part of the female.

The evolutionary evidence would lead to the expectation that during their menstrual periods women might be relatively undesirous of intercourse for purely physiological reasons. But this does not explain the apparent rise in receptivity directly after menstruation, or the heightened responsiveness that precedes the occurrence of bleeding. As indicated earlier, no completely satisfactory explanation is currently available. We wish to suggest, however, that one factor in the situation may be the effect of social conditioning and learning. Since in the vast majority of societies the menstruating woman is deprived of any form of sexual stimulation, it may well be that the premenstrual peak in her curve of desire reflects the effects of anticipated sexual deprivation, and a second rise following the flow may be due to several days of enforced sexual continence. We repeat that this tentative explanation certainly does not account in full for the phenomena under consideration. Nevertheless, we are convinced that the difference between human beings and other primates in this respect is due primarily to the lessening of hormonal control and the pronounced increase in the extent to which social influences govern human eroticism.

EFFECTS OF PREGNANCY

The occurrence of pregnancy is accompanied by a complex series of physiological changes including major modifications in the hormonal balance of the maternal organism. It is established that the urine of pregnant animals of many species, including human beings, contains large amounts of estrogenic material. But it is not known whether this hormone is inactivated before it can produce any effects. Some of the estrogens of pregnancy are ovarian products, but this is not the only point of origin. Pregnant women whose ovaries are removed in the second or third month of gestation continue to exhibit signs of estrogen secretion. And mares that are subjected to the same operation display comparable symptoms. It is generally accepted that the hormone in such cases comes from the placenta, which is known to function as a gland of internal secretion.

Behavior of Subhuman Animals. In view of the fairly common occurrence of high estrogen levels during at least part of the pregnancy period, it might be expected that sexual behavior would appear at these times, and in some species this is the case. Pregnant mice, rabbits, cats, rats, ewes, mares, and cows sometimes permit intercourse by an active male, but their behavior is irregular and unpredictable. Certainly it is not comparable to the performance during normal heat. Furthermore, there are many species in which mating during pregnancy is unknown. Until more information is available concerning the behavioral side of the picture, little can be said with respect to physiological control of sexual activities during gestation.

The pregnancy of subhuman primates is less protracted than that of human females. The rhesus monkey gives birth approximately five and a half months after conception. Within a day or so after impregnation the female shows a decline in sex interest, but three or four weeks later when ovulation would be expected in the non-pregnant monkey there occurs a marked rise in responsiveness, almost as if conception had not taken place. This heightened erotic reactivity appears at the same time as pregnancy bleeding or the "placental sign." Thereafter, according to Ball, sexual excitability dies out more or less gradually and does not rise again during gestation. Zuckerman states that a pair of pigtailed monkeys in the London Zoological Gardens copulated freely throughout the female's pregnancy, mating vigorously just six hours before parturition. The pregnancy of baboons lasts approximately six months (average 169 days), and females rarely copulate during this time, although coition may occasionally occur if it is demanded by the male. Captive gibbons are known to engage in intercourse when the female is pregnant.

Gestation in the chimpanzee covers a period of approximately eight lunar months. During this time some individuals show symptoms similar to those of many pregnant women. The chimpanzee may lose her appetite and react negatively toward food, and vomiting may occur. Bingham says that copulation continues throughout pregnancy, at least in some females. But Yerkes has noted that this behavior is sporadic and not always indicative of sexual desire on the female's part. Occasionally, during early pregnancy, a female may show some swelling of the genital skin which tends to excite the male and may be accompanied by receptive behavior on her part. "In some instances it appears that the receptivity is of considerable strength, while in others mating obviously is due to the expectancy and responsiveness of the male as induced by the visual sign, swelling. Under such circumstances, and lacking opportunity for escape, the female may not safely risk struggle with the male. Instead she responds protectively and accommodatingly, irrespective at times of sexual desire." (Yerkes, 1939, p. 110.)

Behavior of Human Beings. Human couples often continue coital relations for some time after the woman has become pregnant. It appears that the majority of married couples in American society indulge in sexual behavior throughout most or all of the period of pregnancy. Of 1000 American wives studied by Davis, only 11.6 per cent said they never had intercourse while pregnant. Sixty-two per cent reported coitus during at least a part of gestation, and more than one-quarter of the group copulated throughout the entire period. Many medical specialists agree that intercourse can safely be practiced throughout at least the first part of pregnancy. During the last phases of gestation caution is urged against overly vigorous intercourse, particularly that which involves excessive pressure on the female abdomen.

In societies other than that of the United States attitudes toward this problem are highly variable. At one extreme are the peoples who forbid intercourse from the time that pregnancy is first suspected, and at the other end of the scale are the societies that encourage coitus at any time until labor has begun. The Ifugao and Tanala impose no restrictions upon married couples during pregnancy; the wife is expected to receive her husband as long as she can comfortably do so. Among the Chamorro, Kurtatchi, Lepcha, and Pukapukans, intercourse may continue until parturition starts, but the men are warned against allowing too much weight to rest upon the sex partner during the last few weeks of gestation. Some societies which permit mating throughout pregnancy impose the restriction that all such relations must be marital.[4] The pregnant Tswana woman, for example, is warned that copulation with any man save the father of her unborn child will result in illness, possibly fatal, for both herself and her lover.

There are a number of instances in which sexual relations are condoned during most of pregnancy but prohibited for the last few weeks before parturition. This is the case for the Ainu, Ao, Azande, Chenchu, Chukchee, Ila, Jivaro, Kutchin, Quinault, Siriono, and Tarahumara. The Kiwai Papuans insist that the husband copulate with his wife during most of her pregnancy and then cease to do so for the final month or so of gestation. According to the Ainu, coitus should be avoided during the last two months of pregnancy because semen will impair the eyesight of the unborn child or perhaps even choke it to death. More protracted continence is required of the

[4] These are societies that condone certain forms of extramarital liaison when the wife is not pregnant (see Chapter VI).

Crow wife, for she is expected to refuse intercourse from the time she first feels the child move in her womb. The most extreme position is exemplified by the societies which demand cessation of sexual relations as soon as the woman has missed one or two menstrual periods.[5] Figure 9 shows the percentage of peoples permitting coitus during each month of pregnancy.

Prohibitions against intercourse during part or all of pregnancy usually represent attempts to protect the fetus from injury. The Masai state that coitus often causes miscarriage, and the Murngin believe that such activity results in stillbirth. In most of the societies with which we are dealing, natal mortality and the frequency of

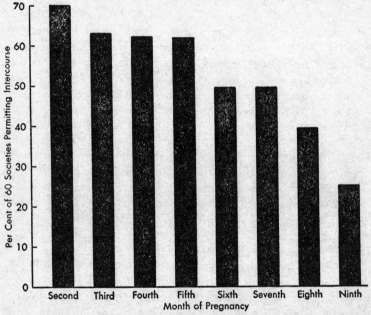

FIG. 9. Attitudes of 60 societies toward the occurrence of marital intercourse during the wife's pregnancy. Since pregnancy is not detected until at least the second month, there are no prohibitions until that time. Thenceforth coitus is subject to taboo in some societies. However, even during the final month of gestation one-fourth of the societies permit continuation of sexual relations.

[5] Abelam, Arikara, Chiricahua, Cuna, Dahomeans, Ganda, Gond, Kongo, Lango, Lesu, Masai, Mataco, Mbundu, Murngin, Nandi, Ramkokamekra, Seniang, Witoto, Wogeo, Wolof, Yapese.

miscarriage may be high enough to account for a common anxiety as to the welfare of the unborn child. The increase in the number of peoples forbidding intercourse toward the end of pregnancy tends to suggest that the majority of societies have become convinced, as a result of centuries of experience, that sexual activities just prior to labor may have unfortunate consequences.

In general, the demand for sexual abstinence during part or all of pregnancy applies exclusively to the wife. Many societies make some provision for alternate sources of outlet as far as the husband is concerned (see Chapter VI). Even though marital intercourse is forbidden, the expectant father is usually afforded opportunity for continuing his own sexual activities. All save two of the twenty-one societies that forbid coitus throughout the greater part of pregnancy are polygynous and the man may have access to other wives who are not pregnant. If the man whose wife is pregnant happens to have only one wife, many societies allow him temporarily to assume the social status of a bachelor and to have access to unmarried girls.

SEXUAL BEHAVIOR AFTER PARTURITION

From the modern medical point of view there appears no physiological contraindication to a woman's resumption of coital behavior as soon after parturition as the vaginal and cervical tissues have repaired themselves and general strength has been regained. This generally requires five to six weeks.

During the first several post-partum months the physiology of the female body is different from what it was before and during pregnancy. This is especially true if the mother nurses her infant. The mammary glands, which have been prepared for milk secretion during the latter stages of pregnancy, do not become fully active until several days after birth. Stewart and Pratt's study of 900 English mothers showed that 87 per cent of them had an adequate milk supply by the fifth day after giving birth. In many women the practice of breast feeding retards or prevents the return of menstrual periods, although this is not inevitable. However, even in those individuals who resume menstruating soon after parturition less than half of the cycles are accompanied by ovulation (45 per cent of 194 cycles; Lass *et al.*, 1938). This greatly reduces the chances of a second pregnancy within a short time after parturition.

Female chimpanzees do not ordinarily begin menstruating for at least four months after giving birth, and according to some observers they are rarely sexually receptive during this period. Yerkes studied a male and a female with one infant and did not discover any evidence of copulation during pregnancy or during the first four months after parturition. However, there is no guarantee that sexual relations did not occur; other records made by the same experimenter show that coitus does occasionally take place during pregnancy. Zuckerman states that one female of this species in the Philadelphia Zoological Park copulated four days after giving birth.

In several species of infrahuman primates the period of lactation is fairly lengthy. It lasts for three or four years in the case of the orangutan, as long as two years in some chimpanzees, and approximately eighteen months in the macaque monkey. Baboons suckle their offspring for nearly a year, and the pigtailed monkey for about half this length of time. Like the human female, most primates do not menstruate during at least the first half of the lactation period, but, according to Zuckerman, if the baby dies and suckling is discontinued the menses return promptly. When the menstrual cycle is re-established during the latter stages of lactation, females again display sex responses of normal frequency and intensity.

Female mammals of several subprimate species come into heat shortly after delivering their young. For larger animals such as the mare and sow the interval is approximately seven to nine days, but in some rodents it is only a few hours. This post-partum estrus is fertile and coition may result in conception. In the event of impregnation the female nurses her first litter while carrying the second, and the gestation period is likely to be prolonged. Rats normally give birth twenty-one to twenty-two days after mating. But Weichart found that pregnant nursing females may carry litters as long as thirty-six days. The stimulus of nursing is believed to delay implantation of the eggs of the second litter.

A few animals including cows and guinea pigs have estrous cycles and mate during lactation; but with the exception of their single post-partum estrous period, the majority of lower mammalian females do not normally become receptive until their young are weaned. The physiological explanation for this retardation in the resumption of reproductive cycles is complex and only partly understood. It is known, however, that the nursing behavior of the young has an effect upon the mother's condition. Nervous stimuli evoked by suckling appear to prevent the anterior pituitary gland from secreting gonadotrophic hormones, and as a result the ovaries do not produce the sex hormones necessary to mating behavior. Female mice normally nurse their young for about three weeks and then estrous cycles and sexual receptivity reappear. However, Selye and McKeown have shown that if a female is periodically given a new foster litter of nursing age, lactation may be prolonged for as long as two months and the resumption of estrous cycles is correspondingly delayed. According to Weisner and Sheard, female rats subjected to comparable treatment may continue to lactate and fail to come into heat for a year.

Although in our own society sexual relations are usually resumed while the mother is still suckling her child and before her menses return, this is not the case for all peoples. Some societies condone the post-partum re-establishment of coital habits after a relatively short delay of one to two weeks.[6] A number of societies insist upon abstinence for a few weeks to a month;[7] for others the period is extended from forty days to six weeks;[8] or two, three, or four months,[9] or eight to ten months.[10]

In a few instances the duration of sexual abstinence is determined by some developmental characteristic of the child. Among the Abelam, for example, husband and wife are supposed to refrain from coitus until the baby can walk. The Alorese wait until the child sits up, and the Yagua delay until it crawls. The Mataco and the Masai are forbidden to have intercourse until the child has cut its teeth. For a number of peoples the duration of the taboo on sexual intercourse extends throughout the lactation period,[11] which may last two[12] to three years.[13]

The reason given for insisting upon sexual abstinence after parturition is the prevention of another pregnancy in the belief that this would be dangerous to the welfare of the present child. Should conception take place while the baby is nursing, the mother's milk supply would diminish and the growing child would have to be prematurely weaned.

[6] Chenchu, Chukchee, Marquesans, Murngin, Tanala, Tswana.

[7] Chewa, Crow, Gond, Kiwai, Koryak, Kutchin, Lamba, Lepcha, Manus, Marshallese, Quinault, Reddi, Sanpoil, Siriono, Witoto.

[8] Arikara, Fez, Hopi, Kababish, Lapps, Riffians, Thompson, Thonga, Walapai.

[9] Ao, Chagga, Chamorro, Haitians, Nandi, Ponapeans, Ramkokamekra, Samoyed, Tubatulabal, Wintu.

[10] Kwakiutl, Yapese.

[11] Abipone, Azande, Bena, Chiricahua, Cree, Dahomeans, Dobuans, Ganda, Ila, Jivaro, Kongo, Kwoma, Lango, Lesu, Tiv, Trobrianders, Wogeo, Wolof, Xosa, Yako.

[12] Azande, Bena, Dahomeans, Kwoma, Tiv, Wogeo, Xosa, Yako.

[13] Abipone, Chiricahua, Ganda, Kongo, Lango.

Although they oppose intercourse for the recently parturient woman, some peoples allow other forms of sexual stimulation. Among the Thonga and the Swazi, for example, the husband and wife may indulge in any type of sexual activity except coitus after the first six weeks of the new infant's life. As is the case during pregnancy, polygynous societies permit the husband of a lactating woman to have intercourse with co-wives, with other legitimate partners, or in some instances with unmarried girls if the social code condones premarital relations for females.

SUMMARY

In this chapter we have assembled evidence revealing a rigid, clear-cut relationship between reproductive fertility and sexual responsiveness in females of lower mammalian species. The relationship is controlled by the periodic secretion of ovarian hormones. The correlation between fertility and sexual receptivity is less well defined in subhuman primates and completely obliterated in the human female. This suggests an evolutionary change involving progressive relaxation of hormonal control of feminine eroticism.

It has been noted, furthermore, that various human societies have divergent rules governing sexual relations during menstruation, pregnancy, and lactation. The two sets of facts seem to be interrelated. If women experienced regular and powerful cycles of sexual desire in which maximal receptivity coincided with the fertile period, it appears probable that this fact would be reflected in social codes pertaining to intercourse. Such rhythms appear to be rare or absent, and therefore different cultures have been able to set up and enforce quite variable socially structured schedules for sexual relations.

In the next chapter we shall consider other aspects of the physiological control of sexual behavior and discuss tentative explanations for the evolutionary changes which have freed the human female's sexual life from strict control by her ovarian rhythms.

Chapter XII

Other Physiological Factors
in Sex Behavior

O NE very important relationship between the chemical content of the blood and sexual behavior was considered at length in the preceding chapter. This is the relationship between erotic excitability and the hormones that are secreted periodically by the ovaries of all female mammals, including the human species. This chapter summarizes additional evidence bearing upon the chemical control of feminine sexuality. Comparable sources of sexual activity in males also are surveyed. Finally, we devote attention to the ways in which the brain and other parts of the central nervous system contribute to the organization and control of sexual responses in human beings and in mammals of subhuman species.

ADDITIONAL EVIDENCE CONCERNING OVARIAN HORMONES

Since Chapter XI contains a great deal of the evidence concerning the behavioral effects of female sex hormones, it is logical to begin the present chapter by considering still other data that bear upon the same problem.

Effects of Removal or Regression of the Ovaries. In the light of previously described findings concerning the importance of ovarian hormones to sexual receptivity in lower mammals it is not surprising to learn that ovariectomy (removal of the ovaries) promptly and permanently abolishes all sexual behavior in females of these species. Ovariectomized rats, rabbits, guinea pigs, cats, dogs, horses, and cows possess no sexual attraction for males of their species and never display sexually receptive behavior.

Ovariectomy in the adult chimpanzee eliminates the usual cycles of sexual responsiveness and drastically reduces the frequency of coital contacts. After this operation females have a relatively low stimulative value for the male and they show little or no desire for intercourse. They behave, in fact, somewhat like a normal animal during the periods when she is not physiologically in estrus. Nevertheless, the ovariectomized chimpanzee may occasionally permit the male to copulate; this occurs most often under circumstances in which sexual acquiescence affords a means of avoiding physical injury. Evidence of this sort reinforces our conclusion that subhuman primates are not completely dependent upon sex hormones for the ability to mate, although the degree of such dependence is much greater than it is in the human female.

Ovariectomy is not uncommonly performed upon human females, but before discussing the effects of this operation we shall review evidence pertaining to the natural regression of ovarian function which takes place during menopause. In most women menopause occurs during the fifth decade of life. Individual differences are marked, however, and this change may take place at any age from the middle thirties to later than the fiftieth year. Menopause marks the cessation of ovarian function. Discontinuation of the periods of monthly flow is merely the outward sign of a complex series of internal changes. In some individuals the onset of the climacteric is dramatic and sudden, but in many others the process is gradual rather than abrupt. The physiological changes involved are more or less the converse of those that take place during adolescence.

Menstrual cycles tend to become anovulatory (lacking ovulation), and intervals between them grow increasingly longer. Eventually the female reproductive glands cease entirely to produce eggs and to secrete hormones. The disappearance of ovarian secretions is accompanied by a pronounced increase in the pituitary substances that previously stimulated the sex glands. Either the decrease in the estrogenic hormone or the increase in pituitary gonadotrophins, or both, produces in most women in our society one or several of the following symptoms: hot flashes, nervousness, morning insomnia, palpitation, sweating, vertigo, headache, depression, crying spells, irritability, and fatigue.

Some women state that their sexual desire and capacity are as great after menopause as they were during the preceding years, but other individuals just as confidently say that the climacteric marked complete and permanent loss of all erotic responsiveness. We consider it extremely unlikely that these two groups represent physiologically distinct populations. It seems more probable that non-hormonal factors are responsible for the changed sexual status of women who become unresponsive following menopause.

Somewhat more conclusive evidence on this score is found in case histories of women who have passed through surgical menopause—the condition resulting from complete removal of both ovaries. Even here, however, the results are not entirely consistent. For example, Heller, Farney, and Meyers examined twenty-seven women before and after ovariectomy. The menopausal symptoms listed above appeared soon after the operation and were most severe between the twenty-seventh and sixty-sixth days after surgery. It is also stated that "loss of libido was common." Generalities of this sort are apt to be misleading; in fact, these authors actually questioned only eleven of their patients concerning this item. Of this number six reported decrease or loss of libido, two said they had no sexual desires prior to the operation, and three described no lowering of the sex drive.

The careful study by Filler and Drezner indicates that the removal of the ovaries need not depress erotic sensitivity. They examined the effects of ovariectomy in forty women, all under 40 years of age. The characteristic menopausal symptoms appeared in 85 per cent of the cases, but sexual urges were not reduced in a single one of these women. Pratt agrees that ovariectomized women are capable of experiencing normal sexual desire and of participating successfully in coital relations. Mansfeld even states that ovariectomy occasionally is followed by an increase in the desire for and enjoyment of intercourse. We suppose that such positive effects are in part referable to removal of the fear of unwanted pregnancy.

In the face of evidence suggesting retention of full sexual responsiveness after natural and surgical menopause, how is one to account for the frequent claims that removal or regression of the ovaries produces a profound decrease in erotic desire? It is our opinion that the explanation rests upon the effects of suggestion, and that physiological changes consequent to ovarian failure are not primarily involved. Daniels and Tauber describe a female patient who experienced a marked decline in erotic sensitivity following ovariectomy. Psychotherapy sufficed to restore this function, indicating that hormonal changes had not been the sole agent in precipitating the sexual depression. As a matter of fact, the patient stated that after psychiatric treatment intercourse became more frequent and satisfactory than it had been during the eight years of marriage preceding the operation.

The major role of nonhormonal factors in controlling the sexual reactivity of human females is apparent in the histories of many of Dickinson's patients. One example will illustrate the point. A young woman, married at 21, engaged in intercourse with her husband once or twice a week for five years until the first child was born. During the first year or two she felt sexual desire but never reached climax. After five years of marriage her desire and responsiveness had grown to be as strong as those of her husband. At this time, however, she discovered that he was unfaithful, and for two years she refused to have intercourse. Following this lapse sexual relations were resumed; but although the wife was easily aroused, she was usually unsatisfied and rarely attained climax. Several years later, after removal of both of her ovaries, her capacity for complete response returned. At that time the habitual pattern of sexual relations included half an hour of foreplay, and a total of an hour to an hour and a half of coitus. She usually had five or six orgasms; less than two left her unsatisfied.

This single case history illustrates several general points, and although some of them have been mentioned earlier they are sufficiently important to justify repeated emphasis. The first is that full sexual responsiveness including regular orgasm may not appear in the physiologically normal woman until she has had a considerable amount of sexual experience. The second point is that normal reactivity to erotic stimulation may be lost under circumstances which have no demonstrable effect upon reproductive physiology. The emotional trauma resulting from discovery of her husband's extramarital affairs created a block in this woman's sexual response, with the result that climax became difficult or impossible to attain even though her ovaries were secreting normal amounts of sex hormones. In a very general way it is probably correct to say that the vast majority of "frigid" or sexually unresponsive women are products of adverse emotional conditioning rather than of an abnormal physiological constitution. Comparable explanations probably apply to the occasional female chimpanzee who never becomes behaviorally receptive although her physiological rhythms are normal (see Chapter XI).

The third and final point illustrated by the example from Dickinson is that complete and satisfactory sexual relations are possible in the human female despite the total absence of ovarian hormones.

Effects of Administering Ovarian Hormones.   The ovariectomized cat or dog is sexually inactive, but if such animals are injected with estrogen they attract males and become highly receptive. This condition continues until the effects of the injected hormone wear off. The spayed dog remains in heat for ten to fourteen days after the injections of estrogen, and spayed cats can be kept constantly in season for months by weekly injections of the same substance. Ovariectomized rodents are similarly responsive to hormone treatment, although in their case it is usually necessary to administer progesterone as well as estrogen. It should be added that when sexually immature female mammals of these subprimate species are treated with the appropriate ovarian hormones they behave sexually in the manner of the adult female in estrus. These findings support the conclusion that for females of lower mammalian species, sexual behavior is strongly conditioned by hormones from the reproductive glands.

Female monkeys become almost totally unresponsive to sexual stimuli after ovariectomy. Ball reports that estrogen injections restore full erotic reactivity in the spayed macaque. Ovariectomized chimpanzees display swelling of the sex skin and desire for intercourse when they are subjected to estrogen therapy. It must be remembered, however, that in this species loss of the ovaries does not completely eliminate the capacity for intercourse.

If human females were as dependent upon ovarian hormones as are the lower mammals, it might be anticipated that low sexual responsiveness could be increased by administration of the appropriate endocrinological preparations. There are a few reports indicating heightened reactivity in postmenopausal women and in sexually frigid individuals following estrogen treatment. In most cases, however, the results are not dependable, and we are led to suspect that positive effects are due primarily to the results of suggestion. Conclusive evidence is wanting; but the survival of normal libido after ovariectomy, the absence of responsiveness in some physiologically normal women, and the lack of a close relationship between rhythms of estrogen secretion and cycles of sexual desire all combine to suggest that impaired or subnormal responsiveness to sexual stimuli cannot be effectively treated by administration of ovarian hormones.

IMPORTANCE OF TESTICULAR HORMONE

In male mammals as in females the degree to which sexual behavior depends upon hormones secreted by the sex glands varies according to the evolutionary status of the species under examination.

Male Sex Cycles. As noted in Chapter XI, many animals are reproductively active for only a brief period of the year, and males of such seasonally breeding species are unresponsive to sexual stimuli at all other times. In some wild rodents and fur-bearing mammals the testes are withdrawn into the body cavity and produce neither sperm nor hormone except in the mating season, at which time they descend into the scrotum and become temporarily functional. Only while the testis is active and the level of its hormone secretion is high do males of this type become aroused by the presence of a receptive female and develop the capacity to copulate with her.

An entirely different situation obtains in the case of male human beings and in most domesticated animals. The adult male dog, cat, horse, pig, rat, or mouse is susceptible to sexual arousal and able to mate at any time. So far as is known, the testes of such animals secrete their hormone at a fairly steady rate and there are no rhythms of sex hormone secretion comparable to those occurring in females of the same species. This does not mean, however, that the male shows no fluctuations in sexual responsiveness. It was pointed out in Chapter IV that males of nocturnal species are more likely to copulate during the dark hours than in the daytime, because their metabolic processes proceed at a faster rate at night when they normally are active. Furthermore, as will be discussed below, human males vary in their sexual responsiveness with changes in physiological condition. Extreme physical fatigue or prolonged inanition, to cite but two examples, exert a profoundly inhibiting effect upon erotic impulses and coital performance.

Regression of the Male Sex Glands. We have already mentioned one type of regression of the sex glands that occurs in male animals of seasonally breeding species. At this point it is desirable to give some attention to the problem of a male climacteric involving permanent testicular regression.

A few clinicians believe that most human males pass through a change of life that resembles the female menopause. Although this opinion is not widely accepted, it is generally agreed that the secretion of testicular hormone does decrease appreciably in later life. One study revealed that the urine of men over 50 years of age contains only one-seventh to one-fifteenth as much male hormone derivative as that of other individuals between the ages of 21 and 29. However, the aging testis, unlike the ovary, does not completely cease to function. Examination of the sex glands of men more than 60 years old shows that although there is an appreciable reduction in the production of sperm, active development of some germ cells is still occurring. It seems likely that spermatogenesis continues at a diminishing rate up to the time of death.

We pointed out earlier in this chapter that the sexual responsiveness of women may outlast the functional life of the ovaries by many years. The opposite situation obtains in some men. Although fertility may never be totally lost, a recognizable proportion of the masculine population in our society becomes impotent with advancing age. Physiological aging is a process that begins in infancy and proceeds steadily to the time of death. And sexual functions, according to some authorities, are no exception to this general rule. In Chapter X it was noted that very young children may be capable of sexual climax without, of course, actual ejaculation. Kinsey, Pomeroy, and Martin state that the capacity for multiple orgasms is higher in infants than in older children and probably higher during pre-adolescence than in the late teens.

Additional information regarding the sexual responses of pre-puberal children is needed, but there are sufficient data to support the conclusion that sexual vigor declines steadily in most American males from the middle teens to extreme old age. On the basis of personal interviews with their subjects, Kinsey and his collaborators report that husbands under twenty years of age attain climax an average of 4.8 times per week. Men in their fifties have an average of 1.8 orgasms per week, and the figure drops to 1.3 per week for sixty-year-old individuals. Men of seventy have an average frequency of 0.9 orgasm per week. Other indicators of erotic power follow a similar curve. The frequency of morning erections drops steadily from early adolescence. With advancing age there occurs a progressive increase in the length of time and the amount of stimulation necessary to produce an erection, and a concomitant decrease in the duration of complete tumescence. The frequency of multiple orgasms is gradually reduced.

Curves representing group averages for all of these functions indicate a steady decline from adolescence, but very rarely is there an abrupt termination of any index of sexual capacity. Some individuals do eventually become totally impotent, however; the age at which this occurs is subject to wide individual variation. In rare instances the onset of impotence is noted at thirty, but at the other extreme are men of eighty who retain some ability to achieve orgasm. One seventy-year-old man interviewed by Kinsey reported an average of more than seven orgasms per week. The proportion of the masculine population in our society that becomes completely impotent amounts to approximately 5 per cent at sixty and nearly 30 per cent at seventy years of age. The gradual increase in incidence of impotence is shown in Figure 10.

It is unfortunate that there are no reliable data to indicate the effects of old age upon sexual performance in male animals of subhuman species. This does not mean, however, that there is no evi-

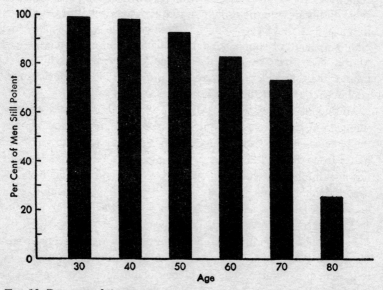

Fig. 10. Per cent of American men retaining erectal potency at different ages. (Based on Table 50 in Kinsey, Pomeroy, and Martin, 1948.)

dence with respect to the importance of testicular hormone in such cases. On the contrary, a number of experiments and observations have dealt with the effects of castration on the mating behavior of animals.

Effects of Removing the Testes.   The behavioral consequences of castration vary with the species of the animal and with the age of the individual at the time the operation is performed. Subhuman mammals that are deprived of the male sex glands during infancy never develop normal degrees of sexual aggressiveness. In adult life they behave much as does the unoperated animal prior to puberty. As noted in Chapter X, however, the prepuberal male does display a recognizable degree of sexual responsiveness, and so does the adult that has been castrated in infancy. Both types of animal make occasional abortive attempts to mount other individuals and display a few weak pelvic thrusts. But the prepuberally castrated mammal of a subprimate species never develops adult coital reactions; instead, it goes through its entire life span displaying nothing more intense than the usual prepuberal responses. It is worth noting here that the castrated male is more active than the ovariectomized female, for the latter exhibits no feminine sexual reactions whatsoever.

The effects of castration during adulthood are different. They have been examined in connection with the behavior of rats, rabbits, guinea pigs, and other rodents. In general the results are about the same in all these species. The ejaculatory response is lost within the first two weeks after removal of the sex glands. Next to disappear is the capacity for erection and therefore the ability to penetrate the receptive female. The tendency to become excited in the presence of estrous females and to mount them without achieving intromission does not disappear for several weeks and may never be completely eliminated. Figure 11 illustrates the mating performance of a group of male hamsters before and after castration. Preoperatively from 85 to 95 per cent of the animals effected intromission during each test with the receptive female. Occasionally, most of these males also executed abortive copulatory attempts which did not result in intromission. It is quite common for a normal male to alternate between successful and unsuccessful mounts. After castration the frequency with which penetration was achieved decreased abruptly, but abortive attempts to copulate continued in approximately 80 per cent of the animals. In other words, during the time

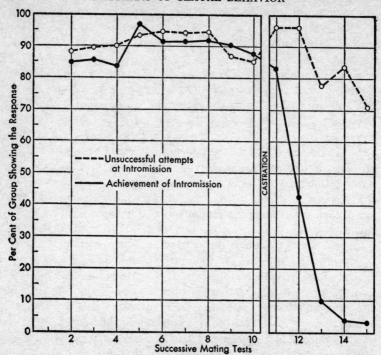

FIG. 11. Effects of castration upon copulatory behavior of male hamsters. (From Beach and Pauker, 1949.)

covered by this experiment loss of the sex glands did not eliminate the capacity for sexual arousal, but it did greatly decrease potency as measured by the ability to copulate.

It is said, without scientific verification, that male farm animals such as cattle and horses continue to display mating responses for years after castration if the operation is performed after the individual has become mature. As this chapter is written, one of us (Beach) is conducting a controlled laboratory investigation of the sexual behavior of male dogs before and after castration in adulthood. It has been found that some males show no decline in sexual aggressiveness for at least two years, and possibly longer, after removal of the reproductive glands. These animals are highly aroused by the receptive female, achieve erection promptly, and copulate as frequently and vigorously as they did prior to the operation. Some other individuals appear to suffer a reduction in the ability to copulate, but none of them have as yet become unable to do so.

Evidence concerning sexual capacities in castrated male primates of subhuman species is scant, but it suggests that these more highly evolved animals are more active in the absence of male hormone than are lower mammals. Hamilton reports frequent and vigorous copulation on the part of castrated male monkeys, although his data are not quantified and the length of the postoperative interval is not specified.

There is in existence one fully mature male chimpanzee that was castrated in infancy. This individual's behavioral development was normal. Masturbation and other forms of sex play appeared at the usual age, and heterosexual experimentation led eventually to the acquisition of a well-defined pattern of coitus with receptive females. This ape's capacity for sexual arousal is strong and the resulting copulatory acts are identical with those of an intact male, with one exception. There is in the castrate no sign of ejaculation, and he copulates much more frequently than normal animals.

The effects of castration upon sexual behavior in the human male vary according to the age at the time of operation. Individuals castrated well in advance of puberty are, so far as is known, never capable of full sexual response. Some are able to produce an erection at will and even to copulate, but Heller, Nelson, and Roth state that in such cases ejaculation never occurs. Of particular interest in this connection is Perloff's claim that some men whose testes have never matured are capable of experiencing sexual orgasm despite their inability to ejaculate. Incomplete and fragmentary as it is, the evidence reviewed thus far suggests that in male as in female mammals, the importance of gonadal hormones for erotic responsiveness decreases with advancing evolutionary status. For most of the lower mammals that have been investigated these hormonal secretions are essential to normal sexual reactivity. Subhuman primates may be able to copulate for years despite castration in adulthood or even before puberty. Human males who lack any source of testicular hormone are able, at least in some instances, not only to cohabit with a woman, but to achieve sexual climax during coitus.

The effects of castration in adult men differ widely from one case to the next. Some patients report gradual reduction in the desire and capacity for intercourse. Others state that although potency is decreased, sexual arousal continues to occur. And a third group of patients claim that the preoperative libido and potency are retained for as long as thirty years after loss of the testes. As in the case of ovariectomized women, individual differences of the type mentioned here probably reflect the importance of psychological factors for a normal sex drive in human beings. It is unlikely that the purely physiological sequelae of castration are as variable as the subjective reports indicate. We consider it more probable that some men, being convinced in advance that the operation will deprive them of potency, actually experience a lessening of sexual ability. Other individuals unprejudiced by such anticipatory effects are able to copulate frequently despite loss of hormonal support.

This interpretation gains support from another type of evidence which shows that some men may become impotent although their sex glands are producing normal amounts of male hormone. Tauber mentions one clinical report describing several unoperated but impotent men who asked for examination because they were convinced that their symptoms were due to deficiencies in testicular hormone. When informed that the assay revealed normal hormone levels, several of these patients promptly became capable of sexual performance. It is known, furthermore, that physiologically normal men may lose all sexual ability as the result of severe emotional disturbance, and in such cases psychotherapy is sometimes effective in restoring potency although it does not alter the hormonal levels of the patient. This sort of evidence strongly indicates that even though testicular hormone plays a definable role in normal human sexuality, it is not indispensable to coital performance.

Effects of Administering Testicular Hormone. The fact that androgen is capable of increasing the male sex drive and performance is most clearly demonstrated in the results of experiments on lower mammals. We stated above that castrated male rodents soon cease to display the ejaculatory response, and later lose the ability to achieve an erection. Failure of erection, in turn, renders the male unable to achieve intromission when tested with a receptive female.

Figure 12 illustrates the results of one experiment on male rats. Three groups of animals were tested several times before castration, and in these preoperative tests from 90 to 100 per cent of the rats copulated with the estrous female. Then all the males were castrated and the mating tests were continued. Males in one group were injected daily with 500 micrograms (1 microgram = 1/1000 milli-

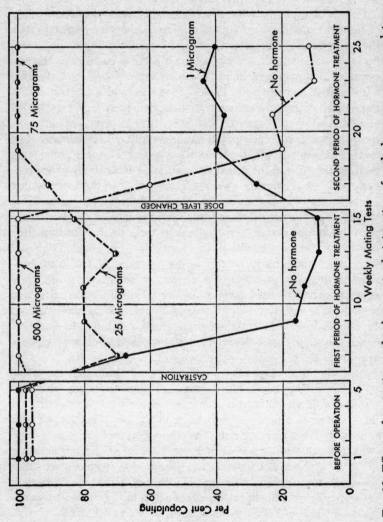

Fig. 12. Effects of castration and subsequent administration of male hormone upon copulatory behavior of male rats. (From Beach and Holz-Tucker, 1948.)

gram) of male hormone. Members of the second group received 25 micrograms of the same substance daily; and the third group was given no hormone after castration.

Figure 12 shows that the animals injected with the highest dose of hormone continued to copulate as frequently after castration as they had before. The rats receiving 25 micrograms per day were less active sexually than they had been prior to castration; and the castrates that were given no hormone rapidly became relatively unresponsive to receptive females. Nine weeks after castration the hormonal treatment was changed. Rats that had been getting 500 micrograms of androgen per day were now deprived of any hormonal support, and their performance rapidly fell off to a very low level. The animals which previously received 25 micrograms were increased to 75, and their behavior improved accordingly. The originally untreated castrates were given daily injections containing 1 microgram of androgen, and this extremely small dose exerted an appreciable effect upon their sexual performance.

As mentioned earlier, some male dogs show no decline in mating behavior for at least two years after castration, but other individuals display a decrease in sexual performance. Dogs of the latter type react to the administration of androgen by returning to their pre-operative level of sexual vigor. It has also been stated that one prepuberally castrated chimpanzee (see page 231) has been proved capable of frequent copulation although he is not able to ejaculate. When this animal was given male hormone the ejaculatory response appeared.

Most significant is the fact that under these conditions the actual frequency of copulatory acts decreased. Prior to hormone treatment the ape often mated ten times in one hour, but under the influence of androgen two or three coital acts in the same amount of time represented his upper limit. The change reflects the temporary exhaustion that follows sexual climax. Because he did not ejaculate or attain orgasm, the untreated chimpanzee was able to copulate time after time without growing tired. But as soon as climax became possible, each coital experience terminated in orgasm and was followed by a period of unresponsiveness to sexual stimuli.

The effects of administering testicular hormone to human males are variable. Pratt has described the response to androgen therapy on the part of one man whose sex glands had never developed. This individual was in his early thirties when treatment first occurred.

By the fourth day [after beginning treatment] penile erections occurred as frequently as once per hour. . . . Several days without treatment resulted in a prompt regression of the turgidity of the genitalia and fewer erections. It was astonishing to observe how promptly the regressive changes appeared when therapy was discontinued. . . . It was noted that erections were rather sharply conditioned [early in the course of treatment] by the size of the dose. [They were] nearly always noted within 12 to 36 hours after the ingestion of the tablets. The patient had a number of seminal emissions during the latter part of the month. . . . Prior to therapy the patient had only the mildest interest in the opposite sex. He . . . had occasional "dates," but only to secure a partner for some social function. He was able to recall about 5 dates in the year before treatment. Contact with the opposite sex was in no way stimulating. The patient rarely indulged in the so-called "necking" because he felt embarrassed. The patient had never had a seminal emission. . . . The increased desire for feminine companionship [during treatment], not based solely on sexual premises, resulted in an almost unbroken succession of "dates." The patient came to enjoy "necking"; close contact frequently resulted in erections and seminal emissions. (Pratt, 1942, pp. 460-462.)

In experiments of this type it is always desirable to control the effects of suggestion by occasionally administering placebos (dummy injections) without the patient's knowledge. This has been done in some instances and the results generally indicate that the effects of androgen do not depend entirely upon the patient's anticipation of an increased sex drive. However, additional and more carefully controlled studies of this matter are badly needed. It is also necessary to realize that a simple increase in the physical indicators of potency is not the only or even the most important aspect of such treatment.

Daniels and Tauber, for example, treated a male patient whose impotence was interfering with his marital adjustment. Administration of large amounts of male hormone rendered the man capable of prolonged periods of erection and of repeated acts of intercourse. It did not, however, particularly increase his desire for coitus save as a means of achieving temporary release from priapism.

On the basis of the available evidence, we are inclined to believe that men are more obviously affected by gonadal hormones than are women. The effects, however, are reliable and predictable only in the case of predominantly physiological functions. Furthermore, in men and women alike, nonhormonal factors are of tremendous importance, and libido and potency are powerfully affected by many influences other than those exerted by glandular secretions. Finally, the cross-species comparisons suggest that the human male's partial independence of testicular hormone as the major source of the sex drive represents the culmination of a progressive evolutionary change. Lower mammals rely heavily upon this source of support, monkeys somewhat less so; anthropoid apes fall at an intermediate point between the lower primates and man.

HORMONES AND SEXUAL INVERSION

When the so-called male and female hormones were first discovered, some authorities concluded that homosexuality is caused by an abnormal amount of female hormone in males or of male hormone in females. There are a few clinicians who still hold this view, but the evidence against it is impressive. Attempts have been made to show that the urine of homosexual men contains an abnormal amount of estrogen. However, the differences between such men and "normal" men have been slight and unreliable, and in many cases no differences at all have been found.

When large amounts of androgen have been administered to male patients diagnosed as exclusively homosexual the result has been merely an intensification of the sex drive with no alteration in its direction. Homosexual patients treated in this manner desired and achieved increased frequency of homosexual contacts. The fundamental error involved in this type of therapy is the unjustified assumption that gonadal hormones determine the character of the sexual drive in human beings. This is not the case. The reproductive hormones may intensify the drive but they do not organize the behavior through which it finds expression.

Cross-cultural evidence reviewed in Chapter VII is of significance to this discussion. Attempts to interpret and treat homosexuality as though it were the product of physiological deviations derive directly from a basic misunderstanding of the phenomenon. When it is realized that 100 per cent of the males in certain societies engage in homosexual as well as heterosexual alliances, and when it is understood that many men and women in our own society are equally capable of relations with partners of the same or opposite sex, and finally, when it is recognized that this same situation obtains in many species of subhuman primates, then it should be clear that one cannot classify homosexual and heterosexual tendencies as being mutually exclusive or even opposed to each other.

Perhaps the most serious logical mistake involved in any attempt to explain homosexuality as the product of hormonal abnormalities is the failure to appreciate the way in which habits of sexual expression are formed. As we previously pointed out, human sexual behavior is controlled and directed primarily by learning and experience. It is possible to begin with a male or female whose physiological constitution is entirely normal and, by a process of cultural or individual conditioning, make that person an exclusive homosexual. And this can be done precisely because human sexuality is so labile, so dependent upon individual experience.

Nonhormonal Factors in Blood Chemistry

The gonadal hormones are by no means the only chemical variables capable of influencing sexual behavior. Other endocrine secretions such as those of the thyroid, parathyroid, adrenal, and pituitary glands are at least indirectly involved. Furthermore, any bodily process that contributes to general health and vigor may be considered to aid normal sexual functions.

Conversely, metabolic deficiencies such as those occurring in semistarvation tend to affect sexual ability adversely.

Stone demonstrated that male rats reared on quantitatively or qualitatively deficient diets do not show mating behavior at the usual developmental age. Their sexual maturation is appreciably delayed. Recent studies of the effects of inanition on human males prove that semistarvation drastically interferes with sexual processes. Keys and his co-workers investigated the behavior of healthy young men who lived for six months on a food intake of 1470 calories per day. Under these conditions the frequency of sex dreams and fantasies was markedly reduced. Masturbation was discontinued and interest in members of the opposite sex was lost.

In view of the widespread belief that certain drugs reliably increase sexual capacity whereas others inevitably reduce it, it is worth while to mention briefly some of the experimental and clinical findings that bear upon this question.

One of the most commonly used drugs in many societies is alcohol, which is physiologically a sexual depressant. Administered in moderate amounts to male dogs, alcohol raises the threshold of the erectile and ejaculatory reflexes. Much more than the normal amount of stimulation is necessary to evoke these reactions in alcoholized animals. Larger doses of the drug completely prevent any sexual response. In human beings this drug has essentially similar effects.

Small to moderate amounts of alcohol interfere with the capacity for erection and for orgasm. Large doses usually produce impotence. The common misconception that alcohol is a sexual stimulant results from the fact that this drug tends to reduce the social inhibitions that normally limit the expression of sexual tendencies.

Morphine and heroin lower erotic responsiveness, and addicts under the influence of these drugs are usually sexually inactive. Abrupt withdrawal of the drugs induces frequent genital erections and ejaculations in male addicts and spontaneous orgasms in women. Morphine addiction has been established in chimpanzees and these animals do not display any signs of hypersexuality during periods of withdrawal. On the contrary, unlike human addicts male chimpanzees appear to be sexually stimulated by the administration of morphine. Shortly after the daily injection is given, the apes display erection and indulge in masturbation to the point of ejaculation. Objects associated with the stereotyped injection procedure tend to acquire a sexual significance. Males have been observed to show copulatory movements toward the box in which the injection syringe is kept.

In many societies certain substances are regarded as capable of increasing sexual vigor or curing impotence. In our own society, for example, it is widely believed that cantharides, or Spanish fly, has aphrodisiac properties. This substance, which is prepared from the dried bodies of a species of beetle, is often employed by animal breeders to evoke mating reactions in farm animals. There is no reliable information with respect to the efficacy of such treatment, but the physiological effects of cantharides are known. They consist in part of irritation of the lining of the urogenital tract. It is possible that the resulting genital sensations may actually increase an animal's tendency to mate, but the evidence is entirely anecdotal and not satisfactory from the scientific point of view. There is little reason to believe that the effect involves anything more than irritation of the peripheral effector organ.

Yohimbine, which is extracted from the bark of the African yohimbine tree, is sometimes used as an aphrodisiac. Although some modern endocrinologists have suggested that this substance acts as a gonadotrophic agent, stimulating the secretion of sex hormones, the weight of the evidence is against any such theory. There is disagreement concerning the response of the genitalia to yohimbine, some specialists asserting that the blood supply to the sex organs is increased, and other authorities denying this assertion. As far as the effects on behavior are concerned, it can be said only that proof of any stimulating action is far from convincing. As a matter of fact, there is no completely satisfactory evidence that any pharmacological agent is capable of directly increasing the individual's susceptibility to sexual arousal and capacity for sexual performance. This is not to say that such agents do not exist. But at present we are limited to the generalization that any chemical compound that reduces the biological efficiency of the organism tends to lower sexual functions, whereas any substance that increases general health and alertness may have a positive sexual effect.

FUNCTIONS OF THE NERVOUS SYSTEM

We have noted that the sexual behavior of human beings resembles that of other animals in many ways and, at the same time, that numerous differences exist. Both the similarities and the differences are best understood as products of certain evolutionary changes that took place while primates slowly differentiated from more primitive mammals and, later, as *Homo sapiens* gradually emerged from the primate stem.

One of the changes already discussed appears to have been a progressive decrease in the importance of sex hormones to mating behavior. In order to interpret this and other evolutionary modifications in the physiology of erotic responses it is necessary to understand something of the way in which various parts of the nervous system contribute to the occurrence of sexual activities.

The Spinal Cord. Several basic sexual reflexes are controlled in part by nervous centers located in the spinal cord. This is just as true of human beings as it is of lower animals. The occurrence of erection and ejaculation in the male depends upon the discharge of nervous impulses from critical spinal and autonomic ganglia and can take place without any control from higher centers in the brain. Male rats, rabbits, and guinea pigs display genital tumescence and ejaculation when a low-voltage electric shock is applied directly to the appropriate segment of the exposed spinal cord. Male dogs in which the cord has been completely severed above the lumbar region (the small of the back) exhibit these genital reflexes in response to manual stimulation of the penis. The sexual activities which can be evoked in animals with severed spinal cords are not limited to isolated reflexes. For example, male dogs with this type of injury react to manipulation of the phallus by extending the hind legs and making shallow pelvic thrusts comparable to those seen in the intact animal during intromission.

Young men with gunshot wounds or tumors that completely interrupt the spinal cord continue to experience nocturnal erections and emissions. Stimulation of the penis in this type of patient sometimes calls forth violent muscular spasms which give the impression of copulatory movements and have been termed "the spinal coital reflex." It is important to recognize that this behavior is entirely involuntary. The men are totally incapable of controlling muscles situated below the point of injury to the cord and they receive no sensation from the affected parts of the body. Nevertheless, they have been known to impregnate their wives.

The Brain. In normal mammals of any species the brain plays an important part in controlling sexual behavior. Experimental and clinical observations like those cited above merely demonstrate that some segments of the total pattern may, under abnormal circumstances, be carried out by relatively primitive nervous mechanisms below the brain. One very important brain region is the hypothalamus, which appears to make essential contributions to the organization of mating responses in female rodents and carnivores. Injury to the anterior third of this area disrupts and may eliminate coital performance in female rats, rabbits, guinea pigs, and cats. There is no evidence concerning the contribution of the hypothalamus to sexual behavior in males of these same species or in primates.

The highest and most recently evolved part of the brain is the cerebral cortex. Primitive cortical tissue first appears in the reptiles. Fishes and amphibia have no cortex, and in birds this brain area is rudimentary. Lower mammals possess a simple but well-defined cortex; in monkeys and apes this part of the brain becomes much larger and more specialized. Man's brain differs from that of other mammals chiefly in the extreme size and complexity of the cerebral cortex. Upon this physical structure depend all the higher psychological capacities such as thought, memory, imagination, and the like. Extreme retardation of the development of the cortex is associated with congenital idiocy, and extensive cortical injury may result in profound interference with behavior.

The cerebral cortex can be surgically removed in some lower mammals without fatal results. Female rats, rabbits, guinea pigs, cats, and dogs which have been subjected to this operation continue to display mating behavior when they come into heat. The reactions are not as well integrated as they are in normal animals, but they are sufficient to permit fertile copulation. It is of the utmost theoretical importance that male rats, cats, and dogs that have been deprived of their cortices immediately become sexually inactive. They appear totally unresponsive to sexually exciting stimuli and display no interest in the receptive female.

It appears that the cortex is essential to effective mating in males of most of the lower mammalian species but is dispensable in the case of females. Additional evidence on this score comes from studies of temporary sexual inversion in female rats. In Chapter VII we described malelike mounting behavior which is shown by normal females of this rodent species. One of us (Beach) has shown that when female rats are deprived of the cerebral cortex they cease to mount other females in masculine fashion, but the same animals continue to react with the feminine pattern of sexual receptivity when they are approached by a male.

We believe that the differential importance of the cerebrum to masculine and feminine sexuality in lower mammals is directly responsible for other differences between males and females at this level of the evolutionary scale. It has been pointed out, for example, that males are more easily inhibited by strange surroundings or by previous unsuccessful sexual experiences than are females. And males may be positively conditioned so that stimuli which originally had no sexual significance become capable of evoking intense erotic arousal. Comparable conditioning has never been observed in lower mammalian females. When the female is fully receptive she is likely to permit any active male to copulate with her. But the sexually aggressive male often displays more discrimination, refusing some females and mating with others that are no more receptive.

We are strongly impressed with the evidence for sexual learning and conditioning in the male and the relative absence of such processes in the female. Inasmuch as learning is known to depend heavily upon the cerebral cortex, the implication is plain that the sex difference derives directly from the unequal role which this part of the nervous system plays in masculine and feminine mating behavior.

Prepuberal sex play is common in young males of subprimate species, whereas immature females show none of the adult feminine mating responses (see Chapter X). This difference might be referred to the fact that some androgen is present in young males, whereas ovarian secretions are not present in the female until puberty. However, castration at birth does not prevent the occurrence of infantile sex play in males. Furthermore, although they do not execute sexually receptive responses, young females often engage in malelike mating responses prior to puberty. Here again, therefore, is a suggestion that the masculine pattern, whether it is exhibited by males or by females, can occur in the absence of testicular hormone, whereas the female mating response is more directly dependent upon sex hormones. We believe that this difference is due to the fact that the cerebral cortex contributes more heavily to the male than to the female response.

No experiments are available to indicate the relative importance of the cortex in the sexual behavior of male and female primates. However, male monkeys and apes are often incapable of copulating effectively without experience, whereas inexperienced adult females of the same species are able to mate the first time they are given an opportunity to do so (Chapter X). Such a difference could conceivably be due to differences in the degree to which masculine and feminine behavior depends upon the functioning of the cortex of the brain.

Physiological Differences in Men and Women

In closing this chapter on the physiological factors affecting sexual behavior we wish to review briefly several lines of evidence that suggest a differential basis for sexual arousal and satisfaction in male and female human beings. We do not insist that our interpretation is valid. The important point is to bring the evidence together to permit formulation of alternative explanations.

Self-Stimulation. In Chapter IX we noted that in all human societies for which there is adequate information males are more likely than females to stimulate their own sexual organs. Of particular importance is the additional fact that the same sex difference exists in many other primate species. Part of the explanation for this difference may be the obvious fact that the shape and location of the male genitalia render them more accessible to stimulation than are those of the female. In other words, it is easier for the male to induce in himself genital sensations closely resembling those derived from coitus. If the female is to achieve a comparable effect she must find and employ a penis substitute that can be inserted in the vagina.

This type of behavior is not beyond the capacities of some sub-human primates, but it occurs very rarely.

We are inclined to believe that the low incidence of vaginal insertions in primates indicates that such practices rarely lead to sexual satisfaction. Observations of heterosexual coitus in monkeys and apes give the impression that the female's satisfaction depends upon repeated intimate and vigorous contact with active males. There are no obvious indications of feminine climax. Reduction of the pressure of the sexual drive seems more dependent on frequent copulation involving continued stimulation. Males that have become satiated are deserted in favor of fresher, more vigorous consorts. The female's coital activity tends to continue until she is exhausted from a series of copulations, or until she emerges from estrus.

It is clear that some human females are capable of achieving orgasm as a result of clitoral stimulation, and this is by far the most common method of masturbation. But many other individuals are not able to bring themselves to climax in this fashion. And even for those women who can achieve this, the resulting sensations may be less complete and satisfying than are those deriving from coitus which involves other forms of stimulation than the purely clitoral ones. Still another factor that may help to account for the relatively low frequency of feminine self-masturbation is the apparent importance of interpersonal relations in feminine sex life. For many male masturbators sexual fantasy accompanies self-stimulation and adds greatly to the satisfaction of the climax thus achieved. The majority of women, in contrast, appear to rely heavily upon the actual presence and behavior of a sexual partner.

Homosexual Behavior.   Like self-masturbation, homosexual activities are more common among males than among females. This holds true for the vast majority of human societies and for all the other primates as well. Here again the relative ease with which the genitals of the two sexes can be stimulated may be important, particularly in the case of subhuman animals. This cannot, however, be the complete explanation. In human beings the relative infrequency of feminine homosexuality probably reflects the fact that for most women sexual satisfaction demands more than simple genital stimulation. It usually rests upon a complex type of interrelationship with the masculine partner. Paradoxically enough, this point of view receives confirmation from the accounts of exclusively homosexual women who affirm that they prefer feminine lovers because the latter are more sentimental, more considerate than men. This simply emphasizes the fact that for the human female, physical climax in and of itself is less sufficient than it is for most men.

Masculine and Feminine Orgasm.   One final difference that deserves mention in this connection involves the frequency and nature of sexual climax in males and females. It has already been noted that external signs of orgasm are present in males of many subhuman primates and lower mammalian species, whereas indicators of a comparable climax are lacking in females. We have also pointed out that sexual satisfaction for the male plainly involves the attainment of orgasm, but that the sources of feminine satisfaction are much more subtle and obscure. One important point is the fact that as far as fertile coitus is concerned the male's orgasm is essential, but that of the female is completely unnecessary. This is true because masculine orgasm is associated with the ejaculation of sperm. No comparable event occurs in the female. This generalization is just as true of human males and females as it is of lower animals.

Some insight into the physiological changes accompanying sexual intercourse is gained from the studies of Pussep. This investigator measured the blood pressure of male and female dogs before, during, and after coitus. As shown in Figures 13 and 14, the reactions of the two sexes differ appreciably. Blood pressure in the female rises sharply when the male licks the vulva, and again when the penis enters the vagina. Pressure remains high until the male withdraws. There are a few irregularities in the curve, but none of them approximate the abrupt rise in the male's blood pressure at the time of ejaculation.

The male dog is a particularly good subject for this type of experiment because, although he ejaculates soon after entering the female, his erection may be maintained for the next half hour, and throughout this period intromission is continued. It will be seen that the male's blood pressure returns to near the resting level shortly after ejaculation and orgasm have occurred, despite the fact that his penis is still in the vagina. The female, in contrast, maintains high blood pressure as long as intromission continues. We conclude from this record that the female's physiological response consists of a more or less steady state of arousal, not marked by any climactic event, and dependent primarily upon vaginal stimulation.

Boas' records of heart rate in a man and woman indicate that

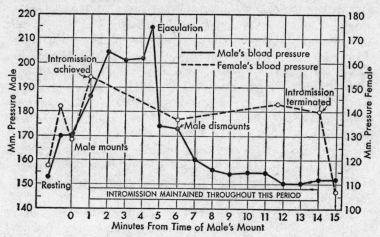

FIG. 13. Comparison of blood pressure changes in the male and female dog during coitus. The animals were not tested simultaneously. Since the mating in which the female was tested was much shorter than that in which the male's pressure was measured, the female's record is distorted, extending over a much longer period of time than was actually involved.

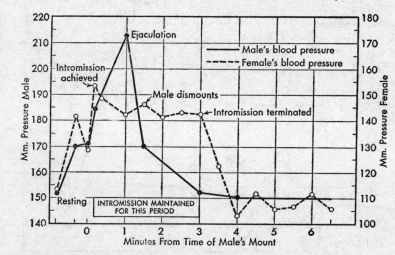

FIG. 14. Blood pressure changes in the male and female dog during coitus. The two animals were not tested simultaneously. In this figure the record of the male has been condensed to fit the time scale of the experiment in which the female was tested.

somewhat comparable results are obtainable in the human species (Figure 15). The curves in this case show that the man's heart rate rises somewhat during precopulatory play and again at the moment of insertion. The obvious point is, however, that ejaculation and orgasm are accompanied by a tremendous increase in heart rate, followed rather promptly by an equally marked decline in this function. For the woman, in contrast, cardiac function changes abruptly with insertion and remains at a high level until the moment of withdrawal. Here again is the suggestion that the primary stimulation accounting for high excitement is derived from penetration and continued insertion (the clitoris also is being stimulated). As long as this stimulation continues, the female's heart rate remains accelerated.

In the human male orgasm is followed rather suddenly by loss of the erection and consequently the feminine partner is suddenly deprived of vaginal stimulation. If men, like male dogs, retained the

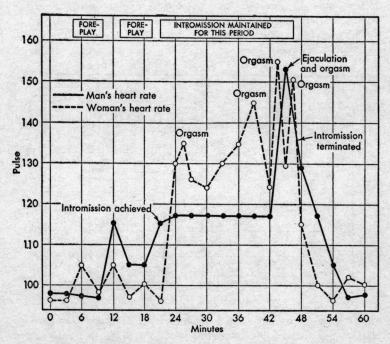

FIG. 15. Effects of sexual intercourse upon the pulse rate in one man and one woman. (From Boas and Goldschmidt, *The Heart Rate.*)

erection after ejaculating, the heart rate records of human beings might be like the curves shown in Figure 16. Here we have simply reversed the man's curve. The resemblance between this record and those taken from dogs is striking. Both suggest that maximal cardiac function in the male is closely associated with orgasm, whereas the condition of the female is controlled primarily by the continuation of intromission.

It remains necessary to account for the four peaks in the woman's heart rate curve, peaks which she identifies as coinciding with subjective sensations of orgasm. These, it appears to us, reflect the effects of experience and learning. Women come to recognize and identify these physiological changes and to call them orgasms. Of course the human male also must learn to identify his climax, but he has an easier task because the subjective event is correlated with the overt and easily observable occurrence of emission.

The difference in physiological concomitants of the male and female orgasm is responsible for several other more generally recognized differences between men and women. One is the female's greater capacity for multiple orgasms. It is true that many women do not recognize their ability to achieve several climaxes in succession. This may be because they have never been stimulated for a sufficient length of time. A woman lacking premarital experience and married to a man whose orgasm occurs within one or two minutes after penetration might easily have one peak in her curve of responsiveness and then fail to have any subsequent ones simply because her partner's loss of erection removes the source of stimulation. Such a woman could easily go through life believing herself capable of but one climax in each coital act.

Since relatively minor physiological changes are sometimes called orgasms, it is not surprising that many women experience some climaxes as being more intense than others. And further, it is understandable that in some instances they may be uncertain as to whether orgasm has occurred. Finally, the fact that some women can find intercourse pleasant and satisfying without experiencing any violent sexual climax may be interpreted as reflecting the primary importance of stimulation which evokes a more or less steady physiological response and may totally lack any climactic features.

In closing this section we wish to say again that the interpretations offered here concerning physiological differences between males and females are speculative in the highest degree. They may meet

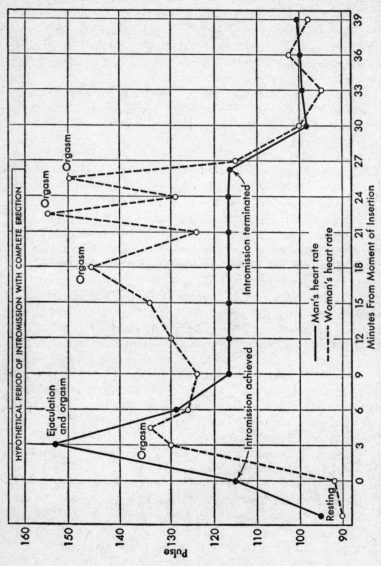

FIG. 16. Pulse rates in a man and woman as they might be affected if the man's orgasm occurred soon after insertion, but erection and intromission were continued for some time. Compare with Figures 13 and 14.

with violent objection from many sides and we are prepared to relinquish or modify them the moment a more inclusive and satisfactory explanation of the facts is advanced. Our primary purpose has been, not to expound prematurely any theoretical point of view, but rather to put before the reader several lines of evidence not previously brought together for consideration.

SUMMARY

This chapter has been devoted to a consideration of the physiological factors involved in the sexual behavior of human beings and lower animals. The role of ovarian hormones, first mentioned in Chapter XI, has been further discussed. The importance of testicular hormones received consideration. In reviewing these topics it became apparent that human beings are less dependent upon sex hormones than are subhuman primates, and that the latter in turn are somewhat freer of hormonal control than are lower mammals. It is therefore proposed that in the course of evolution the extent to which gonadal hormones control sexual behavior has been progressively relaxed, with the result that human behavior is relatively independent of this source of control.

Review of the changes which have taken place in the structure of the brain during mammalian evolution showed that this structure has become increasingly complex and important as the primates and finally our own species developed. In particular, the cerebral cortex has assumed a greater and greater degree of direction over all behavior, including that of a sexual nature. It appears that the growing importance of cerebral influences accounts for the progressive relaxation of hormonal control over sexual responses. At the same time, increasing dominance of the cortex in affecting sexual manifestations has resulted in greater lability and modifiability of erotic practices. Human sexual behavior is more variable and more easily affected by learning and social conditioning than is that of any other species, and this is precisely because in our own species this type of behavior depends heavily upon the most recently evolved parts of the brain.

Chapter XIII

Human Sexual Behavior in Perspective

A S WE explained in the opening chapter, the major purpose of this book has been to describe the general background necessary to a more comprehensive understanding of human sexual behavior. There has emerged from our analysis a fundamental frame of reference which results from examining the subject from three different points of view. This threefold frame of reference serves to assist in the better understanding of human sexual behavior in any society.

One essential way of looking at the evidence involves the achievement of a cross-cultural perspective. Only in this manner can the behavior of men and women in any given society be compared and contrasted with that of peoples belonging to quite different societies. The results of our cross-cultural analysis emphasize the important fact that the members of no one society can safely be regarded as "representative" of the human race as a whole. Although there are many cross-cultural similarities there are also many differences between societies. Both of these must be recognized and interpreted before it is possible to formulate a valid and comprehensive description of human sexuality.

A second perspective developed in this book derives from comparisons between human beings and lower animals. This evolutionary or zoological kind of analysis has revealed the existence of certain common elements in the sexual behavior of many species, including *Homo sapiens*. Man is far from unique in his patterns of sexual behavior. Many of the behavioral items occurring in various human societies are equally characteristic of apes, monkeys, and even lower mammals. Taken together, these broadly distributed types of sexual response may be said to constitute a basic mammalian pattern. Some sexual practices are engaged in only by the human animal. Behavioral differences between man and all other animals are due to two classes of factors. The first comprises the multitude of biological changes that have occurred in the course of human evolution. The second encompasses the profound modifications that every society imposes upon the inherited tendencies of its members.

The third perspective that we have endeavored to develop centers about the relationship between sexual behavior and physiology. Sexual reactions are in part an expression of deep-rooted urges and needs, and the behavior through which these find expression is organized by the physical machinery of the body. The structural and functional capacities of the nervous and muscular systems determine the kinds of behavior that can occur, and, in addition, incline the individual toward certain activities and against others. The chemistry of the blood is particularly important. The presence or absence of certain glandular secretions has far-reaching effects upon susceptibility to sexual arousal and capacity for sexual performance. The chief value of a physiological perspective on human sexual life is that it affords an explanation for many of the differences and similarities between our own and other species.

Evolutionary Changes in the Biology of Sexual Behavior

In most lower animals sexual behavior tends to occur only when fertilization can take place. With relatively few exceptions, the courtship and mating activities of most mammals are tied very closely to reproduction of the species. This obviously is not the case for men and women. On the contrary, in all human societies sexual relations serve a variety of nonreproductive functions. The apparent magnitude of this difference has so impressed many writers that they regard human sexual activities as entirely different from the reproductive responses of all other living creatures.

This view is quite incorrect. Its fallacious nature is at once apparent when one examines the behavior of those animal species whose evolutionary status most closely approximates our own. The infrahuman primates are known to indulge in sexual intercourse under conditions in which such relations cannot possibly result in fertilization. For example, female chimpanzees sometimes offer themselves to the male during the infertile phases of their menstrual cycle. Proffered coitus may be employed to divert an impending attack or to induce the male to share some desired object such as a bit of food. Monkeys are less apt than apes to engage in coitus when the female is infertile but they do so occasionally. Mammals below the primates on the evolutionary scale appear to restrict their copulatory activities to the times when the female is capable of conceiving. One sees, then, evidence for an evolutionary change from strict periodicity of sexual behavior in the female to relative absence of such behavioral rhythms. This change is not an abrupt one. Instead it is progressive, with lower mammals representing one extreme, human beings the other, and infrahuman primates in an intermediate position between the two.

Importance of the Gonadal Hormones. Part of the explanation for the differences between animal species lies in the nature of the physiological factors that control sexual activity. The ease with which erotic arousal occurs and the vigor with which it is expressed depend in part upon the individual's physiological condition. The tendency of men and women to indulge in sexual experiences may be strongly affected by the current state of nourishment, freedom from debilitating disease, chemical composition of the blood, and a variety of other bodily factors. This is equally true of lower animals. There are, however, important physiological differences between species. The most obvious and impressive difference between the physiological control of sexual behavior in human beings and other animals lies in the relative importance of the gonadal or sex hormones.

It is a general rule that females of lower mammalian species are sexually stimulating to the male and are willing to mate with him only when their ovaries are secreting large amounts of estrogenic hormone. In the nonpregnant female this condition obtains only when the ovaries contain ripe eggs and, therefore, when the female can become pregnant as a result of intercourse. Animals that are sexually immature or are past the breeding age, and those from which the ovaries have been removed do not under ordinary circumstances show any sexual activity. In such cases the ovarian hormones are absent, or are present only in very low concentrations. It is entirely feasible to induce sexual behavior in the immature, the ovariectomized, or the aged female of these species by injecting ovarian hormones. Such treatment does not render the animal fertile but causes her temporarily to behave as if she were so.

The sexual activities of monkeys and apes differ from those of lower mammals in that the female's receptivity is less rigidly controlled by blood chemistry. The independence of feminine eroticism from hormonal domination is far from complete, however. It is quite clear, for example, that female chimpanzees are maximally receptive and exciting to the male during that phase of the menstrual cycle when ovulation is imminent, when coitus can result in pregnancy, and when the estrogenic ovarian hormone is being secreted in large quantities. But, as was noted before, some females occasionally invite and accept the male's sexual attentions during other phases of the cycle. Furthermore, female apes from whom the ovaries have been removed sometimes demonstrate a low but recognizable degree of sexual responsiveness. Although distinctly limited, this partial independence of feminine sexual behavior from hormonal support sets the infrahuman primate apart from lower mammals and represents a step toward the much more pronounced freedom that characterizes the human species.

The human female appears capable of marked sexual excitability without the physiological stimulation provided by the ovarian hormones. She may be sexually aroused before puberty and after menopause. Very often the surgical removal of the ovaries has no effect upon the enjoyment of sexual relations. When this operation does depress responsiveness, the change can often be shown to depend upon some other factors, not directly upon the withdrawal of ovarian hormones.

The dependence of men upon testicular hormone for sexual ability is also less marked than that of males of many lower mammalian species. There is evidence to suggest that at least some eunuchs experience sexual arousal and retain the ability to copulate for many years after loss of the reproductive glands. There are other cases in which castration or failure of the testes to develop is accompanied by a decrease in sexual responsiveness and activity. And in some cases desire and capacity can be revived if the missing hormone is supplied by injection. Since replacement therapy is not always effective it is apparent that nonhormonal influences play a major role in regulating the sexuality of men as well as women.

Like some human castrates, the male chimpanzee may continue to show active sexual behavior for years after loss of the testes. But most of the lower animals that have been examined cease to display signs of intense sexual arousal shortly after their reproductive glands have been removed; their sexual performance can be restored if the appropriate hormone is injected at regular intervals. The evolutionary picture is less clear and complete for the male than for the female, but such evidence as is available suggests that a comparable change has taken place in both sexes. For males of species that are relatively low on the mammalian scale, testicular hormone is essential to normal sexual vigor. This hormone is obviously less important for coital behavior in the case of some higher animals, particularly for apes and human beings.

Importance of the Cerebral Cortex. The progressive reduction in hormonal control of sexual behavior is best understood in its relation to another series of evolutionary changes. These are changes in the size and complexity of certain parts of the brain. The most recently evolved part of the nervous system is the cerebral cortex. This structure is absent from the brains of fishes, rudimentary in reptiles, and well developed only in the mammals. In the lowest mammals the cortex is not highly differentiated and constitutes less than one-quarter of the volume of the entire brain. In monkeys and apes the cortex is much larger and is clearly differentiated into a number of complex areas. Ninety per cent of the adult human brain consists of cortical substance, and this mass of nervous tissue is elaborately subdivided into hundreds of different nuclei and tracts, each serving certain functions and all acting together in integrated fashion to produce unified adaptive behavior.

As the cortex has grown in size and complexity its control over behavior has increased. The degree to which cortical activities influence most of the organism's daily responses is lowest in rodents, more marked in carnivores, pronounced in monkeys and apes, and most extreme in the human species. Sexual impulses and responses are no exception to this generalization. We suggest that the evolutionary decrease in the importance of gonadal hormones for sexual behavior reflects a compensatory increase in the degree of control exerted over such activities by the cortex of the brain.

Another consequence of these variations in the structure of the brain deserves special emphasis. In very general fashion it is correct to state that members of the mammalian species that possess a very large and complexly organized cerebral cortex are more susceptible to the effects of learning and personal experience than are other kinds of animals with a simpler and smaller cortex. It is to be expected, therefore, that a high degree of cortical development will be associated with more variable behavior and with more easily modified inherited behavioral tendencies. Because all complex human behavior is heavily dependent upon cortical processes it is automatically open to modification through the influences of previous experience. This explains why, in human beings more than in any other species, sexuality is structured and patterned by learning.

Some Consequences of Man's Mammalian Heritage

Up to this point we have concerned ourselves primarily with differences between man and other animals, but of equal significance are the various points of similarity that reflect the evolutionary heritage of *Homo sapiens*. As we have said, these are sufficiently numerous and important to justify the concept of a basic mammalian pattern of sexual behavior, certain elements of which persist in human beings. Many of these separate items have been pointed out in preceding chapters and only a few need be reviewed here.

Sex Play in Childhood.   Three generalizations can be made with respect to this topic: First, that early sex play occurs in many species other than our own. Second, that the frequency, variety, and completeness of prepuberal sexual reaction tends to increase from the lower mammals to the higher. And third, that species differences in the amount of such behavior are directly related to the physiological differences we have just discussed.

The cross-cultural evidence clearly reveals a universal human tendency for sexual responses to appear in the immature person long before he or she is capable of fertile coitus. Impulses of this nature are condoned and encouraged in some societies, strictly forbidden and punished in others. But regardless of the cultural ideal with respect to sex play in childhood, the underlying drive toward such activity constitutes one feature of the heredity of the human species.

Many years before they are fertile, male and female apes and monkeys indulge in a variety of sexual games which include attempts at heterosexual union. This form of infantile play is no less natural for the young primate than are the chasing, wrestling, and mock fighting that consume much of his waking life. Furthermore, these tendencies are not confined to primates. Although immature females of infraprimate species rarely show the adult mating response, very young males often engage in incomplete coital attempts with other individuals of their own age. This behavior may appear as soon as the young animal is physically capable of performing the necessary responses. For example, some animals such as the sheep are able to stand and walk shortly after birth, and sexual mounting appears in the first few days of life.

Self-Stimulation. Manipulation and stimulation of one's own sexual organs is another item that can be classified as basically mammalian. From the evolutionary point of view this kind of behavior seems to stem from the universal tendency of lower mammals to clean their genitalia by licking and manipulating them with the feet or mouth. Such behavior on the part of such animals as rats and cats cannot be classified as a deliberate attempt at self-excitation. Nevertheless, close observation of the animal's behavior strongly suggests that the resultant sensations have a sexually exciting quality.

In some infrahuman primates, genital manipulation assumes a frankly sexual character and is classifiable as masturbation. Immature and adult apes and monkeys occasionally indulge in stimulation of their own genitalia, and some adult males habitually induce ejaculation by masturbating. It is of considerable importance that this type of behavior is much less common in female primates of infrahuman species. Although a few mature female chimpanzees have been seen to masturbate, this is relatively rare.

Masturbation by captive primates has long been recognized, but most observers have considered the behavior an unnatural response produced by the artificial conditions of cage life. Recently, however, it has been found that self-stimulation is practiced by at least some male monkeys in their native habitat despite ample opportunity for coitus with receptive females. For lower primates, therefore, masturbation does not appear to be an unnatural or abnormal form of sexual activity.

Different human societies maintain widely divergent attitudes toward self-masturbation. Some social codes enforce different rules depending upon the age of the individual involved. There are peoples who condone or even encourage masturbation during childhood, whereas some other societies condemn this form of sexual expression for all individuals from infancy onward. Almost all human groups subject adult masturbation to negative sanctions ranging from mild ridicule to severe punishment. It should be added, however, that regardless of social condemnation, at least some adults in all or nearly all the societies in our sample appear to practice it. In every society self-stimulation seems to be less common among women than among men, and, as was noted earlier, a comparable sex difference is seen in infrahuman primates. The zoological and the cross-cultural evidence leads us to conclude that the tendency toward self-stimulation should be classified as one more item in the basic mammalian sexual repertoire and that masturbation is more likely to occur in the male than in the female.

Homosexual Behavior. Homosexual behavior is never the predominant type of activity for adults in any of the societies covered by this book. Heterosexual coitus is the dominant sexual activity for the majority of the adults in every society. But some homosexual behavior occurs in nearly all the societies comprising our sample. It is generally more common in men than in women. The apparent universality of this form of sexual activity might be due to some equally widespread social influence that tends to force a portion of every group into homosexual alliances. Certain social factors probably do incline certain individuals toward homosexuality, but the phenomenon cannot be understood solely in such terms.

Social codes differ markedly in their treatment of liaisons between members of the same sex. At one extreme are societies such as our own that forbid and punish any homosexual relationship in individuals of any age and of either sex. There are, in contrast, other peoples who are tolerant of homosexual play in childhood but disapprove of the same behavior on the part of adults. Still a third group of societies actively enforces homosexual relations upon all its male members. This is true, however, only for a given age group, and it is usually associated with puberty ceremonials. A number of cultures make special provisions for the adult male homosexual, according him a position of dignity and importance and permitting him to live as the "wife" of some other man.

Our cross-cultural comparisons suggest three generalizations concerning homosexual behavior in human beings: First, there is a wide divergence of social attitudes toward this kind of activity. Second, no matter how a particular society may treat homosexuality, the behavior is very likely to occur in at least a few individuals. Third, males seem more likely to engage in homosexual activity than do females. In order to interpret these facts it is necessary to see their relationships to the zoological and physiological data.

Homosexual behavior is not uncommon among males and females

of several infrahuman primate species. Immature monkeys and apes indulge in a variety of homosexual games which include manipulation of the genitals of a like-sexed partner and may even involve attempts at homosexual coitus. Such relationships tend to occur less frequently after puberty, but in some cases an adult individual may form an enduring homosexual liaison with an immature member of his own sex. It is significant that in other primates, as in human beings, homosexuality is less prevalent among females than among males. It is also important to note the absence of any evidence to justify classifying this behavior exclusively as a substitute for heterosexual relations. Adult male monkeys with ample opportunity for heterosexual intercourse may nevertheless indulge in homosexual relations with younger males. And in some cases the same individual will carry on hetero- and homosexual alliances concurrently.

Male and female mammals belonging to infraprimate species sometimes display mating responses typical of the opposite sex. Adult females often mount other females in masculine fashion, and the females that are thus mounted react as they would to a male. Under certain circumstances males attempt to copulate with males, and occasionally the one thus approached will react in the manner of a receptive female. Such observations reveal the bisexuality of the physiological mechanisms for mammalian mating behavior. Even in such species as the rat or rabbit, the neuromuscular basis for feminine responses is present in males as well as females, and the normal female's physiological capacities include the ability to react as would the male. Temporary inversions of the sexual role are due in these species not to an underlying physical abnormality in the individual but to the nature of the external stimulus situation.

It is our belief that a comparable though much more complex condition obtains in human beings. It seems probable that all men and women possess an inherited capacity for erotic responsiveness to a wide range of stimuli. Tendencies leading to sexual relations with individuals of the same sex are probably not as strong as those leading to heterosexual relations. But the important fact is that all societies enforce some modification of the individual's genetically determined impulses, with the result that the preferred type of behavior is strongly influenced by experience.

Men and women who are totally lacking in any conscious homosexual leanings are as much a product of cultural conditioning as are the exclusive homosexuals who find heterosexual relations distasteful and unsatisfying. Both extremes represent movement away from the original, intermediate condition which includes the capacity for both forms of sexual expression. In a restrictive society such as our own a large proportion of the population learns not to respond to or even to recognize homosexual stimuli and may eventually become in fact unable to do so. At the same time a certain minority group, also through the process of learning, becomes highly if not exclusively sensitive to the erotic attractions of a like-sexed partner. Physical or physiological peculiarities that hamper the formation of heterosexual habits may incline certain individuals to a homosexual existence. But human homosexuality is not basically a product of hormonal imbalance or "perverted" heredity. It is the product of the fundamental mammalian heritage of general sexual responsiveness as modified under the impact of experience.

Types of Foreplay. Comparisons between man and lower animals make it clear that many elements in the human heterosexual coital pattern are directly determined by the species heredity. For example, the male's erection and ejaculation are basic reflexes present in all mammals. Similarly, the tendency to respond to rhythmic stimulation of the genitals with thrusting movement of the pelvic region is a fundamental reaction in the mammalian repertoire.

Somewhat less apparent is the evolutionary generality of several types of behavioral interactions that tend to occur just before heterosexual coitus. For instance, investigation and consequent stimulation of the feminine genitalia by the male are a universal response in all mammals. The manner in which such stimulation is achieved varies from species to species and depends in large measure upon the effector equipment of the animal involved. Application of the male's tongue, teeth, and lips to the vulva and clitoris is extremely common. The forefeet or hands are employed in the same fashion by males of several species. The behavior seems to be investigatory as far as the male is concerned, but the female's bodily responses make it obvious that she is sexually excited by the resultant stimulation.

In all animal species for which adequate knowledge is available, males exhibit much more of this kind of behavior than do females. Nevertheless, females of many if not all species do occasionally investigate and therefore stimulate the sexual organs of the male. This is most likely to occur when the female is sexually aroused and the male is sluggish or slow to respond to her coital invitations.

Some amount of precoital stimulation occurs in nearly every society of which we have record. In certain cases, as in the Ponapeans, the techniques involved are elaborate, involving use not only of the hands but of the mouth as well. There are a few societies which disapprove of any form of genital stimulation except that derived from coitus, but these are rare. Within American society the individual's social stratum partially determines his or her tendency to practice or permit precoital caressing of the sexual organs. Men and women on lower social levels are less likely to indulge in these forms of foreplay than are individuals belonging to a higher socioeducational level. When such behavior is engaged in, it may be mutual or unilateral; but if only one of the partners stimulates the other, the active individual is almost always the male. This is true not only for our own society but also for the vast majority of the remaining ones in our sample. And, as has been pointed out, the same generalizations extend to other animals as well.

Another very common type of prelude to copulation is grooming behavior. This type of activity is characteristic of many human societies and appears in much the same form in every infrahuman primate species that has been studied. In some peoples sexual arousal and expression are enhanced by moderately painful stimulation. Among the Trukese, the Siriono, and certain other tribes, scratching, biting, and hair pulling form a regular part of the coital pattern. Similarly, in several species of lower animals aggressive or assaultive behavior is characteristically incorporated into the mating relationship. One interesting difference between human beings and lower animals is that sexually receptive females of subhuman species rarely bite or otherwise injure the male. Even though, as in the baboon or macaque monkey, the male may severely wound the female, she remains receptive and does not retaliate. But we have found no human society in which such a unilateral relationship exists. On the contrary, if the cultural stereotype of foreplay involves biting or scratching, both partners show this behavior.

The biological functions of preliminaries to intercourse in lower animals are evident. They tend to increase the degree of excitement in both sexes and also to synchronize the behavior of the pair. In this manner foreplay increases the probability of fertile intercourse. Man's capacity for responding to symbolic stimuli such as those involved in language has to some extent reduced the biological necessity for direct physical stimulation prior to copulation, but unless social conditioning imposes inhibitions upon active foreplay it is very likely to occur. And when it does appear it often takes essentially the same forms seen in other mammals and has essentially the same behavioral results.

MAN THE LEARNING ANIMAL

We have said that evolution of the human brain has endowed man with a greater ability to learn from experience than is present in any other animal species. It would, of course, be a mistake to conclude that lower animals cannot learn. In this respect, as in so many others, the human species differs from other mammals more in degree than in kind. The role of learning in sexual behavior varies from species to species in two ways. There are differences in the degree to which learning is necessary for successful coitus, and there are differences in the extent to which learning can suppress, redirect, or otherwise modify the inherited sexual tendencies of the individual.

Learning and practice are apparently not essential for fertile mating in the few species of lower animals that have been carefully studied. If male rats are reared in complete isolation they are nevertheless capable of copulating effectively the first time they are placed with a receptive female. No practice or experimentation is necessary. The behavior is what is ordinarily called "instinctive." This does not mean, however, that experience cannot affect sexual behavior in male rodents. On the contrary, an individual that has repeatedly been presented with receptive females in a particular cage, pen, or experimental room tends to become sexually excited whenever he is returned to the same setting. Under such circumstances sexual attempts may be directed toward any other animal encountered in that particular environment. And conversely, the male may fail to respond sexually to receptive females encountered in surroundings in which he has previously experienced pain or frustration.

Experience and learning appear to be much more important in the sexual performance of the primates. At least some, and perhaps all, male chimpanzees have to learn how to copulate. Adult apes lacking any copulatory experience respond to the receptive female with evident sexual excitement, but they appear to be incapable of carrying out the bodily adjustments necessary for coitus. Their response to the female's sexual invitation is awkward, poorly organized, and inadequately directed. Only after several years of practice and experimentation do male apes of this species become capable of effective and well-integrated coital behavior.

As a result of experimentation some chimpanzees develop highly individualistic methods of mating. For example, the usual method of coitus consists of the male mounting the stooping female from the rear; but some male apes acquire a preference for intercourse in which they remain seated on the ground and the female reclines upon their thighs.

In addition to shaping the physical reactions involved in intercourse, learning exerts other effects upon the sexual habits of infrahuman primates. It contributes to the formation of personal preferences and tastes in sexual matters. Although they occasionally show some selective tendencies, potent males of most of the lower mammalian species will copulate readily with any female who is receptive; and females in estrus are equally undiscriminating. This is much less true as far as monkeys and apes are concerned. Some male chimpanzees show a distinct preference for certain feminine partners and are reluctant or unwilling to copulate with others. Females of these species also tend to seek the company of some potential partners and to ignore or avoid others.

We interpret the increased importance of learning in primates as being due primarily to the evolutionary advance in brain structure and the partial release from rigid hormonal control. From what has already been said concerning the physiological changes associated with human evolution, it might be expected that in our own species learning would have the most marked and far-reaching effects upon sexual activities. This expectation is amply verified by the facts. Human sexuality is affected by experience in two ways: First, the kinds of stimulation and the types of situations that become capable of evoking sexual excitement are determined in a large measure by learning. Second, the overt behavior through which this excitement is expressed depends largely upon the individual's previous experience.

Human beings can learn without tutelage. That is to say, they can learn by trial and error in much the same fashion as a rat learns to traverse a maze or a cat to open a puzzle box. And to a certain degree, unguided trial-and-error learning may influence the development of the individual's sexual patterns. But this is exceptional. By far most of what people learn to feel and to do in the realm of sex is learned from or with other individuals. Human learning, in other words, customarily occurs in a social context. For this reason the impact of learning upon human sexuality is best understood within the frame of reference provided by the society of which the individual is a member.

Man the Social Animal

Human infants are always born into extensive social groups, or societies. And the things that children and adults learn are governed to a considerable extent by the social structure and culture of their societies. Every society has accumulated, over centuries of experience, preferential ways of behaving, habits and codes that are transmitted from one generation to the next. Each new member of the society finds pressures brought to bear upon him to behave in the traditional manner, to conform to custom. Cultural precepts define for the individual when and where it is proper to behave in a certain manner, and they even specify the types of activities in which he may engage. In a word, the culture provides, through the habits of its members, the major learning conditions for the maturing individual.

The social structure and culture of a society have special significance with respect to sexual behavior. The position occupied by the individual in the social group carries with it definitions of the sexual activities expected of him. Some of these definitions are taken so seriously that severe punishment awaits the person who fails to perform his role in the traditionally accepted manner. Other rules are regarded more lightly, and the individual who varies his behavior may run only the risk of ridicule. But in any case cultural pressure is constantly exerted on all members of any society to express their sexual impulses in socially accepted fashion.

Intercultural Similarities Produced by Learning. There are many general similarities between human cultures in respect to sexual behavior. Some of these cultural universals cannot be explained solely in terms of the species heredity. Instead, they seem to be the products of common learning experience on the part of the members of all societies. An outstanding example is seen in the universal prohibition against primary incest.

Animals of infrahuman species freely interbreed with their own offspring, parents, and siblings. And in human beings consanguinity is no barrier to erotic attractiveness. Analyses of the fantasies and dreams of people in our own and many other societies plainly reveal the existence of unconscious sexual desires directed toward offspring, parents, and siblings. One must therefore look to social learning rather than to biological factors for an interpretation of incest taboos. The tentative explanation which we have offered involves the assumption that such taboos have arisen and persisted during societal evolution because they serve as a protective device against disintegration of the nuclear family—disintegration which would result if intrafamilial sexual jealousies and conflicts were not held at a minimum. We do not suppose that this device has been rationally conceived and instituted. On the contrary, it seems best understood as a product of natural selection. Societies lacking this protective regulation could not long endure. Survival of the larger social group depends too heavily upon preservation of its basic unit, the nuclear family. It is true that close inbreeding sometimes has biologically unfortunate or maladaptive consequences. And it might be surmised that this in itself would result in the eventual extinction of any society that failed to forbid incestuous relations. However, the evidence in this direction is scant, and it seems to us that the universality of incest taboos is more adequately explained on social-psychological grounds.

Another illustration of the way in which learning and societal evolution may produce widespread channelization of sexual impulses is the almost universal prohibition against intercourse with a menstruating woman. There is no evidence to suggest that these restrictions rest upon a biologically controlled absence of desire for sexual stimulation or capacity to respond to it on the part of either the woman or the man. On the contrary, the taboo appears to reflect common attitudes toward menstrual blood as a substance somehow associated with disease or physical injury.

Intercultural Differences Produced by Learning. Socially controlled learning is responsible not only for a number of intercultural similarities but also for many of the differences that exist between societies. It is generally agreed that all human races belong to the same species. They will, therefore, possess essentially the same species heredity. Whether or not there are important genetic differences between races—difference directly affecting behavior—is a matter of some dispute. However, no one has suggested, and we do not believe, that members of separate societies are sufficiently different genetically so that the variations in their sexual codes and habits can be explained on the basis of heredity. It follows, then, that marked intersocietal variations in such matters must be referable to differences in the cultural modification of inherited sexual impulses.

The full extent to which social forces can influence the behavior of the individual is not immediately obvious. It should be apparent that the attitude of members of a given society toward masturbation or toward homosexuality will be shaped to a large degree by early training. The result is that many members of our own society, for instance, look upon such phenomena with loathing and disgust and tend to classify the behavior as "abnormal" or "perverted." But the Keraki of New Guinea regard a man as "abnormal" if he abstains from homosexual relations prior to marriage. The importance of learning and culture in the formation of attitudes toward various sexual practices becomes fairly obvious after the evidence is reviewed and reflected upon, but there are still other effects that are less likely to be recognized. For example, various aspects of the heterosexual relationship are also influenced by training.

Certain elements in the coital pattern appear to be so completely reflexive that their control by voluntary means might seem impossible, but in fact some of them are powerfully affected by experience. One of these is the occurrence of man's ejaculation within a relatively short time after the penis has entered the vagina. Data presented in Chapter II indicate that for the majority of men in our society, ejaculation and orgasm occur within two minutes or less after the beginning of intercourse. Among the Marquesans, in contrast, the habitual copulatory pattern involves reservatus, and every man learns early in life to control his ejaculatory reflexes in such a manner as to permit maintenance of an erection and continuation of coitus for as long as the woman desires.

Both the tendency to incorporate painful stimulation in the culturally accepted pattern of precoital play and the type of response to such stimulation are strongly influenced by learning. From early life the Siriono or the Trobriand man or woman has learned to associate sexual excitement with the experience of being scratched or bitten. Accordingly, such sensations acquire erotic value and are subjectively experienced as pleasantly stimulating. Most members of other societies in which love-making lacks such aggressive components are likely to find physical pain a deterrent to sexual arousal and satisfaction.

Social learning and experience powerfully affect the extent to which a man or woman adopts and enjoys a passive or an active role in the sexual relationship. We have pointed out that in every infra-human species the distribution of sexual initiative is bilateral. Both the male and the female may extend the sexual invitation and both have an active share in the continuation of the relationship until coitus is completed. The wide divergence between different human societies in this regard is probably due, not to biological differences between males and females, but to the lifelong effects of early training.

The societies that severely restrict adolescent and preadolescent sex play, those that enjoin girls to be modest, retiring, and submissive appear to produce adult women that are incapable or at least unwilling to be sexually aggressive. The feminine products of such cultural training are likely to remain relatively inactive even during marital intercourse. And, quite often, they do not experience clearcut sexual orgasm. In contrast, the societies which permit or encourage early sex play usually allow females a greater degree of freedom in seeking sexual contacts. Under such circumstances the sexual performance of the mature woman seems to be characterized by a certain degree of aggression, to include definite and vigorous activity, and to result regularly in complete and satisfactory orgasm.

Individual Differences Produced by Learning. Personal experience, operating through learning, is one important source of variation in the sexual practices followed by different members of the same society. We have noted, for instance, that at least a small proportion of every society engages in homosexual behavior even though the social code may strongly condemn such activities. It is our opinion, as expressed earlier in this chapter, that the occurrence of exclusive homosexuality in the face of severe disapproval is due primarily to learning rather than to constitutional factors. In other words, men and women who are exclusively homosexual become so because of personal experience rather than because of some imperative, inherited urge. Of equal importance is the point that total absence of any conscious response to homosexual stimuli probably reflects the inhibiting effects of social conditioning.

The amount and kinds of foreplay which the individual finds satisfying and stimulating depend in part upon learning. Some American women are sexually aroused if the partner manipulates the vulva and clitoris before coitus, whereas other individuals find the same techniques unpleasant. These individual differences might be due in part to variations in the sensitivity of the organs involved, but we consider it much more likely that learned attitudes toward this type of behavior play the major role in determining its effects.

The ability of a man to perform the coital act depends not solely upon his physical condition, but also upon emotional attitudes toward the general subject of sex and toward the particular feminine partner involved. As a result of personal experience, some men become unable to achieve and maintain an erection or to reach climax under certain conditions, although they may be potent in other circumstances. The feminine orgasm is an especially sensitive indicator of experience. Many women have to learn to recognize orgasm when it occurs; and others, as a result of learned inhibitions, may go through life without ever experiencing a satisfactory sexual climax.

A FINAL WORD

If we have achieved our original objective, the reader of this book will have gained an appreciation of the necessity of viewing sexual behavior in broad perspective, and of interpreting the habits of any particular group of human beings in terms of the broad background provided by the cross-cultural and cross-species evidence. The pressing need for some such frame of reference is particularly obvious in a society such as our own which, until quite recently, has refused to deal with sexuality in objective terms. The traditional reserve with respect to sexual matters has, with a few notable exceptions, inhibited American scientists almost as strongly as laymen. This book is addressed, therefore, to all serious students of human behavior, be they professional specialists or otherwise.

It is most regrettable that an area of inquiry having such fundamental importance in both its practical and its theoretical aspects should have been so inadequately studied and so incompletely understood. Hesitancy to attack basic problems in this field cannot today be excused on grounds of public disapproval or moral censorship. Intelligent people everywhere are eager for information that will help them to understand their own sexual lives and those of their associates. This information must be gathered and interpreted by social and biological scientists.

It is our hope that the present volume will serve as a useful step toward the development of a sound understanding of the sexual behavior of human beings as it is affected by their evolutionary heritage and by the conditions imposed upon them by their social environment.

Glossary

Abelam. Sepik district, northern New Guinea. Subsist on garden products and flesh of domesticated pigs. Head-hunting formerly practiced. Polygyny permitted but rare.

Abipone. Gran Chaco, central South America. Gatherers and nomadic hunters. Simple technology. Once numbering 5000, they are now extinct. Polygny permitted but rare.

aborigines. The native inhabitants of a region; synonymous with indigenous peoples.

accessory sex structures. Technical term for certain parts of the reproductive system, including the sexual organs and associated parts. The female accessories are the vaginal labia, clitoris, vagina, uterus, and Fallopian tubes. The masculine sex accessories are the penis, scrotum, seminal vesicles, prostate gland, and the tubes leading from the testes.

adolescence. The period between puberty and full reproductive maturity. Defined in detail in Chapter X.

adolescent sterility. Period immediately following puberty before complete fertility is achieved. Heterosexual coitus during this developmental stage is less likely to result in pregnancy than is the same behavior somewhat later in life.

adrenals. A pair of glands situated just above the kidneys and consisting of two parts. One part secretes hormones that are closely related to the hormone of the male sex glands.

Ainu. Yezo, Sakhalin, and Kurile Islands, north of Japan. Controlled by Japanese since 1000 A.D. Formerly warlike, now peaceful. Polygyny practiced.

Aleut. Aleutian Islands, southwest of Alaska. Fishers, hunters, and gatherers. Simple technology. Polygyny restricted to the more well-to-do.

Alorese. Indonesia, directly north of central Timor. Live in small villages in mountainous interior. Sedentary planters. Some hostile contacts with coastal Mohammedan population. Polygyny permitted and common.

American chameleon. A small lizard.

amphibian. Any animal belonging to a class of vertebrates, most species of which reproduce and develop in the water and spend the adult phase

268

of their life on land. Representative amphibians are frogs, toads, and salamanders.

anal copulation. Copulation in which the penis is inserted into the rectum of the partner. May be either heterosexual or homosexual.

Andamanese. Andaman Islands in the Bay of Bengal, southeast Asia. Seminomadic gatherers, hunters, and fishers. Simple technology. Strictly monogamous.

androgen. A generic term for chemical substances secreted by certain endocrine glands. Androgenic hormones are commonly referred to as "male sex hormones." One form of androgen known as testosterone is produced by the male sex glands. The first androgenic material identified was that associated with the testes; this is the reason for calling it "male hormone." More recent studies have shown that similar secretions are produced by the cortex of the adrenal gland and also by the ovary.

anovulatory. Refers to the absence of ovulation. In some menstrual cycles (in primates) or estrous cycles (in lower mammals) all the external signs of ovarian activity are present, but no egg or eggs are released from the ovary. In such cases sexual relations cannot result in pregnancy.

anthropologist. Professional investigator of different peoples, their social organization and ways of life, their arts and crafts, and their history.

anus. Rectum.

Ao. Naga Hills, Assam. Population 30,000. Primarily agriculturalists, but they also keep domestic animals, hunt, and fish. Strictly monogamous.

Apache [western group]. Eastern Arizona. Farmers; they go on extended gathering and hunting trips. Polygyny permitted but confined mainly to the rich.

ape. This primate group is more highly evolved than monkeys and belongs just below man on the evolutionary scale. Also called anthropoid apes. See *Primate.*

Apinaye. North-central Brazil. Population 4000. Planters and nomadic hunters. Primitive technology. Peaceful. Monogamous.

Aranda. Central Australia. Population 2000. Very primitive technology. Hunters and gatherers. Generally polygynous, occasionally sororal.

Arapaho. Wyoming, Colorado, Montana, and Saskatchewan. Hunters. Polygyny, always the sororal form, is common.

Arikara. North Dakota. Agricultural. Polygyny general, sororal form preferred.

Ashanti. Guinea coast, Africa. Agriculturalists and hunters. Complex social and political organization. Advanced technology. Polygynous.

autoerotic. Any type of behavior that results in production of sexual excitement within oneself.

autogenital stimulation. Stimulation of one's own genitals.

axillary. Pertaining to the armpit.

Aymara. Lake Titicaca in western Bolivia and southern Peru. Subsist on products of animal husbandry and agriculture. Now number about 4000. Polygyny permitted but rare.

Azande. Eastern Sudan, central Africa. Population 2,000,000. Predominantly agriculturalists and hunters. Skilled craftsmen. Generally polygynous.

baboon. One type of Old World monkey.

Balinese. Bali Island, off the coast of Java. Population over 1,000,000. Mixture of Hindu Javanese and aboriginal Indonesians. Agricultural economy. Polygyny permitted but rare.

Barama. Barama River, British Guinea. Population about 300. Hunters, fishers, and farmers. Formerly warlike. Generally polygynous, sororal form preferred.

bate. Name given by the Crow Indians to homosexual men who have affairs with young boys.

Bena. Tanganyika, East Africa. Population over 15,000. Agriculturalists. Generally polygynous, sororal form preferred.

berdache. Name given by some societies to any male who dresses like a woman, performs women's tasks, and plays a feminine sexual role with male partners.

bestiality. Sexual intercourse between a human being and an animal of a different species.

buggery. Usually refers to heterosexual or homosexual anal copulation between human beings; can also apply to intercourse between a man and some other animal, in which the vagina is penetrated.

bull. A term applied to the adult males of several mammalian species including domestic cattle, their wild relatives, and some sea animals such as seals.

carnivore. The meat-eating animals including dogs, cats, lions, etc. They are classified separately from the herbivores which eat plants (cows, horses, etc.).

castration. Removal of the reproductive glands from either sex. More commonly applied to removal of the testes, the term is nevertheless correctly employed to designate removal of the ovaries.

Cayapa. Northwestern province of Esmeraldas, Ecuador. Population between 1500 and 2000. Sedentary agriculturalists who also hunt, gather, and fish. Technology quite well developed. Monogamous.

cetacean. An order of mammals living exclusively in the sea, such as whales, dolphins, etc.

Chagga. Tanganyika, Africa. Population 60,000. Advanced agriculturalists. Generally polygynous.

Chamorro. Marianas Islands, south of Japan. Population 3000. Fishers and agriculturalists. Polygyny permitted, but monogamous unions prevail.

Chenchu. Hyderabad, India. Seminomadic hunters and gatherers. Number 3000, but only 400 cling to aboriginal way of life. Monogamous.

Cherente. Central Brazil. Hunt, fish, and gather, but also raise maize and tubers. Monogamy prevails, but sororal polygyny occurs occasionally.

Cherokee [eastern group]. North Carolina. Remnants of the once-powerful Cherokee of the southeastern United States. Monogamous.

Chewa. British Central Africa. Primarily agriculturalists. Technologically quite advanced. Generally polygynous.

Cheyenne. Colorado and Montana. Live mainly by hunting buffalo and other game. Polygyny, always sororal, is general.

chimpanzee. One species of anthropoid ape.

Chiricahua. Arizona. Important division of the warlike Apache. Primarily hunters and gatherers, supplemented by some agriculture. Sororal polygyny permitted, monogamy more common.

Choroti. Gran Chaco, central South America. Population 2000. Live by hunting, fishing, and gathering, limited amount of agriculture. Predominantly monogamous.

Chukchee. Northeastern peninsula of Asia. Population 12,000. Three-fourths are nomadic reindeer-breeders; remainder are sedentary sea-mammal hunters. Polygynous.

circumcize. To remove the prepuce, the loose skin surrounding the end of the penis.

climacteric. The time when menstrual cycles permanently cease. Also called menopause. Existence of a climacteric in men has been suggested by some authorities but is not generally agreed upon.

climax. See *orgasm.*

clitoris. Part of the feminine sexual organs. Described in detail in Chapter II.

coitus. Copulation. Sexual intercourse.

coitus interruptus. Heterosexual copulation in which the penis is withdrawn from the vagina before ejaculation occurs.

Colorado. Base of the western Andes in Ecuador. Agriculture, supplemented by hunting and fishing, provides subsistence. Generally monogamous.

Copper Eskimo. Arctic coast of North America in region of Coronation Gulf and part of Victoria Island. Population 700, split up in bands of 20 to 100. Follow caribou, seal, and fish. Polygyny permitted but not common.

copulate. Usually refers to the act of inserting the penis into the vagina and the subsequent discharge of seminal material from the penis into the female organs. However, various other activities may be subsumed under this term. Thus "anal copulation" sometimes occurs. Alternate usages are defined at the appropriate points in this glossary.

cortex [cerebral]. The outermost layer and the most recently evolved part of the forebrain.

cover. A verb referring to assumption of the copulatory position by male animals.

cow. Generic term for females of several mammalian species including domestic cattle, their wild relatives, and some others such as the fur seal.

Cree [Plains]. Saskatchewan, Alberta, and Montana. Mainly hunters. Formerly prosperous fur traders. Generally monogamous, although polygyny, preferably sororal, is practiced.

Creek. Formerly Alabama and Georgia, today Arkansas. Hunters and agriculturalists. Formerly very warlike. Sororal polygyny permitted, but rare.

cross-cultural. Involving comparisons between two or more cultures or societies.

cross-species. Involving comparisons between two or more species.

Crow. Northern Wyoming and Montana. Seminomadic hunters and gatherers. Sororal polygyny general.

culture. Patterned and customary ways of behaving and acting which characterize the members of a society; sometimes broadened to include the products of their behavior, e.g., artifacts, paintings, clothing.

Cuna. Mountainous interior of San Blas coast of Isthmus of Panama. Predominantly agriculturalists. Population 20,000. Arts and technology well developed. Generally monogamous, sororal polygyny permitted.

Dahomeans. Dahomey, West Africa. Agriculturalists and fishers. Once an important slave-trading center. Generally polygynous.

deflower. To insert an object into the vagina in such a way as to stretch or nick the hymen. This may occur during intercourse or may be achieved in virgins by the use of the fingers or some foreign object (see *hymen*).

Delaware. Formerly Canada, New York, New Jersey, Pennsylvania, and Delaware. Depended on agriculture as well as hunting, fishing, and gathering. Skilled in manufacture of beadwork and feather mantles. Polygyny formerly permitted.

detumescence. Reduction of swelling.

Dieri. Eastern part of South Australia. Less than 200 persons. Subsistence provided by hunting and fishing. Simple technology. Sororal polygyny common.

distance receptors. Sense organs which are affected by stimulation coming from a distance. They include the eyes, the ears, and the nose.

diurnal. Occurring during the daytime or every day. Diurnal animals are animals that are active in the day and inactive at night.

Dobuans. Dobu, an island off the coast of New Guinea. Subsist mainly on garden products. Villages permanently hostile toward one another. Strictly monogamous.

dog fox. The adult male fox.

dolphin. Synonym for porpoise, a mammal that lives exclusively in the ocean.

Dusun. British North Borneo. Agriculturalists and fishermen. Skilled craftsmen. Head-hunting formerly practiced. Polygyny permitted but rare.

Easter Islanders. An island about 2000 miles west of South America. Agriculture, fishing, and a few domestic animals provide subsistence. Mainly monogamous, although polygyny permitted.

ejaculation. The reflexive act of expelling certain secretions from the masculine sex organs. The ejaculate, termed "semen," consists of a mixture of sperm cells, fluid from the prostate gland, and fluid from the seminal vesicles. Ejaculation does not occur in immature males, or in males that have been castrated. It has no direct counterpart in the female. In adult male mammals ejaculation usually occurs in close relationship to climax or orgasm, but the two events are not totally interdependent.

engorge. To become swollen, usually with blood.

epididymis. Very small coiled tube leading from the male sex gland to the prostate gland and seminal vesicles. Through the epididymis pass the sperm cells which mature in the testes and are ejaculated during coitus.

erection. Attainment of an erect state. As used in this book, the term refers to reflexive filling of the penis or clitoris with blood which transforms these organs from flaccid structures to rigid, rodlike pillars.

erogenous. Having the quality of sexual excitability.

estrogen. A generic term for a group of closely related hormones. All of them are similar to estrone, which is a hormone produced by the ovary. Often called the "female sex hormone."

estrus. Refers to the physiological condition of a female at the time when she can become pregnant as a result of copulation. The bodily changes occurring at this time are described in Chapter XI. Some authors differentiate behavorial from physiological estrus, using the former term to cover all the periods in which the female will copulate, even though she may not be susceptible to impregnation.

eunuch. A term most commonly applied to a castrated male. Less often used to refer to females whose ovaries have been removed, or to individuals of either sex in whom the sex glands have never developed.

extramarital.   Relations of married individuals with partners other than the spouse.

Fallopian tubes.   Tubes leading from the ovary to the uterus. Also called "oviduct."

fellatio.   Stimulation of the penis with the lips and tongue.

femoral copulation.   Sexual intercourse in which the penis is inserted between the thighs rather than in the vagina. Can be either heterosexual or homosexual. Also called "interfemoral."

fertile.   Capable of impregnating a female or of becoming pregnant. Can be used to differentiate between individuals or for the same individual at different times. Thus, some men are not fertile at any time; all normal women are fertile only at a particular stage of each menstrual cycle.

Fez.   French Morocco. Population nearly 100,000. Manufacture clothes, saddlery, and weapons which they trade for farm products.

fisher.   Small, fur-bearing mammal related to the mink, sable, and marten.

Flathead.   Western Montana. Seminomadic hunters and gatherers. Formerly warlike, much intertribal raiding and horse stealing. Polygyny general, sororal form usual.

foreplay.   Any form of sexual stimulation indulged in immediately before complete sexual relations (i.e., intercourse) begin.

foreskin.   Prepuce. Loose skin covering the end of the penis. When the foreskin is retracted the glans penis is exposed. Circumcision consists of removing the foreskin.

Fox.   Formerly Wisconsin. Agricultural; raise corn, beans, and squash. Fairly primitive technology. Restless and warlike. Polygyny general, sororal form preferred.

free-living.   Refers to wild animals living in their native habitat.

Futunans.   Two islands in western Polynesia, not far from Fiji. Cultivate coconut, breadfruit, and taro; fish and raise pigs. Monogamy general, but polygyny is occasional.

Ganda.   Uganda Protectorate, Africa. Population 1,000,000. Primarily agriculturalists who also hunt and fish. Wars formerly frequent. Polygyny general.

genital swelling.   Filling of the skin adjacent to the vaginal opening with certain body fluids. Occurs in apes and in some monkeys. Is coincidental with the period of physiological estrus, the time at which the female is maximally attractive to the male and when she is most eager for sexual relations (see Chapters V and XI).

genitalia.   The external sexual organs of males and females. Includes the penis and scrotum of the male, and the vaginal lips, the clitoris, and the vagina of the female.

germ cell.   Sperm cells in the male; eggs in the female.

gestation.   Pregnancy.

Gilbertese. Gilbert Islands, Pacific Ocean. Cultivate yams and taro, and are expert fishermen. Both monogamy and polygyny occur.

gilt. A young sow.

Gilyak. Northeastern Asia and northwestern shore of Sakhalin, an island off the coast. Principal source of food is fish. Sororal polygyny common.

glans. The head or tip of the penis. Ordinarily covered by the foreskin in uncircumcised males.

Goajiro. Goajiro Peninsula, Colombia. Population 18,000. Nomadic cattle raisers. Suspicious and warlike. Generally polygynous.

golden hamster. A small rodent used in experimental investigations.

gonad. A sex gland, either the testis or the ovary.

gonadotrophin. Hormones produced by the pituitary gland or the placenta which cause development of the ovaries or testes.

Gond [Maria group]. Bastar State in the Central Provinces, India. Information mainly concerns Hill Maria, peaceful and industrious agricultural people. Polygyny, preferably sororal, is common.

gorilla. One species of anthropoid ape.

Gros Ventre. Reservation in Montana. Seminomadic buffalo hunters. Apparently sororal polygyny is permitted.

Haitians. Information concerns people of Mirebalais, a valley in central Haiti. Agricultural region. People greatly influenced by their religion, a mingling of Catholicism and the *vodun* of West African Negroes. Polygyny exists but is not legally sanctioned.

Havasupai. Northwest Arizona. A small isolated tribe. Cultivate the land by irrigation, also hunt and gather. Obtain utensils by barter with Hopi. Monogamy customary, although polygyny permitted.

heat. Nontechnical term referring to the condition of females when they are willing to copulate with males. Usually applied only to lower mammals in which heat or estrus coincides with the period of fertility in the female.

hermaphrodite. A male or female whose external genitalia are modified in such a manner that they resemble those of the opposite sex. Usually the sex glands are abnormal. Described in detail in Chapter VII.

heterosexual. Involving individuals of the opposite sexes.

Hidatsa. North Dakota. Now number 500. Seminomadic agriculturalists and hunters. Polygyny common, preferably sororal.

Homo sapiens. Scientific name for the human species.

homosexual. Involving individuals of the same sex.

Hopi. Northeastern Arizona. Farmers; subsist mainly on corn. Skilled in weaving, basketry, and woodcarving. Strictly monogamous.

howler monkey. Central and South America. A New World type and therefore classified as somewhat more primitive than the Old World monkeys such as the macaque or baboon.

Huichol. Sierra Madre region, Mexico. Subsist on products of animal husbandry and agriculture. Polygyny formerly practiced occasionally, but now monogamous.

hymen. Commonly referred to as the "maidenhead," this structure is found in human females and in no other species of mammal. It consists not of a membrane but of a fold of tissue that may partially obstruct the opening of the vagina. Its size and thickness vary greatly from one individual to the next. The hymen is not "ruptured" during the first penetration of the vagina, as is so often stated. It is usually simply stretched, although in some cases it may actually be nicked.

hypothalamus. Part of the brain which is thought to play an important role in sexual behavior and also influences the activity of the pituitary gland with which it is connected.

hysterectomy. Removal of the uterus, leaving the ovaries intact.

Ifugao. Central Luzon, Philippine Islands. Population 80,000. Cultivate rice and raise a few domestic animals. Head-hunting commonly practiced. Monogamous.

Ila. North of Victoria Falls, Northern Rhodesia. Population 60,000. Subsist on products of hunting, fishing, cattle raising, and a crude form of agriculture. Polygyny common.

implantation. The process that occurs early in pregnancy by which the fertilized egg becomes attached to the wall of the uterus.

impotent. Lacking potency. See *potent.*

impregnate. To make pregnant.

inanition. Wasting of the body from starvation.

incest. Sexual relations between closely related individuals. Primary incest refers to sexual relations between parent and child, or between brother and sister. Each society extends incest prohibitions beyond the nuclear family and forbids intercourse with certain other relatives. See Chapter VI.

in copulo. During copulation.

infrahuman. Refers to any species belonging below our own on the evolutionary scale.

infraprimate. Refers to any mammalian species below the primates.

inseminate. To introduce male germ cells into the female and thus fertilize the eggs produced by her ovaries.

intercourse (sexual). Refers primarily to copulation between males and females. May also be applied to certain kinds of homosexual relations and to contact between two individuals of different species.

interfemoral intercourse. See *femoral copulation.*

intromission. Insertion of the penis into the vagina. In some cases the same term is applied to introduction of the penis into the anus.

jack. A male donkey.

jennet. A female donkey.

Jivaro. Southern Ecuador and northern Peru. Agriculture and technology quite highly developed. Also raise domestic animals, hunt, and fish. Polygyny, often sororal, is common. Head-hunting generally practiced.

Jukun. Nigeria, Africa. Population 25,000. Primarily agriculturalists, but also raise animals, hunt, and fish. Hostile to foreigners. Polygynous.

Kababish. Anglo-Egyptian Sudan. Richest and most powerful of camel-raising Arab tribes. Nomads with a simple technology. Polygynous.

Kaingang. Southern Brazil and Uruguay. Semimigratory. Live by hunting, farming, fishing, and gathering. Polygyny and polyandry permitted.

Kamilaroi. Interior of New South Wales, Australia. Primitive hunters and gatherers who practice no agriculture. Polygyny permitted but rare.

kangaroo rat. A small desert-living rodent.

Kansa. Formerly Kansas but now northern Oklahoma. Population in 1850 was 1700, but remnants of tribe now number 200. Nomadic buffalo hunters. Polygyny common, but always sororal form.

Kazak. Central Asia. Population 3,000,000. Nomadic horsemen whose main occupation is herding. Polygyny permitted but confined to the wealthy.

Keraki. Southwestern Papua, New Guinea. Seminomadic. Formerly victims of head-hunting raids, but now protected by the government. Generally polygynous.

Khasi. Khasi Hills, Assam. Population 100,000. Predominantly agricultural. Various skilled crafts well developed. Exclusively monogamous.

Kickapoo. Formerly Wisconsin and Michigan, now Illinois and Missouri. Hunters, trappers, gatherers, and planters. Material and social culture quite well developed. Polygynous.

kinship system. In every society people are believed to be related by ties of kinship to some members of the group and not related to others. The system by which such relationships are determined is the kinship system.

Kiowa Apache. Southwestern Oklahoma, but formerly ranged over territory from Texas to Nebraska. Hunters and gatherers. Sororal polygyny common.

Kiwai. Kiwai Island and other islands on southeastern coast of New Guinea. Primarily agriculturalists. Simple technology. Generally monogamous, but polygyny permitted.

Klamath. Eastern Oregon. Population 1200. Seminomadic hunters, fishers, and gatherers. Sororal polygyny permitted but rare.

Kongo. Lower Congo region, Africa. Subsist on products of farming and animal husbandry. Technology relatively advanced and religious ritual highly developed. Polygyny general, sororal form preferred.

Koniag. Alaskan peninsula and island of Kodiak off the coast. Hunters, fishers, and gatherers. Most numerous and powerful tribe on Alaskan coast. Polygyny formerly common.

Koryak. Northeastern Asia. Maritime Koryak are sedentary fishers and hunters. Reindeer Koryak are nomadic reindeer herders. Polygyny permitted but not common.

Kurd [Rowanduz group]. Kurdistan in northeastern Mesopotamia. Population 5,000,000. Northern Kurd are semimigratory pastoralists; southern Kurd are sedentary agriculturalists. Polygyny common.

Kurtatchi. Northern Bougainville, one of the Solomon Islands. Subsist mainly on garden products and fish. Polygyny, exclusively sororal, is common.

Kusaians. Eastern Carolines, Pacific Ocean. Subsistence based on cultivation supplemented by great variety of fish. Polygyny practiced by aristocrats.

Kutchin. Northwest Canada and eastern Alaska. Depend for subsistence on fishing, hunting, and collecting. Skilled woodworkers. Polygyny permitted, but monogamy general.

Kutenai. Northwestern Montana, northern Idaho, and part of British Columbia. Hunters and gatherers who migrate seasonally. Marriage generally polygynous.

Kwakiutl. Northeast coast of Vancouver Island. Primarily fishermen who also hunt and gather. Generally polygynous.

Kwoma. Mandated Territory of New Guinea. Live on garden products and small game. Head-hunting practiced. Polygyny common.

labia. The labia majora are the outer lips of the vagina; the labia minora, the inner lips. See Chapter II for detailed description.

lactation. The formation of milk in the breast.

Lakher. Southern Assam and western Burma. Population 10,000. Predominantly agricultural. Technology quite well developed. Exclusively monogamous.

Lamba. Northwestern Rhodesia and tongue of Belgian Congo. Population over 100,000. Intricate agricultural and hunting culture. Polygyny permitted by monogamy general.

Lango. Uganda, East Africa. Population 200,000. Agriculturalists and cattle breeders. Complex ritual and ceremonial culture. Technology well developed. Polygynous.

Lapps. Northern Scandinavia. Population 30,000. Mountain and Woodland Lapps are nomadic reindeer herders; Maritime Lapps fish and hunt sea mammals. Strictly monogamous.

Lenge. Gazaland, Portuguese East Africa. Subsist mainly on agricultural products. Polygyny generally practiced.

Lepcha. Sikkim on the slopes of the southeastern Himalayas. Population

25,000. Principally agriculturalists who also hunt, trap, collect, and fish. Industrious and cheerful. Polygyny permitted, but monogamy more common.

Lesu. New Ireland. Population 200. Subsistence derived from hunting, fishing and primitive form of agriculture. Lack advanced technology. Polygynous.

Lhota. Naga Hills, Assam. Population 20,000. Predominantly agriculturalists, also fishers and hunters. Polygynous.

liaison. One type of sexual partnership without marriage. Some types of liaisons are approved by many societies (see Chapter VI).

libido. Sexual desire.

lingual. Effected with the tongue.

lower mammals. All mammalian species below the primates on the evolutionary scale.

Loyalty Islanders. Loyalty Island, situated east of Australia. Population 10,000. Expert fishermen and canoe builders. Cultivate yams, coconuts, and various vegetables. Polygyny permitted but confined to well-to-do.

macaque. One species of Old World monkey. Also referred to as rhesus macaque, or simply rhesus.

Macusi. British Guiana. Population 3000. Farmers, hunters, gatherers, and fishers. Technology relatively simple. Polygyny permitted but rare.

Mailu. Toulon (Mailu) Island, off southern coast of Papua. Live by fishing, hunting, and tending gardens. Considerable trade with neighboring people. Strictly monogamous.

mammals. Warm-blooded vertebrates that suckle their young. The human species is included in this class.

mammary glands. The glands in the breast that secrete milk.

Mandan. North and South Dakota. Agricultural; raise corn, beans, and squash. Seminomadic. Sororal polygyny common.

mangabey. An Old World species of monkey.

Mangarevans. Eastern edge of Polynesian culture area, Pacific Ocean. Ruling classes own all cultivable land; commoners depend on fish and wild plants. Wars between islands formerly frequent. Polygynous.

Manus. Admiralty Islands, north of New Guinea. Population 2000, distributed in eleven villages. Primarily fishermen who trade fish for garden products and implements from other tribes. Polygyny permitted but rare.

Maori. New Zealand. Population 100,000. Agriculturalists. Formerly warlike. Polygyny permitted, but incidence low.

Maricopa. Central southern Arizona. Primarily planters, because semi-desert environment provides little large game. Monogamy general, although polygyny permitted.

marital. Pertaining to relations between married individuals.

Marquesans. Series of high mountainous islands in central Pacific. Subsist on tree crops and fish. Generally polyandrous.

Marshallese. Marshall Islands, Pacific Ocean. Chief nourishment from fish, breadfruit, coconuts, and taro. Excellent sailors and shipbuilders. Polygyny permitted but rare.

marten. A small fur-bearing mammal related to the mink, fisher, and sable.

Masai. Uganda, Kenya, and northern Tanganyika in Africa. Population 15,000. Nomadic cattle herders. Feared by neighboring tribes, whose herds they often raid. Polygynous.

masturbation. Manipulation of the sexual organs in such a way as to produce sexual excitement.

Mataco. Bolivian and Argentine Gran Chaco, South America. Population 20,000. Originally seminomadic hunters, fishers, and gatherers. Polygyny permitted, but monogamous unions prevail.

mateship. A stable, enduring sexual partnership accompanied by mutual economic and domestic responsibilities (see Chapter VI).

Mbundu. Central part of Angola, Africa. Subsist on products of agriculture supplemented by game and wild plants. Generally polygynous.

menarche. The time of the first menstruation.

Menomini. Inhabit reservation in Wisconsin. Population 2000. Harvest wild rice in fall, carry on lumbering industry in winter, migrate to maple-sugar camps in spring. Formerly polygynous, now strictly monogamous.

menopause. The permanent cessation of menstruation in women and other primates. Also called "climacteric."

menstruation. The period of hemorrhage from the lining of the uterus in female primates. The physiology of the process is described in Chapter X. The phrase "menstrual cycle" refers to the events occurring from the first day of one period of flow until the beginning of the following one.

mid-interval. The point in the menstrual cycle between two periods of bleeding at which ovulation is most likely to occur and during which a woman or other female primate is capable of conceiving.

Miriam. Murray Islands in Torres Straits between Australia and New Guinea. Planters, who also hunt and fish. Skilled in manufacture of bamboo articles. Polygyny permitted but quite rare.

Mongols. Steppes of Mongolia in central Asia. Pastoral people who live in tents and move with their herds. Monogamy universal, although concubinage permitted.

monkey. Generic term including, among other species, the baboon, macaque (or rhesus), Moore monkey, bonnet monkey, howler monkey, green monkey, etc. Monkeys are less highly evolved than apes, but more highly so than infraprimate forms such as cats, dogs, horses, cows, etc. See *primate*.

monogamy. One form of mateship in which each man and woman has only one spouse. See Chapter VI for full definition.

mores (pl.; mos, sing.). The customs of a people which seem most important to them. Deviation from a mos generally is followed by severe punishment and often is believed to bring supernatural disfavor.

Murngin. East Arnhem Land, on coast of Northern Territory, Australia. Seminomadic hunters and gatherers. Simple technology. Polygyny general, sororal form preferred.

Nama. Important branch of Hottentots, Southwest Africa. Formerly nomadic herders, but introduction of agriculture has affected their mode of life. Many disputes and quarrels between tribes. Polygyny permitted but rare.

Nandi. Nandi plateau in Anglo-Egyptian Sudan, Africa. Formerly nomadic cattle herders, they have recently settled down and adopted agriculture. Generally polygynous.

Naskapi. Tribe of twenty bands living on Labrador peninsula. Subsistence based on hunting, trapping, and fishing. Simple technology. Polygyny common.

Natchez. Aborigines of Natchez, Mississippi. Agricultural economy which included some hunting and fishing. Population once 3500, but only a few still survive. Sororal polygyny permitted but rare.

Nauruans. Island of Nauru, west of Gilbert Islands in the Pacific. Population 1000. Subsist on fish and tree crops. Polygyny common, sororal form perferred.

Navaho. Northwestern New Mexico and northeastern Arizona. Once agriculturalists, now a pastoral society, rearing sheep, goats, cattle. Polygyny, always sororal, is common.

New World monkeys. Monkeys such as the howler and spider that are found in Central and South America. They are regarded as more primitive, less highly evolved than the Old World monkeys such as the baboon and macaque.

nocturnal emission. Discharge of semen without coition during sleep.

nocturnal species. Animals that normally are active at night and not during the day.

nuclear family. The social group consisting of a man and woman and their offspring. Polygynous families consist of several nuclear families with the man participating in each as husband and father.

Oceania. The vast area of the Pacific Ocean including the islands lying between the American continents and Asia.

Ojibwa. Region of Lake Superior. Formerly very numerous. Vigorous and warlike. Polygyny common, sororal form preferred.

Old World monkeys. Species native to Africa, India, and other non-American countries. They include the macaque and baboon and are classified as more highly evolved than the New World (howler and spider) monkeys which inhabit Central and South America.

Omaha. Nebraska. Seminomadic buffalo-hunting and agricultural people. Highly formalized social and religious organization. Well-developed technology. Sororal polygyny permitted but infrequent.

onanism. Genital stimulation by oneself or by a partner that does not involve heterosexual coitus.

oral. Performed with the mouth.

orangutan. One of the anthropoid apes. More highly evolved than monkeys.

orgasm. Also called "climax." These terms refer primarily to subjective sensations accompanying the peak of sexual arousal and usually followed by a release of emotional tension as well as partial or complete loss of responsiveness to sexual stimulation. The occurrence of sexual climax in others than oneself, or in other animals, is not directly observable and can only be inferred.

Orokaiva. North coast of New Guinea. Divided into six subtribes among whom raids are common. Agriculturalists, who also hunt and fish. Polygyny permitted but monogamy common.

os penis. A bone that is found in the shaft of the penis of several species of mammals including the rat, dog, monkey, and ape.

Osset. Ossetia, country near center of Caucasus mountain range. Rounded agricultural and animal-raising economy. Simple technology. Exclusively sororal polygyny common.

Oto. Formerly Iowa, later moved to Kansas and Nebraska. Peaceful agricultural and hunting people. Monogamy preferred, but sororal polygyny frequent.

ovariectomize. To remove the ovaries.

ovary. The female sex gland. It produces eggs and secretes certain hormones.

ovulate. To release ripe eggs from the ovary into the Fallopian tubes. An essential precursor to conception.

Palauans. Palau, archipelago in western part of Caroline Islands. Natives raise breadfruit, rice, coconuts, and dates. Monogamy characteristic but polygyny permitted.

Palaung. Tawnpeng in Burma. Population 50,000. Agricultural, raising mainly rice and tea; latter is traded for various implements. Polygyny permitted but rare.

Papago. Three reservations in southwestern Arizona. Economy changed from that of primitive hunters and gatherers to intensive agricultural and cattle-raising economy. Mainly monogamous, but polygyny, preferably sororal, permitted.

parathyroid.   Small gland lying beside the thyroid.

parturition.   The act of giving birth to young.

pederasty.   Homosexual anal intercourse.

Pedi.   Transvaal, South Africa. Agriculturalists and stock farmers, raising cattle and goats. Polygynous marriages quite common.

penis.   The male organ of copulation.

Penobscot.   Region of Penobscot Bay and River in Maine. Hunting the dominant economy; game and fish abundant. Polygyny permitted but not frequent.

perversion.   A term without scientific meaning. It refers to any form of sexual activity which a given social group regards as unnatural and abnormal. Activities that are classified as perversions by one society may be considered normal in another.

phallus.   Penis.

pigtailed monkey.   An Old World species.

Pima.   Two reservations in southern Arizona. Sedentary agricultural and gathering people. Good-natured and unaggressive. Generally polygynous.

pituitary.   An endocrine gland located in the skull directly beneath the brain. It secretes a variety of hormones which in turn control several important bodily processes. Some of the pituitary hormones stimulate activity in other glands including the ovaries, testes, adrenals, thyroids, and parathyroids.

placenta.   Organ on the wall of the uterus to which the embryo is attached by means of the umbilical cord and from which it receives its nourishment. At parturition the placenta makes up a large part of the "afterbirth."

polyandry.   Form of mateship in which more than one man is associated with the same woman. See Chapter VI for full description.

polyestrous.   Refers to animal species in which the female is fertile and sexually active at regular intervals throughout most or all of the year. These species are distinguished from others called "monestrous" in which the female has a single breeding season each year.

polygyny.   Form of mateship in which one man is permitted to have more than one permanent sexual partner. See Chapter VI for full description.

Ponapeans.   Atoll in eastern part of Caroline Islands, Pacific Ocean. Natives cultivate yams and breadfruit, spend much time fishing. Monogamy prevails, but polygyny permitted.

Ponca.   Nebraska and Oklahoma. Closely affiliated with the Omaha. Present population about 800. Originally hunters and gatherers but have lately made feeble attempts at agriculture. Peaceful and law-abiding.

porpoise. A sea-living mammal. Also called "dolphin."

postpartum. Following the birth of young.

postpuberal. Following puberty.

potent. Term used variously by different authors to describe the sexual capacity of males. In some cases it refers to the ability to carry out the physical act of copulation. This depends upon achievement and maintenance of erection in the penis and upon the occurrence of orgasm. Potency has nothing to do with fertility. That is to say, a man may be potent but sterile. In other instances the word describes the capacity to experience sexual arousal. Most commonly, *impotence* refers to a condition in which the male cannot perform the coital act even though he desires to do so.

precocious puberty. Puberty at a very early age.

preliterate. Adjective describing the fact that a people have not developed a written language.

prepuberal. Before puberty.

present. Verb describing the bodily actions of a female animal in preparation or invitation for intercourse.

priapism. Persistent erection of the penis, usually unaccompanied by sexual desire.

primary relatives. The members of one's own family. For an unmarried person primary relatives consist of father, mother, sister, brother. For a married person the spouse and the resulting children are primary relatives.

primate. The name of the most highly evolved order of mammals. The order is subdivided in the following fashion, beginning with the lowest suborder and proceeding to the highest:

Suborder Lemuroidea } very primitive primates not mentioned in
Suborder Tarsioidea } this book.

Suborder Pithecoidea—includes monkeys, apes, and man.

- Infraorder Platyrrhini—New World, or American monkeys, including the spider and howler.
- Infraorder Catarrhini—Old World monkeys and apes.
  - Family Cercopithecidae—monkeys, e.g., macaques, baboons.
  - Family Hylobatidae—gibbons and siamang.
  - Family Pongidae—orangutan, gorilla, chimpanzee.
  - Family Hominidae—man.

In common terminology the families Hylobatidae and Pongidae are referred to as anthropoid apes, and are next to man on the evolutionary scale. All groups below the apes are classifiable as monkeys. Catarrhine monkeys are less primitive than platyrrhine species.

progesterone. Hormone secreted by the ovary and by the placenta which prepares the uterus for implantation of fertilized eggs. It is essential to mating behavior in some mammalian species.

prostate gland. An organ surrounding the neck of the bladder and the beginning of the urethra in the male.

pseudocoitus. Sexual relations in which the penis is stimulated by contact with the partner's body but is not inserted in the vagina.

pubertas praecox. Puberty at a very early age.

puberty. The stage of bodily development at which the signs of sexual maturity first appear as a result of changes in the sex glands. Some of the more obvious indications of puberty in human females are the occurrence of menstruation and growth of the breasts. In boys the change of voice and beginning of beard growth are comparable indicators. The physiology of puberty is described in Chapter X.

pubic. Pertaining to the pubes, the region just above the penis or vagina.

pudenda. External sexual organs of the female.

Pukapukans. Atoll of Pukapuka, three islands in eastern Polynesia. Population 600. Subsistence economy based on fishing, horticulture, and trapping of birds. Strictly monogamous.

Purari. Purari delta in Papua, New Guinea. Mainly a hunting, fishing, and collecting people, practice agriculture in rather haphazard fashion. Crabs very important item in food supply. Marriage usually monogamous, but polygyny occurs.

Quinault. Quinault River, northwestern Washington. Population 800. Seminomadic hunters, fishers, and gatherers. Monogamy general, although sororal polygyny permitted.

Ramkokamekra [Timbira]. Northeastern part of central Brazilian steppe area. Of late they have been confined within boundaries, thus have become sedentary farmers rather than seminomadic gatherers. Strictly monogamous.

rear entry. Heterosexual copulation in which intromission is achieved while the woman's back is turned to her partner.

receptive. Pertaining to the condition in the female when she is willing to copulate with the male.

Reddi. Hyderabad, India. Traditionally an agricultural and gathering people, migrating to a fresh location every few years. Polygyny permitted but quite rare.

Rengma. Naga Hills, Assam. Greatly preoccupied with agriculture, but also hunt, fish, and raise animals. Head-hunting practiced. Strictly monogamous.

rhesus. Also referred to in this book simply as "macaque." A species of Old World monkey.

Riffians. Spanish Morocco. Population 200,000, distributed in 200 villages. Agriculture the basis of subsistence, but various animals raised. Technology quite well developed. Polygyny permitted but rare.

rodent. Class of mammals which includes mice, rats, squirrels, chipmunks, and the like.

Rossel. Island in Louisiade Archipelago off southeast coast of Papua. Natives subsist on garden products, wild fruits, fish, and domesticated pigs. Population 1500. Polygyny permitted, but rare.

Rucuyen. Tumuc-Humac mountain range between Brazil and the Guianas. Raise yams, sugar cane, and maize, but also hunt and fish. Polygyny and polyandry permitted but uncommon.

rut. In lower animals, the time of ovulation in the female and the time when the male is capable of inseminating. Synonyms in the female: "heat" or "estrus."

Rwala. Bedouin tribe of northern Arabian desert. Lead strenuous nomadic life. Camel meat and milk form basic diet; lack of water a problem. Monogamy general although polygyny permitted.

sable. A fur-bearing mammal related to the mink, fisher, and marten.

Samoans. Samoa, group of islands in western Polynesia. Natives cultivate various plants and trees, also raise pigs and poultry. Wars between villages frequent. Monogamy the rule for all except chiefs.

Samoyed. Northwestern Russia. Nomads who live by hunting reindeer and sea mammals, fishing and selling furs. Live in tents despite severe, cold winters. Monogamy prevails, but polygyny permitted.

Sanpoil. Northeastern Washington. Seminomadic on seasonal basis. Hunters, fishers, and gatherers. Peaceful. Polygyny common.

sarombavy. Name used in some societies for men who adopt the feminine sexual role.

scrotum. Sac of skin in which the testicles are located.

sea lion. A sea-living mammal.

seasonal breeders. Species of animals which are capable of fertile copulation only during a restricted season in each year.

secondary relatives. The primary relatives of one's father, mother, spouse, sibling, or child—e.g., grandparents, uncles and aunts, spouse's parents and siblings, grandchildren.

secondary sex characters. In the human male these include the growth of facial, axillary, and pubic hair, the deep voice, and certain aspects of body form such as broad shoulders and relatively narrow hips. The secondary sex characters of human females include the breasts, wide hips, and axillary and pubic hair.

self-stimulation. The handling or otherwise stimulating of one's own genitals or other erogenous zones.

Sema. Naga Hills, Assam. Subsist primarily on products of animal husbandry and agriculture, supplemented by hunting and fishing. Polygyny permitted but confined to wealthy.

Semang. Interior of the Malay Peninsula. Hunters, fishers, and gatherers who move to a new site every few days. Peaceful. Primitive technology. Monogamy general but polygyny occurs occasionally.

semen. The material discharged from the penis in ejaculation. It consists of sperm and a mixture of secretions from the testes, the seminal vesicles, and the prostate gland.

seminal vesicles. Two small sacs at the base of the bladder. They secrete a fluid which forms part of the semen and are connected to the testes by the epididymis.

Seminole. Everglades, Florida. Population of 200 separated into five widely scattered settlements. Live on agricultural products as well as wild fruits and game. Polygynous.

Seniang. Island of Malekula, New Hebrides. Natives cultivate yams and raise pigs. Materialistic people who like to bargain, borrow, and lend. Polygyny, preferably sororal, common.

sex skin. Specialized areas of skin adjacent to the feminine sexual organs. In some species of apes and monkeys the sex skin is markedly swollen during the fertile period and in others it becomes brilliantly colored.

sexual behavior. Defined in Chapter I. As employed in this book, the phrase refers to behavior involving stimulation and excitation of the sexual organs.

sexual cycle. In women and other female primates one sexual cycle lasts from the beginning of a period of menstrual flow until the start of the next bleeding. In lower mammals the cycle is timed from the opening of one period of fertility and receptivity until the occurrence of the subsequent one. Loosely synonymous with this term are the phrases "estrous cycle" and "menstrual cycle."

sexual locking. A phase of the normal copulatory pattern in dogs and their wild relatives (foxes and wolves) during which one region of the penis becomes so greatly swollen that it cannot be withdrawn from the vagina without physical injury to the female. This "locking" persists from five to six minutes to as long as half or three-quarters of an hour.

shaman. A religious specialist believed to possess supernatural power.

shrew. Includes several species of small, insect-eating mammals.

sibling. Offspring of the same parents, i.e., brothers or sisters.

Sinkaietk. North-central Washington and British Columbia. Aboriginally a seminomadic fishing-hunting-collecting people. Polygyny general, sororal form preferred.

Siriono. Eastern Bolivia. Wander about in small bands living on wild roots and animals. Strenuous and difficult nomadic life. Little contact with other tribes. Polygynous, favoring sororal form.

Siwans. Siwa valley in North Africa. Population 3000. Live by raising various crops, domestic animals, and fowls. Simple technology. Polygyny permitted, but monogamy more common.

society. A group of people constituting a unit characterized by a common culture. Usually, but not always, the members of a society live in a contiguous geographical area. By "our society" we mean "American society" which, although exhibiting social class, regional, and ethnic differences, may be considered for purposes of comparison to be characterized by a common culture.

sodomy. Anal intercourse. May be heterosexual or homosexual or may involve a human being and an animal of a different species.

soixante-neuf. One form of human sexual behavior in which the man and woman simultaneously stimulate the genitalia of the other with their mouths.

sororal. Relating to sisters; e.g., sororal polygyny refers to the marriage of one man to two or more women who are sisters.

sperm. Male sex cells, produced by the testes. Join with the female sex cells (eggs) in fertilization.

spermatogenesis. Formation of sperm in the testis.

spider monkey. A New World species.

spontaneous orgasm. Orgasm that occurs without apparent physical stimulation.

steatopygia. Excessive deposits of fatty tissue on the buttocks.

subadult. Young animals nearing puberty.

subhuman. Pertaining to all animals other than man.

subincize. To cut the underside of the penis so that the urethra is opened.

subprimate. All mammals below primates on the evolutionary scale. Synonym: infraprimate.

Swazi. Swaziland and Transvaal, South Africa. Population 200,000. Predominantly cattle raisers, but also horticulturalists. Generally polygynous, sororal form preferred.

symphysis. Bony projection beneath the pubes.

tactile stimulation. Involving the sense of touch.

Tanala. Southern Madagascar. Agriculturalists who seem to represent an archaic cultural type in Madagascar. Warfare and slave raids formerly common. Marriage generally polygynous.

Taos. Pueblo of Taos on plateau in New Mexico. Farmers. Peaceful. Strictly monogamous.

Tarahumara. Sierra Madre region, southern Chihuahua, Mexico. Planting and herding nomads. Live in isolated households. Strict monogamy.

Tasmanians. Tasmania, island off southeastern coast of Australia. Tribe now extinct. Nomads who lived by hunting, fishing, and collecting. Polygyny permitted but practiced mainly by older men.

Taulipang. Northern coast of South America. Fishing more important than hunting in their economy. No tribal organization, much rivalry between villages. Polygyny frequent.

technology. Techniques by means of which a people carry on their arts and crafts; synonymous with material culture.

Tehuelche. Southern Patagonia, South America. Wander over wide areas in search of wild game and vegetables. Simple technology. Horse indispensable in their culture. Polygyny permitted but monogamy prevails.

terrestrial. Residing on land.

territorial. Refers to animals which characteristically establish and maintain possession of a given geographical area.

testicular hormone. Produced by the male sex glands.

testis. Male sex gland; testicle. Plural: testes.

Thompson. British Columbia. Live along river valleys in winter; in summer hunt deer and gather roots and berries in mountains. Formerly polygynous, now mostly monogamous.

Thonga. Mozambique, Africa. Raise many varieties of cereals. Agriculture relatively backward, surrounded by superstition and ritual. Polygyny general, sororal form preferred.

thyroid gland. Endocrine organ lying in the neck in front of the windpipe.

Tikopia. Small island east of Solomons in Pacific Ocean. Population 1000. Peaceful agricultural people. Devote much attention to ceremonial and religious affairs. Polygyny, preferably sororal, is general.

Tinguian. Northwestern Luzon, Philippine Islands. Predominantly agricultural. Population 20,000. Technology well developed. Head-hunters. Ceremonial life quite complex. Exclusive monogamy.

Tiv. South of River Benue, Nigeria, Africa. Population 500,000. Practice shifting agriculture, moving to new site whenever land is exhausted. Polygynous.

Tlingit. Islands and coast of southeastern Alaska. Population 4000 in 1890. Livelihood comes chiefly from the sea, although they hunt and gather from the land. Display much mechanical skill.

Toba. Gran Chaco, South America. Hunt and collect in certain seasons, but subsist mainly on fish. Agriculture has now been adopted. Simple technology. Monogamy general, but polygyny permitted.

Toda. Nilgiri Hills, southern India. Population 800. Buffalo herders who trade dairy products for agricultural goods and artifacts of neighboring tribes. Polyandry, usually fraternal, common.

Tokelauans. Tokelau group of four islands in northwest Polynesia. Fish ing and canoe building most important occupations; islands not well suited to agriculture. Warfare formerly common. Strictly monogamous.

Tolowa.   Northwestern California. Subsistence depends on fishing, hunting and gathering. Much time spent on carefully finished artifacts. Polygyny permitted but quite rare.

Tongans.   Western Polynesian island of Tonga. Agricultural people. Excellent sailors. Formerly warlike. Sororal polygyny permitted, but monogamy prevails.

transvestite.   An individual who dresses like a member of the opposite sex and plays the latter's sex role with other individuals of the same sex.

Trobrianders.   Group of islands in eastern Melanesia, western Pacific. Primarily gardeners and fishermen. Accomplished at wood carving and basket making. Monogamy general, although polygyny permitted.

Trukese.   Truk, islands in central Carolines. Excellent fishermen who also cultivate taro and breadfruit. Generally monogamous.

Tswana.   Bechuanaland Protectorate, South Africa. Population 250,000. Subsist on products of farming and animal husbandry. Generally polygynous, sororal form preferred.

Tuareg.   An elevated oasis in Sahara Desert. Nomadic camel herders. In dry season, prosper by transport work between cities of Nigeria. Polygyny permitted, but monogamy general.

Tubatulabal.   East central California. Originally numbered 300. As they migrate seasonally, they live by hunting, fishing and gathering. Exclusively monogamous.

tumescent.   Descriptive of various body tissues when filled with fluid. The tumescent penis is engorged with blood. The tumescent sex skin of female apes is filled with lymphatic fluid.

Tupinamba.   Near Rio de Janeiro in Brazil. Mainly agricultural people, but hunting is principal occupation of men. Polygyny permitted, but monogamy more common.

urethra.   The canal through which urine is discharged, extending from neck of bladder to the external sexual organs.

uterus.   The part of the feminine reproductive tract in which the embryo normally develops. Commonly called the "womb."

vagina.   Opening of the feminine reproductive tract in which the penis is inserted during copulation and in which sperm are deposited. Opening into the inner part of the vagina is the cervix which constitutes the lower end of the uterus.

Vedda.   East central Ceylon. Three groups, of which Jungle Veddas represent original culture. Seminomadic hunters. Strictly monogamous.

Venda.   Northern Transvaal, Africa. Population 150,000. Economy both agricultural and pastoral, with warfare and hunting main occupations of men. Generally polygynous, sororal form preferred.

vixen. Female fox.

Vulva. Term used in this book as a synonym for vagina.

Walapai. Along Colorado River from the Great Bend into the interior of Arizona. Live chiefly by hunting and gathering but are beginning to practice agriculture. Marriage usually monogamous, but polygyny permitted.

Wapisiana. British Guiana, South America. Population 15,000. Mainly agricultural, but also hunt, fish, and collect. Marriage generally monogamous.

Wappo. Central California. Subsist on acorns, small game, wild roots and nuts. Live in villages of 100 persons in winter, camp by river in summer. Strictly monogamous.

Wintu. Sacramento valley in California. Seminomadic hunters, fishers, and gatherers. Marriage generally monogamous, but sororal polygyny permitted.

Witoto. Remote country claimed by both Colombia and Peru. Population 15,000. Hunt, fish, gather, and practice a simple form of agriculture. Suspicious and hostile. Strictly monogamous.

Wogeo. Wogeo, in the Schouten Islands off north coast of New Guinea. Population under 1000. Live along coast; principal foods grow all year round. Polygyny, preferably sororal, common.

Wolof. Senegal and Gambia, Africa. Predominantly agricultural; supplement diet by hunting and fishing. Technology well developed. Polygyny general.

Xosa [Bomvana group]. Eastern coast of Cape Province, Union of South Africa. Population over 30,000. Cattle very important in their culture; they are also agriculturalists. Polygyny common, sororal form preferred.

Yagua. Lowland Amazon basin in northeastern Peru and western Brazil. Hunt, trap, fish, and carry on simple form of agriculture. Peaceful. Apparently monogamous.

Yako [Umor group]. Umor, an independent village in southern Nigeria, Africa. Population over 10,000. Self-sustaining agriculturalists; collect fruit and sap wine from oil palms. Polygyny common.

Yakut. Northeastern Siberia. Population over 200,000. Turkish tribe driven north by Mongols, carried with them comparatively high culture of central Asiatic horsemen, modified to suit needs by adopting reindeer breeding. Polygynous.

Yapese. Yap, large island in western part of Caroline group, Pacific Ocean. Diet depends largely on skill as fishermen; also raise water taro. Monogamy customary, although polygyny permitted.

Yaruro. South and east of the Venezuelan Andes. River nomads who drift up and down rivers gathering daily food. Practice no agriculture. Peaceful. Strictly monogamous.

Yukaghir. Northeastern Siberia. Once numbered 15,000 but rapidly becoming extinct. Seminomadic, dependent on hunting, fishing, and gathering. Very severe climate. Polygyny permitted but rare.

Yuma. Arizona and southeastern California. Sedentary, remaining close to their villages where they practice simple form of agriculture. Mainly monogamous, but polygyny permitted.

Yungar. Southwestern coast of Western Australia. Population 3000. Hunting-fishing-gathering people. Seminomadic, living in groups of about fifty. Primitive technology. Polygyny prevails.

Yurok. Region of Klamath River, northwestern California. Live in towns along river and coast. Salmon most important food. Marriage generally polygynous.

Zulu. Zululand and Natal, Union of South Africa. Breeding of cattle most important economic activity, but corn and other vegetables also cultivated. Polygyny general, sororal form preferred.

Zuñi. Large pueblo in central western New Mexico. Population almost 2000. Peaceful and good-natured farmers. Strictly monogamous.

Bibliography

The following list of references includes all books and articles specifically mentioned in this book, but it represents only a small fraction of the works consulted during the preparation of our volume. The list is in no sense an exhaustive bibliography of the subject. Instead it consists of a representative sample of the types of literature on which this book is based. The list is divided into the following four sections: 1) Human Societies, 2) Human Physiology, 3) Primates, and 4) Lower Mammals.

HUMAN SOCIETIES

Barton, R. F. *Philippine Pagans, The Autobiographies of Three Ifugaos.* London: G. Routledge and Sons, Ltd., 1938.

Basedow, H. *The Australian Aboriginal.* Adelaide: F. W. Preece and Sons, 1925.

Beaglehole, E. and P. "Ethnology of Pukapuka." *Bulletins of the Bernice P. Bishop Museum,* No. 150, 1-419, 1938.

Best, E. *The Maori.* 2 vols. Wellington: H. H. Tombs, Ltd., 1924.

Blackwood, B. *Both Sides of Buka Passage.* Oxford: The Clarendon Press, 1935.

Bogoras, W. "The Chukchee." *Memoirs of the American Museum of Natural History,* Vol. XI, 1904-1909.

Coudreau, H. A. *Chez nos Indiens.* Paris: Hachette et Cie, 1893.

Covarrubias, M. *Island of Bali.* New York: Alfred A. Knopf, Inc., 1937.

Culwick, A. T. and G. M. *Ubena of the Rivers.* London: G. Allen and Unwin, Ltd., 1935.

Davis, K. B. *Factors in the Sex Life of Twenty-Two Hundred Women.* New York: Harper & Brothers, 1929.

Deacon, A. B. *Malekula, A Vanishing People in the New Hebrides.* Edited by C. H. Wedgwood. London: G. Routledge and Sons, Ltd., 1934.

Dennis, W. *The Hopi Child.* New York: Appleton-Century-Crofts, Inc., 1940.

Deutsch, H. *Psychology of Women.* 2 vols. New York: Grune and Stratton, 1944-45.

Dickinson, R. L. and L. Beam. *A Thousand Marriages.* Baltimore: The Williams and Wilkins Co., 1931.

DuBois, C. *The People of Alor.* Minneapolis: The University of Minnesota Press, 1944.

Earthy, E. D. *Valenge Women.* London: Oxford University Press, H. Milford, 1933.

Ellis, H. *Studies in the Psychology of Sex.* 2 vols. New York: Random House, Inc., 1936.

Emenau, M. B. "Toda marriage regulations and taboos." *American Anthropologist*, n.s., Vol. XXXIX, 103-112, 1937.

Evans, E. P. *The Criminal Prosecution and Capital Punishment of Animals.* New York: E. P. Dutton and Co., Inc., 1906.

Evans-Pritchard, E. E. "Heredity and gestation, as the Zande see them." *Sociologus*, Vol. VIII, 400-413, 1932.

Fejos, P. "Ethnography of the Yagua." *Viking Fund Publications in Anthropology*, No. 1, 1943.

Firth, R. *We, The Tikopia.* London: G. Allen and Unwin, Ltd., 1936.

Fortune, R. G. *Sorcerers of Dobu.* New York: E. P. Dutton and Co., Inc., 1932.

Fürer-Haimendorf, C. von. *The Chenchus.* London: Macmillan and Co., Ltd., 1943.

Fürer-Haimendorf, C. von. *The Reddis of the Bison Hills.* London: Macmillan and Co., Ltd., 1945.

Gifford, E. W. "Tongan society." *Bulletins of the Bernice P. Bishop Museum*, Vol. LXI, 1929.

Gillin, J. "The Barama River Caribs of British Guiana." *Papers of the Peabody Museum of American Archaeology and Ethnology, Harvard University*, Vol. XIV, No. 2, 1936.

Gorer, G. *Himalayan Village.* London: Michael Joseph, Ltd., 1938.

Guttmann, B. "Die Frau bei den Wasdchagga." *Globus*, Vol. XCII, 1-4; 29-32; 49-51; 1907.

Hamilton, G. V. *A Research in Marriage.* New York: A. C. Boni, 1929.

Henry, G. W. *Sex Variants.* 2 vols. New York: Paul B. Hoeber, 1941.

Henry, J. *Jungle People.* New York: J. J. Augustin, 1941.

Herskovits, M. J. *Dahomey: An Ancient West African Kingdom.* New York: J. J. Augustin, 1938.

Hogbin, H. I. "Puberty to marriage: a study of the sexual life of the natives of Wogeo, New Guinea." *Oceania*, Vol. XVI, 185-209, 1946.

Holmberg, A. R. *Nomads of the Long Bow.* Washington, D. C.: Smithsonian Institution, 1950.

Holmberg, A. R. *The Siriono.* Unpublished Ph.D. dissertation, Yale University, 1946.

Jenness, D. "The life of the Copper Eskimo." *Report of the Canadian Arctic Expedition*, 1913-1918, Vol. XII, pt. A, 1-277. Ottawa, 1922.

Jochelson, W. *The Yukaghir and the Yukaghirized Tungus.* Leiden: E. J. Brill, Ltd., New York: G. E. Stechert, 1926.

Junod, H. A. *The Life of a South African Tribe.* London: Macmillan and Co., Ltd., 1927.

Karsten, R. "The head-hunters of western Amazonas." *Societas Scientiarum Fennica, Commentationes Humanarum Litterarum*, Vol. VIII, No. 1, Helsingfors: Centraltryckcriet, 1935.

Kinsey, A. C., Pomeroy, W. B. and Martin, C. E. *Sexual Behavior in the Human Male.* Philadelphia: W. B. Saunders Co., 1948.

LaBarre, W. "The Aymara Indians of the Lake Titicaca Plateau, Bolivia." *Memoirs of the American Anthropological Association*, No. 68, 1948.

Lagae, C. R. "La Naissance chez les Azande." *Congo*, Vol. I, No. 2, 161-177, 1923.

Landes, R. *The Ojibwa Woman*. New York: Columbia University Press, 1938.

Landis, C. and Bolles, M. M. *Personality and sexuality of physically handicapped women*. New York: Paul Hoeber, 1942.

Landtman, G. *The Kiwai Papuans of British New Guinea*. London: Macmillan and Co., Ltd., 1927.

Linton, R. "Marquesan culture." *The Individual and His Society*, by A. Kardiner, 137-196, New York: Columbia University Press, 1939.

Malinowski, B. *The Sexual Life of Savages in North-Western Melanesia*. 2 vols. New York: Harcourt, Brace and Co., Inc., 1929.

Mead, M. *Coming of Age in Samoa*. New York: William Morrow and Co., 1932.

Mead, M. *Growing Up in New Guinea*. London: William Morrow and Co., 1930.

Merker, M. *Die Masai*. Berlin: D. Reimer, 1904.

Mills, J. P. *The Ao Nagas*. London: Macmillan and Co., Ltd., 1926.

Morris, J. *Living with Lepchas*. London: William Heinemann, Ltd., 1938.

Murdock, G. P. *Social Structure*. New York: Macmillan Co., 1949.

Musil, A. *The Manners and Customs of the Rwala Bedouins*. Published under the patronage of the Czech Academy of Sciences and Arts and of Charles R. Crane, New York: 1938.

Nimuendajú, C. "The Apinayé." *The Catholic University of America, Anthropological Series*, No. 8, 1939.

Nimuendajú, C. "The Eastern Timbira." *University of California Publications in American Archaeology and Ethnology*, Vol. XLI, 1-358, 1946.

Parsons, E. C. "Zuñi conception and pregnancy beliefs." *Proceedings of the Nineteenth International Congress of Americanists*. Held at Washington, December 27-31, 1915. Prepared by the Secretary, edited by F. W. Hodge. Washington, 1917. Pp. 378-383.

Powdermaker, H. *Life in Lesu*. New York: W. W. Norton and Co., 1933.

Rasmussen, K. "Intellectual culture of the Copper Eskimos." *Report of the Fifth Thule Expedition*, Vol. IX, 1-350, Copenhagen: Gyldendalske Boghandel, Nordisk Forlag, 1932.

Rattray, R. S. *Ashanti*. Oxford: The Clarendon Press, 1923.

Raum, O. F. *Chagga Childhood*. London: Oxford University Press, 1940.

Rivers, W. H. R. *The Todas*. London: Macmillan and Co., Ltd., 1906.

Rodd, F. R. *People of the Veil*. London: Macmillan and Co., Ltd., 1926.

Roheim, G. "Women and their life in Central Australia." *Journal of the Royal Anthropological Institute of Great Britain and Ireland*. Vol. LXIII, 207-265, 1933.

Schapera, I. *The Khoisan Peoples of South Africa*. London: G. Routledge and Sons, Ltd., 1930.

Simmons, L. W. *Sun Chief*. New Haven: Yale University Press, 1942.

Spencer, B. and Gillen, F. J. *The Arunta: A Study of a Stone Age People*. 2 vols. London: Macmillan and Co., Ltd., 1927.

Stayt, H. A. *The Bavenda.* London: Oxford University Press, H. Milford, 1931.

Strehlow, C. "Die Aranda- und Loritja-Stämme in Zentral-Australien," Pt. 4, "Das soziale Leben der Aranda und Loritja." *Veröffentlichungen aus dem Städtischen Völker-Museum,* Vol. I, pt. 4, sect. 1, pp. 1-103; Sect. 2, pp. 1-78. Frankfurt am Main: Joseph Baer und Co., 1915.

Steytler, J. G. *Ethnographic Report on the Achewa Tribe of Nyasaland.* Unpublished manuscript, 1934.

Terman, L. M. *Psychological Factors in Marital Happiness.* New York: McGraw-Hill Book Company, Inc., 1938.

Tessmann, G. *Die Indianer Nordost-Perus.* Hamburg: Friederichsen, de Gruyter and Co., 1930.

Thompson, L. "Guam and its people." *Studies of the Pacific,* No. 8, San Francisco, New York, Honolulu; American Council Institute of Pacific Relations, 1941.

Warner, W. L. *A Black Civilization.* New York: Harper & Brothers, 1937.

Whiffen, T. *The North-West Amazons.* London: Constable and Co., Ltd., 1915.

Whiting, J. W. M. *Becoming a Kwoma.* New Haven: Yale University Press, 1941.

Williams, F. E. *Orokaiva Society.* London: Oxford University Press, H. Milford, 1930.

Williams, F. E. *Papuans of the Trans-Fly.* Oxford: The Clarendon Press, 1936.

HUMAN PHYSIOLOGY

Beach, F. A. *Hormones and Behavior.* New York: Paul Hoeber, 1948.

Boas, E. P. and Goldschmidt, E. F. *The Heart Rate.* Springfield, Ill.: Charles C. Thomas, 1932.

Corner, G. W. *Ourselves Unborn.* New Haven: Yale University Press, 1944.

Corner, G. W. *The Hormones in Human Reproduction.* Princeton: Princeton University Press, 1942.

Daniels, G. E. "An approach to psychological studies or urinary sex hormones," *Am. J. Psychiat.,* Vol. C, 231-239, 1943.

Daniels, G. E. and Tauber, E. S. "A dynamic approach to the study of replacement therapy in cases of castration." *Am. J. Psychiat.,* Vol. XCVII, 905-918, 1941.

Dickinson, R. L. *Human Sex Anatomy.* 2nd edition. Baltimore: The Williams and Wilkins Company, 1949.

Ellis, A. "The sexual psychology of human hermaphrodites." *Psychosomat. Med.,* Vol. VII, 108-125, 1945.

Filler, W. and Drezner, N. "Results of surgical castration in women over forty." *Am. J. Obst. & Gynec.,* Vol. XLVII, 122-124, 1944.

Heller, C. G., Farney, J. P. and Myers, G. B. "Development and correlation of menopausal symptoms, vaginal smear and urinary gonadotrophin changes following castration in 27 women." *J. Clin. Endocrinol.,* Vol. IV, 101-108, 1944.

Heller, C. G., Nelson, W. O. and Roth, A. A. "Functional prepuberal castration in males." *J. Clin. Endocrinol.,* Vol. III, 573-588, 1943.

Keys, A. B., Brožek, J., Henschel, A., Mickelson, O., Taylor, H. L. *The Biology of Human Starvation*, 2 vols. Minneapolis: University of Minnesota Press, 1950.

Landis, C., Landis, A. T., Boles, M. M., Metzger, H. F., Pitts, M. W., D'Esopo, D. A., Moloy, H. C., Kleegman, S. J., Dickinson, R. L. *Sex in Development*. New York: Paul B. Hoeber, 1940.

Lass, P. M., Smelser, J. and Kurzrok, R. "Studies relating to time of human ovulation." III. "During lactation." *Endocrinology*, Vol. XXIII, 39-43, 1938.

Mansfeld, O. P. "Eirstock und Geschlechtrieb," *Arch. f. Gynak.*, Vol. CXVII, 294-310, 1922.

Perloff, W. H. "Role of the hormones in human sexuality." *Psychosom. Med.*, Vol. XI, 133-139, 1949.

Pratt, J. P. "A personal note on methyl testosterone in hypogonadism." *J. Clin. Endocrinol.*, Vol. II, 460-464, 1942.

BEHAVIOR AND PHYSIOLOGY OF APES AND MONKEYS

Ball, J. "Sexual responsiveness and temporally related physiological events during pregnancy in the rhesus monkey." *Anat. Rec.*, Vol. LXVII, 50-512, 1937.

Ball, J. and Hartman, C. G. "Sexual excitability as related to the menstrual cycle in the monkey." *Am. J. Obst. & Gynec.*, Vol. XXIX, 117-119, 1935.

Bingham, H. C. "Sex development in apes." *Comp. Psychol. Monogr.*, Vol. V, 1-165, 1928.

Buffon, Comte De. *Natural History*. Translated by W. Kendrick and J. Murdoch. Vol. IV. London: T. Bell, 1775.

Carpenter, C. R. "A field study of the behavior and social relations of howling monkeys (*Alouatta palliata*)." *Comp. Psych. Monogr.*, Vol. X, 1-168, 1934.

Carpenter, C. R. "Behavior of red spider monkeys in Panama," *J. Mammal.*, Vol. XVI, 171-180, 1935.

Carpenter, C. R. "A field study in Siam of the behavior and social relations of the gibbon (*Hylobates Lar*)." *Comp. Psychol. Monogr.*, Vol. XVI, 1-212, 1940.

Carpenter, C. R. "Sexual behavior of free ranging rhesus monkeys (*Macaca mulatta*) I. Specimens, procedures and behavorial characteristics of estrus. II. Periodicity of estrus, homosexual, autoerotic and non-conformist behavior." *J. Comp. Psychol.*, Vol. XXXIII, 113-142 and 143-162, 1942.

Fox, H. "The birth of two anthropoid apes." *J. Mammal.*, Vol. X, 37-51, 1929.

Hamilton, G. V. "A study of sexual tendencies in monkeys and baboons." *J. Anim. Behav.*, Vol. IV, 295-318, 1914.

Kempf, E. J. "The social and sexual behavior of infrahuman primates with some comparable facts in human behavior." *Psychoanalytic Review*, Vol. IV, 127-154, 1917.

Maslow, A. H. "The role of dominance in the social and sexual behavior of infra-human primates. I. Observations at the Vilas Park Zoo." *J. Genet. Psychol.*, Vol. XLVIII, 261-338, 1936.

Montane, L. "A Cuban chimpanzee." *J. Anim. Behav.*, Vol. IV, 330-333, 1916.

Nissen, H. W. "A field study of the chimpanzee. Observations of chimpanzee behavior and environment in Western French Guinea." *Comp. Psychol. Monogr.*, Vol. VIII, 1-122, 1931.

Pratt, J. P. "Sex functions in man." *Sex and Internal Secretions* (ed. Edgar Allen). Baltimore: The Williams & Wilkins Company, 1939.

Simpson, G. G. *The Meaning of Evolution*. New Haven: Yale University Press, 1949.

Sokolowsky, A. "The sexual life of anthropoid apes." *Urol. Cutan. Rev.*, Vol. XXVII, 612-615, 1923.

Tinklepaugh, O. L. "Fur-picking in monkeys as an act of adornment." *J. Mammal.*, Vol. XII, 430-431, 1931.

Yerkes, R. M. "The mind of the gorilla. III. Memory." *Comp. Psychol. Monogr.*, Vol. V, 1-92, 1928.

Yerkes, R. M. "Genetic aspects of grooming, a socially important primate behavior pattern." *J. Soc. Psychol.*, Vol. IV, 3-25, 1933.

Yerkes, R. M. "Sexual behavior in the chimpanzee." *Human Biology*, Vol. II, 78-110, 1939.

Yerkes, R. M. *Chimpanzees*. New Haven: Yale University Press, 1943.

Yerkes, R. M. and Elder, J. H. "Oestrus, receptivity and mating in the chimpanzee." *Comp. Psychol. Monogr.*, Vol. XIII, 1-39, 1936.

Yerkes, R. M. and Yerkes, A. W. *Social Behavior in Infrahuman Primates*. Worcester, Mass.: Clark University Press, 1935.

Young, W. C. and Orbison, W. D. "Changes in selected features of behavior in pairs of oppositely sexed chimpanzees during the sexual cycle and after ovariectomy." *J. Comp. Psychol.*, Vol. XXXVII, 107-143, 1943.

Young, W. C. and Yerkes, R. M. "Factors influencing the reproductive cycle in the chimpanzee; the period of adolescent sterility and related problems." *Endocrinology*, Vol. XXXIII, 121-154, 1943.

Zuckerman, S. "The menstrual cycle of the primates." *Proc. Zool. Soc.*, 691-754, 1930.

Zuckerman, S. *The Social Life of Monkeys and Apes*. London: Kegan Paul, Trench, Trubner, Ltd., 1932.

BEHAVIOR AND PHYSIOLOGY OF LOWER MAMMALS

Aronson, L. R. "Behavior resembling spontaneous emissions in the domestic cat." *J. Comp. Physiol.*, Vol. XLII, 226-227, 1949.

Asdell, S. A. "The reproduction of farm animals." *Cornell Extension Bulletin*, No. 305, 3-27, 1934.

Beach, F. A. "Sex reversals in the mating pattern of the rat." *J. Genet. Psychol.*, Vol. LIII, 329-334, 1938.

Beach, F. A. "Effects of cortical lesions upon the copulatory behavior of male rats." *J. Comp. Psychol.*, Vol. XXIX, 193-244, 1940.

Beach, F. A. "Female mating behavior shown by male rats after administration of testosterone propionate." *Endocrinology*, Vol. XXIX, 409-412, 1941.

Beach, F. A. "Analysis of factors involved in the arousal, maintenance and manifestation of sexual excitement in male animals." *Psychosom. Med.*, Vol. IV, 173-198, 1942.

Beach, F. A. "Central nervous mechanisms involved in the reproductive behavior of vertebrates." *Psychol. Bull.*, Vol. XXXIX, 200-225, 1942.

Beach, F. A. "Effects of injury to the cerebral cortex upon the display of masculine and feminine mating behavior by female rats." *J. Comp. Psychol.*, Vol. XXXVI, 169-199, 1943.

Beach, F. A. "Relative effects of androgen upon the mating behavior of male rats subjected to forebrain injury or castration." *J. Exp. Zool.*, Vol. XCVII, 249-295, 1944.

Beach, F. A. "Bisexual mating behavior in the male rat: Effects of castration and hormone administration." *Physiol. Zool.*, Vol. XVIII, 391-402, 1945.

Beach, F. A. "A review of physiological and psychological studies of sexual behavior in mammals." *Physiol. Rev.*, Vol. XXVII, 240-307, 1947.

Beach, F. A. "Evolutionary changes in the physiological control of mating behavior in mammals." *Psychol. Rev.*, Vol. LIV, 297-315, 1947.

Beach, F. A. *Hormones and Behavior.* New York: Paul B. Hoeber, 1948.

Beach, F. A. "A cross-species survey of mammalian sexual behavior." *Psychosexual Development in Health and Disease.* Hoch and Zubin ed. New York: Grune and Stratton, 1949.

Beach, F. A. "Sexual behavior in animals and men." *The Harvey Lectures, 1948,* 254-280. Springfield, Ill.: C. C. Thomas, 1950.

Beach, F. A. and Gilmore, R. W. "Response of male dogs to urine from females in heat." *J. Mammal.*, Vol. XXX, 391-392, 1949.

Beach, F. A. and Holz-Tucker, M. "Effects of different concentrations of androgen upon sexual behavior in castrated male rats." *J. Comp. Psychol.*, Vol. XLII, 433-453, 1949.

Beach, F. A. and Levinson, G. "Diurnal variations in the mating behavior of male rats." *Proc. Soc. Exp. Biol. Med.*, Vol. LXXII, 79-80, 1949.

Beach, F. A. and Pauker, R. "Effects of castration and subsequent androgen administration upon mating in the male hamster (Cricetus auratus)." *Endocrinol.*, Vol. XLV, 211-221, 1949.

Cooper, J. B. "An exploratory study on African lions." *Comp. Psychol. Monogr.*, Vol. XVII, 1-48, 1942.

Darling, F. F. *A Herd of Red Deer.* London: Oxford University Press, 1937.

Enders, R. K. "Induced changes in the breeding habits of foxes." *Sociometry*, Vol. VIII, 53-55, 1945.

Hamilton, J. E. "The southern sea lion (*Otaria byronia DeBlainville*)." *Discovery Reports*, Vol. VIII, 268-318, Cambridge University Press, 1938.

Hinsey, J. C. "The relation of the nervous system to ovulation and other phenomena of the female reproductive tract." *Cold Spring Harbor Symposia on Quant. Biol.*, Vol. V, 269-279, 1937.

Hodgson, R. E. "An eight generation experiment in inbreeding swine." *J. Hered.*, Vol. XXVI, 209-217, 1935.

McBride, A. F. and Hebb, D. O. "Behavior of the captive bottle-nose dolphin, *Tursiops truncatus.*" *J. Comp. Physiol. Psychol.*, Vol. XLI, 111-123, 1948.

McKenzie, F. F. and Berliner, V. "The reproductive capacity of rams." *U. S. Department of Agriculture Research Bulletin*, No. 265, 5-143, 1937.

Macirone, C. and Walton, A. "Fecundity of male rabbits as determined by 'dummy matings.'" *J. Agricul. Sci.*, Vol. XXVIII, 122-134, 1938.

Marshall, F. H. A. and Hammond, J. "Fertility and animal breeding." *Ministry of Agriculture and Fisheries Bulletin*, No. 39, 1-42, 1943.

Montagu, M. F. Ashley, *Adolescent Sterility*. Springfield, Ill.: C. C. Thomas, 1946.

Murie, A. "The wolves of Mount McKinley," *U. S. Department of the Interior, Fauna Series*, No. 5, 1-238, 1944.

Pearson, O. P. "Reproduction in the shrew (*Blarina brevicauda Say*)." *Am. J. Anat.*, Vol. LXXV, 39-93, 1944.

Pussep, L. M. "Der Blutkreislauf im Gehern beim Koitus." *Sexualreform und Sexualwissenschaft. Vortrage gehalten auf der I. Internationalen Tagung für Sexualreform auf sexualwissenschaftlicher Grundlage in Berlin (in 1921)*, pp. 61-85. (Herausgegeben von Dr. A. Weil.) Stuttgart: Julius Puttman, 1922.

Reed, C. A. "The copulatory behavior of small mammals." *J. Comp. Psychol.*, Vol. XXXIX, 185-206, 1946.

Schwab, G. R. "Raising chinchillas in Canada." *Fur Trade Journal of Canada*, Vol. XXIII, No. 8, pp. 17, 47-48, 53, 1936.

Selye, H. and McKeown, T. "Further studies on the influence of suckling." *Anat. Rec.*, Vol. LX, 323-332, 1934.

Shadle, A. R. "Copulation in the porcupine." *J. Wildlife Management*, Vol. X, 159-162, 1946.

Shadle, A. R., Smelzer, M. and Metz, M. "The sex reactions of porcupines (*Erethizon D. dorsatum*) before and after copulation." *J. Mammal.*, Vol. XXVII, 116-121, 1946.

Stone, C. P. "A note on 'feminine' behavior in adult male rats." *Am. J. Physiol.*, Vol. LXVIII, 39-41, 1942.

Stone, C. P. "Counteracting the retarding effects of inanition on the awakening of copulatory ability in male rats by testosterone propionate," *J. Comp. Psychol.*, Vol. XXXIII, 97-105, 1942.

Weichert, C. K. "The experimental shortening of prolonged gestation in the lactating albino rat." *Anat. Rec.*, Vol. LXXV, Suppl., 72-73, 1939.

Wiesner, B. P. and Sheard, N. M. *Maternal Behavior in the Rat*. Edinburgh: Oliver and Boyd, 1933.

Authors' Note

We have written this book in such close collaboration that it is impossible for either of us to state with certainty which sentences he composed and which were written by his co-author. And although we have not examined the evidence statistically, it is unlikely that the volume contains a single sentence that has not been rewritten at least once by both of us. As a matter of fact, when it became necessary to decide whose name would appear as senior author there was no logical method of assigning more credit (or onus) to one than to the other. The matter was finally settled by one hand of showdown poker dealt by John Fischer. Not a single pair turned up, but on the last card Ford won the senior authorship with Ace high over a Jack high for Beach.

Despite this facetious way of solving what in some cases is presumably a vexing problem, it should be stated that there was an initial division of labor in collecting the data that appear in the book. Ford was responsible for surveying and organizing all the material on human societies other than our own. Beach covered the zoological evidence and the published studies of sexual behavior in the United States, as well as the physiological material. However, once the first draft of each section had been written it immediately changed hands, and more often than not was revised and rewritten several times until it met with the approval of both authors.

We wish to acknowledge special thanks to Mark A. May, Director of the Institute of Human Relations, for his support and continued interest in our research, and also to our colleagues at Yale University in the Departments of Anthropology and Psychology. For assistance in compiling the data and in preparing the manuscript we are indebted to Carol Johnson, Anne Palmer, Katherine Schlesinger, and Joan Clark.

Before the final draft of the manuscript was written, a tentative and incomplete version was submitted to a number of readers for criticism. We feel that their comments and suggestions have added appreciably to the value of the book and we wish to acknowledge our appreciation to them here. These persons are: C. R. Carpenter, George C. Corner, Robert L. Dickinson, Robert Enders, Earl T. Engle, Isabelle Hahn, Donald O. Hebb, Allan Holmberg, Lawrence Kubie, David M. Levy, Ralph Linton, Mark A. May, Carmen Murdock, George P. Murdock, John S. Murphy, David M. Rioch, Mary Mikami Rouse, Amram Scheinfeld, Henry Silverthorne, Abraham Stone, Thomas Waldron, Jane Whiting.

Acknowledgment is made to the following publishers from whose publications tables and figures have been reproduced: Harper & Brothers, McGraw-Hill Book Company, Inc., Princeton University Press, W. B. Saunders Company, Charles C. Thomas, Williams and Wilkins Company, and Yale University Press.

CLELLAN S. FORD
FRANK A. BEACH

Departments of Anthropology and Psychology and
  Institute of Human Relations

Yale University
11 October 1950

Index of Names

Aristotle, 31
Aronson, L. R., 165
Asdell, S. A., 202

Ball, J., 204, 214, 225
Beach, F. A., 13, 140, 230, 233, 241
Beam, L., 32, 33
Berliner, L., 93
Bingham, H. C., 26, 27, 28, 29, 49, 50, 52, 80, 81, 98, 103, 135, 137, 138, 149, 150, 162, 163, 214
Blackwood, B., 93, 94
Boas, E. P., 244, 246
Buffon, C., 149

Carpenter, C. R., 26, 30, 36, 37, 44, 48, 61, 80, 91, 93, 97, 98, 103, 110, 111, 119, 120, 121, 135, 159, 162, 193, 204
Corner, G. W., 200
Covarrubias, M., 49

Daniels, G. E., 223, 235
Darling, F. F., 161
Darwin, C., 90
Davis, K., 33, 126, 127, 154, 155, 156, 196, 208, 215
Deutsch, H., 62, 63
Dickinson, R. L., vii, 20, 21, 32, 33, 40, 46, 49, 50, 77, 87, 154, 156, 158, 159, 181, 196, 224, 225
Drezner, N., 223
DuBois, C., 48
Duncan, J. M., 172

Elder, J. H., 20, 42, 91, 102, 103, 194, 195, 206, 207, 208
Ellis, A., 134
Enders, R. K., 111
Evans, E. P., 144, 145

Farney, J. P., 223
Filler, W., 223

Fox, H., 204
Freud, S., 63

Goldschmidt, E. F., 244, 246
Gorer, G., 46, 47, 79

Hamilton, G. V., 29, 30, 53, 60, 92, 98, 116, 120, 121, 127, 135, 136, 138, 143, 149, 150, 154, 159, 162, 231
Hamilton, J. E., 50
Hammond, J., 93, 202
Hartman, C., 204
Hatfield, D. M., 46
Hebb, D. O., 139, 160
Heller, C. G., 223, 231
Henry, G. W., 126, 128
Henry, J., 109
Hodgson, R. E., 118
Hogbin, H. I., 88
Holmberg, A., 44, 55, 56, 69, 88, 89, 130
Holz-Tucker, M., 233

Junod, H. A., 174, 175

Kempf, E. J., 29, 30, 53, 98, 134, 135, 136, 150, 159
Keys, A. B., 237
Kinsey, A. C., vii, 2, 7, 23, 24, 32, 41, 46, 49, 50, 51, 52, 73, 78, 116, 117, 126, 141, 145, 153, 154, 164, 179, 185, 186, 210, 227, 228

Landis, C., 21, 33, 41, 116, 127, 154, 185
Lass, P. M., 217
Linton, R., 131

McBride, A. F., 139, 160
McKenzie, F. F., 93
McKeown, T., 219
Malinowski, B., 56, 57, 70, 89, 94, 157
Mansfeld, O. P., 223
Marshall, F. H. A., 93, 202

Martin, C. E., vii, 2, 7, 23, 32, 41, 50, 51, 52, 73, 78, 116, 126, 141, 145, 153, 164, 179, 185, 210, 227, 228
Maslow, A. H., 137
Merker, M., 87
Metz, M., 31, 35, 42
Meyers, G. B., 223
Montagu, M. F. A., 172
Murdock, G. P., 107, 112
Murie, A., 111

Nelson, W. O., 231
Neumann, H., 50

Orbison, W. D., 205

Pauker, R., 230
Pearson, O. P., 165
Perloff, W. H., 231
Pomeroy, W. B., vii, 2, 7, 23, 32, 41, 50, 51, 52, 73, 78, 116, 126, 141, 145, 153, 164, 179, 185, 210, 227, 228
Powdermaker, H., 158
Pratt, J. P., 223, 234, 235
Pussep, L. M., 244

Rasmussen, K., 148
Reed, C. A., 46, 49
Roheim, G., 133
Roth, A. A., 231

Selye, H., 219
Shadle, A. R., 31, 35, 42, 160
Sheard, N. M., 219
Simpson, G. G., 11
Smelzer, M., 31, 35, 42
Sokolsky, A., 118
Steytler, J. G., 178
Stone, C. P., 140, 237
Strehlow, C., 132
Struthers, P. H., 49

Tauber, E. S., 223, 232, 235
Terman, L. M., 117, 186, 187, 208
Tinklepaugh, O. L., 91, 92

Ulmer, F. A., 26, 27

Weichart, C. K., 218
Weisner, B. P., 219

Yerkes, A. W., 109
Yerkes, R. M., 20, 35, 42, 45, 80, 91, 92, 102, 103, 109, 148, 149, 160, 173, 192, 194, 195, 206, 207, 208, 214, 218
Young, W. C., 173, 205

Zuckerman, S., 21, 29, 44, 53, 60, 92, 98, 110, 119, 135, 136, 137, 138, 150, 151, 159, 160, 162, 192, 201, 204, 214, 218

Index of Topics

Abortion, 188
Adolescence, Chapter X
  bestiality, 145
  homosexual behavior, 127-128, 136, 178, 191
  masturbation, 154-157
  nocturnal emissions, 164
  sterility, 172
Adrenal gland, 237
Adultery, 108, 111-118
Alcohol, 237-239
Androgen, 141, 168, 226-236, 241-242
Animals, classification of, 11
Apes, classification of, 13
Aphrodisiacs, 237-239
Autoeroticism. See Masturbation

Bate, 133
Berdache, 130-131
Bestiality. See Cross-species matings
Birth control. See Contraception
Bisexual behavior. See Homosexual behavior
Biting, 40, 55-65
Brain, 240-242
Breasts, 41, 46-48, 87-89, 94, 101, 126, 128, 170, 182, 217
Breeding season, 202-203, 226

Castration, 141, 177, 226-236, 242; see Testis
Change of life. See Climacteric, Menopause
Childbirth. See Parturition
Childhood, 129
Circumcision, 177, 182
Climacteric,
  female, 94, 221-222
  male, 226-229
Climax. See Orgasm
Clitoris, 20-24, 30, 34, 38, 40, 50-55, 86, 88, 128-129, 133, 156, 158, 162, 176, 243, 246

Coitus, Chapter II
  anal, 126, 130-135, 146-147, 177-178
  during lactation, 217-219
  during menstruation, 211-213
  during pregnancy, 213-217
  frequency, 75-82
  interfemoral, 126, 182, 188
  interruptus, 182, 188
  invitations to, 93-105
  place of occurrence, 68-72
  premarital and extramarital, 69, 108, 111-118
  pseudo, 41, 126, 182
  time of occurrence, 73-75
  See also Incest
Conception. See Fertility, Pregnancy
Concubines. See Mateships
Contraception, viii, 132, 173-174, 182, 188, 191
Copulation. See Coitus
Cortex, cerebral, 240-242
Courtship, Chapter III, 93-105
Cross-species matings, Chapter VIII, 120-121
Cunnilinctus, 40, 128, 188-189, 191-192

Defloration, 51, 63, 174, 176, 184
Delousing, 44-46; see also Grooming
Dominance, social, 60-62, 91-93, 110, 119, 122, 135-139, 206
Dreams, 14, 97, 113, 164, 237
Drugs, 237-239

Ejaculation, 22, 29, 30, 32-33, 35-38, 44, 80-81, 139, 154, 159, 161, 164-166, 170, 177, 179, 186, 193, 229, 231-240, 244-247; see also Orgasm
Emission. See Ejaculation
Epididymis, 169
Estrogen, 141-142, 168, 199-213, 221-226, 236, 242
Estrus, 202-207, 207-213, 218, 221-226, 243
Extramarital intercourse. See Coitus

Fallopian tubes, 169, 200

Fellatio, 40, 52, 54, 126, 132-133, 146, 188-189, 191

Female hormone. *See* Estrogen, Progesterone

Fertility,
   female, Chapter XI, 172-176
   male, 226-227

Foreplay, Chapter III

Frequency of intercourse. *See* Coitus

Frigidity, 133, 203, 205, 224, 225

Gestation. *See* Pregnancy

Gifts, 98-100

Gland. *See* Adrenal, Ovary, Parathyroid, Pituitary, Prostate, Testis, Thymus, Thyroid

Gonadotrophins, 167-169, 199-202, 218, 222, 238

Grooming, 40, 44-46, 135, 138, 166

Heat. *See* Estrus

Hermaphroditism, 134

Heterosexual behavior. *See* Coitus

Homosexual behavior, Chapter VII, 121, 128, 141, 178, 187, 191-192, 236-237, 241, 243

Hormones. *See* Adrenal gland, Androgen, Estrogen, Gonadotrophins, Parathyroid gland, Thyroid gland

Hymen, 21, 51, 184; *see also* Defloration

Hypothalamus, 240

Impotence. *See* Potency

Incest, 112-113, 118, 190, 192

Infancy, 217-220, 225

Initiative, distribution of, 101-103

Intercourse. *See* Coitus

Inversion. *See* Hemosexual behavior

Invitations to coitus, 93-105

Jealousy, 112, 119, 121

Kissing, 30, 49-50, 127-128

Labia, vaginal, 20-21, 50-51, 86-87, 138, 158, 161, 169, 176, 181

Lactation, 217-220

Learning, Chapter X, 255-267

Liaisons, 106, 111-122, 131

Libido. *See* Sexual desire

Love magic, 100-101

Maidenhead. *See* Hymen

Male hormone. *See* Androgen

Marriage, 107-109, 195-197

Masochism. *See* Painful stimulation

Masturbation, 112, 126-129, 132-133, 136, 138, 145-146, 148-149, 179-181, 188-193, 207, 231, 237-240, 242-243

Mateships, 106-111, 131

Mating calls, 97

Mating season. *See* Breeding season

Menarche, 169, 173-174, 181, 191; *see also* Puberty

Menopause. *See* Climacteric

Menstruation, 131, 170, 172, 174, 176, 199-202, Chapter XI

Monkeys, classification of, 13

Monogamy. *See* Mateships

Mouthing, 49-50

Music, 96-98

Nervous system, 179, 201, 203, 218, 239, 242

Nursing. *See* Suckling

Odors, 96

Old age, 78-79, 221-229

Oral contacts. *See* Cunnilinctus, Fellatio, Soixante-neuf

Orgasm, 21-22, 24, 30, 31-34, 37-38, 46-47, 50, 56, 64, 78-81, 84, 126, 128-129, 134, 140, 145, 153-159, 164-165, 170, 177, 179, 186, 196, 224, 227-228, 231, 234, 238, 243-244, 246-247

Ovarian hormone. *See* Estrogen, Progesterone

Ovariectomy, 213, 221-226

Ovary, 134, 167-168, 199-213, 218, 221-226

Ovulation, 59-60, 141-142, 191, 199-213, 217, 222

Painful stimulation, 55-65

Parathyroid gland, 237

Parturition, 217-220

Pederasty. *See* Coitus, anal

Penis, 20, 22-23, 26, 29, 31, 37, 40, 50-55, 89, 92, 95, 101, 126, 129, 133, 135, 147, 150-151, 154, 157-161, 165, 169, 178, 180-181, 192, 203, 235, 239-240, 242, 244

Phallus. *See* Penis

Pinching, 55-65

Pituitary gland, 167, 199, 218, 222, 237

Placenta, 213

Polyandry. *See* Mateships

Polygyny. *See* Mateships

Potency, 226-236, 238

Pregnancy, 33, 187, 190-191, 213-217, 223

Premarital intercourse. *See* Coitus
Primates, classification of, 13
Progesterone, 199-213, 221-226
Prostate gland, 169
Prostitution, 98, 130
Psychotherapy, 223-224, 232
Puberty, Chapter X

Rape, 59, 63, 102

Sadism. *See* Painful stimulation
Sarombavy, 131
Scratching, 40, 54-65, 102
Self-stimulation. *See* Masturbation
Seminal vesicles, 169
Sex characters, 90, 169-173
Sex hormones. *See* Androgen, Estrogen, Progesterone
Sex organs. *See* Clitoris, Labia, Penis, Vagina
Sex skin, 90-91, 95, 102, 201, 204, 207, 214, 225
Sexual attraction, Chapter V, 113, 118, 151, 202, 206-207, 221-222
Sexual desire, Chapter XI, 226, 236
Societies, distribution of, 8-10

Sodomy. *See* Coitus, anal
Soixante-neuf, 40, 52
Spinal cord, 239-240
Starvation, 237-239
Sterility, 172, 212
Subincision, 177
Suckling, 46-48, 218-219

Territorialism in animals, 57-58, 72
Testicular hormone. *See* Androgen
Testis, 134, 141, 167-168, 226-236; *see also* Castration
Thymus gland, 169
Thyroid gland, 169, 237
Transvestite, 130, 134

Urine, 34-35, 51, 96, 168, 180, 236
Uterus, 169, 199; *see also* Menstruation and Pregnancy

Vagina, 20-22, 26, 28, 29, 31, 34, 37, 43, 50-55, 89-90, 94, 129, 147, 150, 156-158, 161, 163, 169, 188, 201-203, 242-244

Wife lending or exchange, 114